Goodbye to the Vikings?

Goodbye to the Vikings?

Re-reading Early Medieval Archaeology

Richard Hodges

Duckworth

First published in 2006 by
Gerald Duckworth & Co. Ltd.
90-93 Cowcross Street, London EC1M 6BF
Tel: 020 7490 7300
Fax: 020 7490 0080
inquiries@duckworth-publishers.co.uk
www.ducknet.co.uk

A catalogue record for this book is available
from the British Library

ISBN 0 7156 3429 1

Typeset by Ray Davies
Printed and bound in Great Britain by
CPI Bath

Contents

To the memory of John Hurst (1927-2003)

Preface

Indeed it must be confessed that the historian and the archaeologist of the Dark Ages are very like two men clutching each other in mid-air to prevent themselves from falling (Wheeler 1935: 3).

This collection of essays reflects my interests in using archaeology to re-read the main lines of early medieval European history. Based in part upon my doctoral research on North Sea commerce, and then upon my long-term excavations at Butrint (Albania), Montarrenti (Italy) and San Vincenzo al Volturno (Italy), this book uses recent archaeological research to shape a narrative that, above all, places emphasis upon inter-connections in space and time. Throughout, the archaeological evidence is used as a source with which to reassess a familiar textual history. If there is an underlying methodology, it could be said to follow one pursued with great purpose by the ancient historian, Moses Finley: 'The historian... narrates, moving from one concrete datum of experience to the next. The importance of the experiences, together with their mass and their inter-connections, evokes the general ideas' (Finley 1960: 528; see Shaw and Saller 1983: xxvi-xviii).

The book focusses upon the period between the sixth and tenth centuries in western Europe. If it has a goal it is to argue the case for a new historical paradigm for the period. The ethno-histories on which the familiar story of European origins is based need overhauling in the light of modern archaeological research. Accepted stories, for these are what they are, about migratory tribes, King Arthur, Charlemagne, the Vikings and many others, stand in as much need of reappraisal as the Illyrian history constructed by Albania's post-war communist government (see Chapter 4). Particular emphasis is placed on the changing settlement types in this period. The end of Roman towns, for instance, is considered through the prism of the Butrint excavations, while the rise of new forms of medieval towns is examined using the North Sea emporia. The changing role of regions is also considered. Fundamental in this respect, it is argued, is the part played by monastic cities, once best known from the schematic drawing known as the Plan of St Gall dating to c. 820. The excavations at San Vincenzo al Volturno (Italy) are interpreted not only to show what a monastic city might have consisted of, but how it operated within the ninth century as the legacy of Charlemagne was translated by regional authorities into many new and sustainable forms. The role of trade, too, is a theme

vii

of the book. The exciting new work of the historian Michael McCormick is considered in the context of the breakdown of Roman trading systems in the Mediterranean, the eighth-century significance of Carolingian contact with the Abbasid caliphate, and new evidence for North Sea exchange in the Viking age.

Some essays have been either partially rewritten or modified for this book; others, such as those relating to the ongoing excavations at San Vincenzo al Volturno (Italy), are unaltered. Even where the essays have been altered, I have not attempted to provide amplified bibliographies. To do this would be to belie the purpose of the book as impressionistic sketches about general historical themes.

In writing this book I owe a great debt to Cassy Payne, the erstwhile administrator of the Institute of World Archaeology at the University of East Anglia, Norwich, who has helped me to prepare the essays for publication. Thanks, too, to William Bowden for permitting me to include our joint essay on 'Balkan ghosts' (Chapter 4). Particular thanks, as ever, to Deborah Blake of Duckworth, who once again has encouraged and guided me on this venture. Finally, a special word of gratitude to Riccardo Francovich and John Mitchell who have debated many of these issues with me over the past twenty-five years. Their friendship has been priceless.

Norwich

Richard Hodges

Sources

Chapter 1 is a substantially revised version of 'The not-so-Dark Ages', *Archaeology* September/October 1998: 61-5.

Chapter 2 was published in R. Hodges and W. Bowden (eds) *The Sixth Century. Production, Distribution and Demand*, E.J. Brill, Leiden, 1998: 3-14.

Chapter 3 is an unpublished lecture given to the Arkeolan conference held at Pisa in November 2003.

Chapter 4 was written with William Bowden and published in Neil Christie (ed.), *Landscapes of Change. Rural Evolution in Late Antiquity and the Early Middle Ages*, Ashgate, Aldershot, 2004: 195-222.

Chapter 5 was written for the *festschrift* for W.A. van Es: H. Sarfati, W.J.H. Verwers and P.J. Woltering (eds), *Discussion with the Past. Archaeological Studies Presented to W.A. van Es*, ROB, Zwolle, 1999: 227-32.

Chapter 6 was published in *History Today,* December 50 (12) 2000: 21-7.

Chapter 7 was published in R. Hodges (ed.) *San Vincenzo al Volturno 2.* British School at Rome, London, 1995: 153-75.

Chapter 8 was published in the *festshrift* for Cecil Lee Striker: Judson Emerick (ed.), *Archaeology in Architecture. Essays in Honour of Cecil Lee Striker.* Von Zabern, Mainz, 2005.

Chapter 9 was published in *I Longobardi dei Ducati di Spoleto e Benevento,* Centro Italiano di Studi sull'Alto Medioevo, Spoleto, 2003: 1077-98.

Chapter 10 was published in *History Today* 54 (9) 2004: 29-30.

Chapter 11 was published in *Il Secolo di Ferro: Mito e Realtà del Secolo X, Settimane di Studio del Centro Italiano di Studi sull'Alto Medioevo,* Spoleto, 1991: 125-57.

Illustrations

1

Introduction: new light on the Dark Ages?

> If we are fully to understand the historical past, we must seek out the details of the way in which people, in historically specific contexts, used, manipulated and confronted both texts and objects. We have to reconstruct the details of their entanglements with words and things, and write the kind of 'thick descriptions' which allow the variety and ingenuity of human creativity, and the difference of the past, to shine through (Moreland 2002: 97).

> One must face the fact that, when it comes to the historical record, there are no grounds to be found in the record itself for preferring one way of construing its meaning rather than another .... We can tell equally plausible, alternative, and even contradictory stories ... without violating rules of evidence or critical standards (White 1973: 5-7).

High up in the oak woods of western Tuscany, where today only hunters go, the University of Siena is currently excavating the abandoned early medieval village of Miranduolo. The scene is almost surreal. A toppled twelfth-century tower dominates the exposed hilltop. Around it are the tell-tale post-holes, cut into the rock, revealing the presence of substantial post-built structures pre-dating the tower (Valenti 2004: 50-6). But the jumble of holes, some filled with carbonised botanical remains and microscopic fragments of hemp sacks, is not what catches the eye. Improbable as it seems in this unlikely location, a huge u-shaped ditch perhaps 5 metres deep and 6 metres across, similar to one recently found around the contemporary Lombard monastery Nonantola (Gelichi, Librenti and Gabrielli 2004: fig. 3), separates the core of an outcrop on which the later tower sits from the little tongue of land beyond. The meaning of the ditch at first perplexed the excavators. Such is its vaunting ambition that it could not have been for defence. Rather, they concluded, its intention was to reinforce the status of the Carolingian era lord who made a manor within the earlier hilltop ensemble of timber and sunken-floored buildings. It was a gesture consistent with the parvenu feudal authority that Tuscan lords were beginning to exhibit elsewhere in this region.

Carolingian intervention is just as evident far to the east at the monastery at Mosaburg in south-western Hungary. The settlement, located in the marshes along the Zala river, was built by Priwina of Nitra who had been expelled from Moravia in 830 (Szöke, Wedepohl and Kronz 2004). He had escaped across the Danube with the Frankish prefect Ratbod and around 838-40, Louis the Pious granted him land to build. The settlement

1

was dominated by a great church dedicated in 850. About five years later 'builders, carpenters, smiths and artists' were sent to Priwina by Liupram, archbishop of Salzburg, to construct a church at the burial site of the martyr, Hadrian. Beyond the apse of the great church recent excavations revealed the remains of a glass workshop that in form and production bears so many similarities to the early ninth-century glass workshop found to one side of San Vincenzo Maggiore, the great abbey-church of the Benedictine monastery of San Vincenzo al Volturno on the northern limits of the Principate of Benevento (Hodges 1997a: 134). Separated by huge distances, the similarities, best illustrated in a table of chemical composition of early medieval soda-lime glass, could not be more telling.

No less improbable are the broadly contemporary remains from Borg on the Lofoten Islands, well into the Arctic circle. The great timber long hall, now gloriously rebuilt for visitors, when excavated in the 1980s revealed connections far and wide: Frankish glass, a tin-foil decorated Tating ware pitcher, south Norwegian whetstones best known from the ninth-century Danish emporium of Hedeby, and gold filigree metalwork of the finest Baltic smithing. Judging from these finds, Borg, in as unlikely a location as Mirandolo in Tuscany, exhibited its Viking-age affluence in the ninth century with pride. The excavated evidence provides tangible evidence of a place sympathetically described by the Lofoten islander Ottar, when he visited King Alfred's West Saxon court in the 890s (Munch, Johansen and Roesdahl 2003).

New archaeological investigations throughout Europe show that such acts of grandiosity are not uncommon and take different forms. One further example merits mentioning: the Vrina Plain – the southernmost experiment in Albania by Chinese engineers during the cultural revolution to make featureless maize-growing lands out of the seemingly timeless salt marshes (Fig. 1.1). Here, new excavations by the Butrint Foundation show that the marshes were probably first drained by order of the irrepressible Emperor Augustus shortly after his victory over Mark Anthony at the battle of Actium in 31 BC to serve a new veteran colony at Butrint. In the ruins of the late antique colony an elegant aisled church with a fine mosaic was made here. The discovery of the church should not surprise us. Here as in many regions of the Mediterranean, the Church exhibited a strong hold in the changing social dynamics of the later Roman community (Bowden 2003). However, while most of Butrint was abandoned – a history consistent with all other Adriatic sea ports – this church was partially maintained almost certainly to mark a crossing-point in the marshes on the route into the mountainous interior (Hodges, Bowden and Lako 2004; McCormick 2001: 534). Within its narthexes and aisles the excavators found ninth- to eleventh-century dwellings and workshops, conspicuously rich in Byzantine bronze *folles*, simple metalwork and imported pottery from the Salento peninsula of Italy. Like the tell-tale material culture of Borg in the earlier ninth century, these finds conform

2

1. Introduction: new light on the Dark Ages?

1.1. View of Butrint and the Vrina Plain beyond.

to a pattern familiar from other places. Notably, the histogram of coins from Butrint resembles that from Corinth with a striking revival of Byzantine coins dating from the later ninth century (Sanders 2003). More remarkably, this pattern, an expression no doubt of Byzantine revival under the Macedonian emperors (Harvey 1989; Laiou 2002), is mirrored by a similarly striking incidence of Byzantine *folles* – from the new excavations undertaken in the 1990s at the middle Swedish emporium of Birka (Ambrosiani and Clarke 1992).

What do all these places with their farflung connections have in common? Firstly, they belong to a new age in which medieval archaeology is no longer designed to illustrate history. These are sites that need to be read like books: places like chronicles that make up the fabric of the transformation of the Roman world and the beginning of the Middle Ages. Secondly, with our minds daily opened to the muse of globalism, it is no longer difficult to envisage a past which needs to be read in terms of the rise and fall of connections rather than the isolation of regions. Much of the history written in the twentieth century owed its genesis to the need for nationalist order (cf. Geary 2002). Archaeology tended to serve this history in providing a regional rhythm for the past. Now, the archaeology of unlikely places like Miranduolo, Mosaburg, Borg and Butrint provides compelling reason to re-read the history of our teachers, taking account of our great fortune to be the first generation to witness the discovery of so

3

many new places that shed light on the first millennium. It is as if a new library of chronicles and lives has been chanced upon.

This book aims, through a series of snapshots taken across western Europe, to re-examine the sixth to ninth centuries. If there is one thrusting contention, it is that the discontinuity between antiquity and the early Middle Ages, coupled with the development afterwards, punctuated by the intervention of remarkable individuals such as Charlemagne, led to the formation of a sustainable European economy based upon a shared culture. This thesis, as will be already apparent, takes a very particular approach to the past. Emmanuel Le Roy Ladurie commented wryly that there are two kinds of historian: parachutists and truffle-hunters. The former observe the past from afar, slowly floating down to earth. The latter, transfixed by the discovery of buried treasures, keep their noses close to the ground. Not unnaturally, these two kinds of historian often find it difficult to work together. This book comprises several examples of parachuting as well as three examples of truffling at the monastery of San Vincenzo al Volturno. In each case, the intention is to re-read a historical issue using newly acquired archaeological data.

Time's arrow

A word of caution: as we seek out connections, one further generalisation on methodology must be mentioned. Historians are invariably seduced into linking one point in their texts with another. Finding connections through time makes sense. As a result, texts inevitably favour continuities as opposed to discontinuities, especially in the ethno-histories of pre-modern times. In the absence of quantified data of the kind provided by censuses, for example, it is difficult though of course not impossible to chart discontinuities and changing rhythms. Archaeology, on the other hand, gives emphasis to discontinuities: one layer is replaced by another; one measured building form is abandoned in favour of another; one quantifiable type of pottery is succeeded by another.

Now, of course, numerous historians of early medieval Europe have recognised the importance of measuring their data (cf. Devroey 2003; McCormick 2001). A telling illustration is Paolo Delogu's (2000) important quantification of the references in the *Liber Pontificalis* to prestige or luxury items registered as gifts to Rome's eighth- and ninth-century churches. The quantification shows a palpable rise in the consumption of such items by the later eighth and early ninth centuries, dropping off sharply in the mid-ninth century. Equally, archaeologists have been commonly seduced into interpreting long occupation of a site as an index of continuity, and only in recent years have started to measure the evolving and changing scale of each settlement episode. For example, the Iron Age village of Vorbasse in Jutland was occupied for almost a millennium, but the arrangement of the many settlement episodes culminating in the

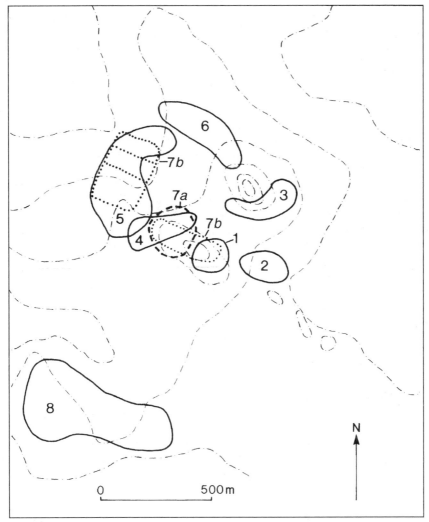

1.2. Vorbasse: phases of the shifting settlement. Area 1: first century BC; Area 2: first century AD; Area 3: second century AD; Area 4: third century AD; Area 5: fourth-fifth centuries AD; Area 6: sixth-seventh centuries AD; Area 7a: eighth-ninth centuries AD; Area 7b: eleventh century AD; Area 8: the village of Vorbasse after the eleventh century.

major Viking Age community altered remarkably over the course of the forty or fifty generations that lived here (cf. see Hamerow 2002: 55-7) (Fig. 1.2).

In the chapters that follow, a central tenet of the many hypotheses is that time's arrow must be measured by archaeologists, as best we can. Continuity, a theme of most archaeological research in the 1970s and

1980s, is now redundant; our role is to punctuate the chronological patterns of sites, making measured sense of our explicit samples of regions, communities and households through time. These measures then provide an invaluable foothold on the familiar histories, often motivated by political reasoning.

The rise of medieval archaeology

In 1945 the archaeology of the period between the fall of the Roman empire and the High Middle Ages (*c.* AD 1000), familiarly known as the Dark Ages, effectively did not exist. The material culture of post-Roman Europe was for the most part known only by a miscellany of brooches and funerary pots from unscientifically excavated cemeteries and an array of liturgical objects kept in church treasuries. Added to this, there were architectural studies of churches where archaeologists had made rather poor excavations to elucidate their histories. Sixty years on and early medieval archaeology is a standard course in European universities, and well-represented in countless museums. Today, archaeological evidence compiled from many research excavations and numerous salvage sites is used by historians to reconstruct all aspects of the transformation of the Roman world.

New light on the Dark Ages owes much to the transformation of Europe itself since 1945. The rebuilding of war-torn European towns provided an unparalleled opportunity to excavate bombed sites to investigate the layers of history stretching back to their foundation. By the 1970s, as the European Union took shape, it was clear that archaeology illuminated crucial centuries embracing the fall of the Roman empire and the makings of medieval nation states.

Until recently the history of Dark Age scholarship has taken one of two different approaches since the beginning of the century: either an art historical or an economic history approach. Up until the 1970s the commonplace portrayal of the Dark Ages owed everything to an art historical paradigm rather than a historical one. Art historians emphasised the contrasting notions of a civilised Roman world and a barbaric medieval one. They tended to be awe-struck by classical antiquity – by its architecture, fine art, sculpture, and its monumental scale, and deeply unimpressed by its demise leading to a world bereft of monumentality. This approach resulted in catalogues of buildings and objects: for example, corpuses of Anglo-Saxon churches and Early Christian churches in Rome as well as corpuses of Anglo-Saxon funerary pots, Byzantine ivories and Merovingian (Frankish) jewellery. The buildings and objects, in effect, were deployed to illuminate the margins of a cultural history described by a miscellany of contemporary early medieval sources.

Nevertheless, a number of historians, since the early years of this century, have described the period from a different point of view. Inter-war

6

1. Introduction: new light on the Dark Ages?

historians such as Marc Bloch and Henri Pirenne attempted to reassess the transformation of the Roman world and the making of the Middle Ages. Their essential conclusion was that in the eclipse of the Roman empire the foundations of modern European culture were laid. Bloch and Pirenne, for example, deployed the documentary sources assiduously published in the nineteenth century to show that the early Middle Ages were anything but primitive. While the original written texts (mostly chronicles charting early monastic histories) described primeval conditions, with an emphasis upon pagan migrants, brutal pirates and the like, the historians, making use of land charters and administrative texts, stressed the complex social organisation of Europe's new villages and the far-reaching effects of a new class of merchant-adventurers.

Even before 1945 certain archaeologists were influenced by this innovative historical approach. Two figures merit mention. In 1937 Holger Arbman, then in Stockholm Museum, published an important account of the impact on Viking-age Sweden of the ninth-century Carolingian Renaissance using archaeological evidence (Arbman 1937), principally from nineteenth-century excavations at the central Swedish emporium of Birka. At much the same time the young German scholar, Herbert Jankuhn, used the excavations of the Danish trading town of Haithabu (now in Germany) – a classic Dark Age site – to illustrate how Carolingian, Slavic and Viking merchants participated together in the complex ninth-century Baltic Sea economy.

Of course, these first attempts to interpret the archaeological evidence invariably perpetrated a primitive view of early medieval society. For example, the excavators of Hamwic, Anglo-Saxon Southampton – a 40-hectare eighth- to ninth-century trading town – were actively seeking the traces of pit-dwelling townsfolk in the excavations of bomb-sites made in the late 1940s. Indeed, ten years later, the first volume of the distinguished British scientific journal *Medieval Archaeology* contained an essay suggesting that the Anglo-Saxons lived, more or less like troglodytes, in pit-houses (see now Hamerow 2002: 46). (In fact, archaeologists would soon recognise that the pit-houses were annexes, invariably for storage, to large timber halls which could only be identified when the post-settings of the structures were revealed in large area excavations as opposed to the confines of narrow trenches. They exist from Scandinavia to the Salento peninsula in south-east Italy: cf. Arthur 2004: 117.) Puzzled by such revelations, one provocative Viking-period historian commented that archaeology was merely an expensive way of illustrating what historians already knew.

Academic attitudes to the early Middle Ages altered as a number of large-scale excavations revealed the extraordinary ability of the people of this age to forge a new identity for Europe. Of the many major research excavations, a few certainly became benchmarks, convincing historians that the written sources merited re-evaluation (cf. Duby 1974). In each case the excavations brought to life the complex nature of European society – this was a world that was rather different to the brief written descriptions. Among the most notable excavations are W.A. van Es's of the seventh- to ninth-century emporium at Dorestad at the confluence of the Lek and Rhine (van Es 1990; see Chapter 5 below); Brian Hope-Taylor's excavations of the seventh-century Northumbrian royal palace at Yeavering (Hope-Taylor 1977); and the painstaking excavations of an insula of (central) Rome, the Crypta Balbi (Manacorda 2001). These are not Pompeiis in the strict sense, but places characterised by post-holes, rudimentary walls, beaten earth floors and rubbish pits. These sites test the archaeologist's ability to interpret vestigial evidence, and infuse it with historical significance. But the archaeology of each of these places invariably fleshes out the bald written record, and, together with countless studies of ceramics, glassware and other objects, as well as systematic field surveys of regions as diverse as western Brittany and the Libyan pre-Sahara, have together constituted a body of information that in some respects is now more revealing than any contemporary account.

Archaeology, as the recent European Science Foundation workshops on 'The Transformation of the Roman World' showed, is compelling historians to re-read their texts (Christie 2004b: 1-2). The loss of innocence is, perhaps, most apparent in three areas.

The collapse of the Roman empire

Texts seek to ascribe the end of the Roman empire to the invasions and migrants – tribal peoples like the Angles, Goths, Huns and Lombards who travelled from central Europe (outside the Roman empire) to settle in niches inside the Roman frontier. Edward Gibbon's eighteenth-century enlightenment saga of the decline and fall reinforced this dramatic history. The paradigm still has its supporters, puzzling though this is to archaeologists like Helena Hamerow, who recently concluded: 'Are there really archaeologists who still envisage mass Germanic invasions of a depopulated Britain, or who believe that people who buried their dead in a style originating on the European mainland were invariably immigrants? Current views seem to... accept that the roles played by migration and endogenous processes in the formation of what we have come to call early Anglo-Saxon England were highly complex and varied regionally, and that generalising models, while useful, are by themselves inadequate to explain what really happened' (2004: 311).

Of course there are still archaeologists who conclude that new brooch types equate to new cultures and, then, equate these cultures with historic migrants that sustain origin myths for modern nations. Archaeologists in Albania, a country cut off from western Europe between 1945 and 1991, have made much of the sub-Roman Komani culture (see Chapter 4 below). These (undocumented) peoples, they deduced on the most tenuous grounds, were a link between the prehistoric Illyrians and the Albanians first mentioned in an eleventh-century Byzantine chronicle. The type fossils in question are decorated metalwork that, it is now clear, belong to a pan-European phase of jewellery production extending from the Adriatic coast to the Caucasus (Daim 2000; see also Schutz 2004). With strong Byzantine elements, like the so-called Slavic pottery of the same period, these pieces show the connections that existed in the sixth to tenth centuries across the breadth of the Balkans. As for the migrations and the movements of peoples, as Hamerow acknowledged, the picture is complicated. One illustration reinforces this point: excavations in the Crypta Balbi, Rome, found discarded moulds for seventh-century fibulae in the rubbish middens of the church of S. Pensilis (Delogu 1997: 429-30). Fibulae from these moulds, meanwhile, are known from the archetypal Lombard cemeteries two hundred kilometres away at Nocera Umbra. In short, the archaeology warns us not to draw simple conclusions, equating peoples with objects, but to seek to construct measured models of relations in an age when new social conditions were taking shape.

The context for these new social conditions was the bewilderingly catastrophic collapse of the Roman empire. Before the Second World War emphasis was given to the great phase of classical sites spanning the first century BC and first century AD when the empire was shaped by the Emperor Augustus and his immediate descendants. In the past thirty years the emphasis has changed: thanks to well-dated ceramics, the final episodes of places as diverse as Antioch, Athens, Carthage, Ephesus and Rome, when examined as part of changes around the Mediterranean as a whole, show Edward Gibbon's *Decline and Fall* to be essentially a caricature (see now Hordern and Purcell 2000). The economic crisis of the western Roman empire in the third century – an age typified by intense inflation, civil unrest and political instability – was not only a stimulus to invest in the eastern empire focussed upon Constantinople (modern Istanbul), but, inevitably, created problems for the peoples beyond the frontiers. These peoples had counted upon long-standing relations with the well-run Roman provinces. Klavs Randsborg's seminal study, *Europe in the First Millennium* (1991), vividly illustrates how the civil unrest and economic tensions experienced in the western provinces duly impacted upon an arc of barbarian communities from southern Scandinavia to the Caucasus. Such seismic circumstances also had an impact upon the kingdoms east of the empire with which the Romans had increasingly strained relations. Not surprisingly, hoarding practice beyond the Roman frontiers, for example, invariably correlates to economic or social upheaval within it. Put under pressure as trade and exchange with the empire diminished, those peoples beyond the frontier reacted by forcing their way into the provinces to benefit, as best they might, from any dwindling opportunities such as gaining entitlement to land.

The archaeology of the fourth to seventh centuries in much of Europe

9

traces the synthesis of two very different cultures, Roman and Germanic. New rural communities were created in marginal areas, many of them introducing the essential architectural and material characteristics of the German peoples (see Bowden, Lavan and Machado 2004; Christie 2004a; Hamerow 2002 for overviews). The wealth of archaeology charting the transformation of the European landscape and its communities is now impressive. No less impressive is the evidence for the transformation of many later Roman towns from Spain to the Near East and from Carthage to York where the rise of churches appears to have gone hand in hand with the end of the so-called Roman house and the introduction of more modest buildings made of cheap materials (wood, rubble or pisé), initially described by archaeologists as the homes of squatters. The new configurations of urban communities after the later fourth century tend to pre-figure medieval towns, although it is now clear that virtually every Roman centre was either reduced to small-scale elite homesteads by the later seventh century (if not before) or totally deserted (as described in the celebrated Anglo-Saxon poem, 'The Ruin').

The pattern of new rural colonisation, the steady deterioration of imperial standards of civic life, the rhythms of Mediterranean and pan-European trade and so on conjure up a picture of decline and fall that, for example, bears comparison with the dismal collapse of the ex-Soviet Union into a mosaic of impoverished (and politically confused) states. Yet many of those living beyond the frontiers of the old Roman empire were far from primitive. One compelling illustration is fifth-century Denmark. Modern excavations have revealed a great deal about the later Roman period in this region. For example, the region boasted emporia such as Lundenborg on the island of Funen, an expansionist agrarian regime and Baltic-wide trading connections (Nielsen, Randsborg and Thrane 1994). Recent archaeology shows that this was far from a primitive region, abandoned by destitute tribesmen who sought greener pastures in Britain. On the contrary, the Jutes, who quit western Denmark and sailed to sub-Roman Britain, discovered primitive conditions by their standards: a ruinous countryside, deserted towns, and a political system that had devolved in cartographic terms into a patchwork quilt of tribes.

Coupled with economic and social instability was demographic change. The archaeological evidence controversially emphasises that the later Roman population declined dramatically. This is most conspicuous in Italy where many scholars have sought an explanation for such change in the documented plagues of the sixth century, but this may be only half the story. Long before the plagues in Britain, for example, the population was in headlong decline: an estimated three to six million Roman Britons in *c.* AD 300 had dwindled to no more than about half a million so-called Anglo-Saxons by *c.* AD 600. Miles of abandoned Roman fields and countless farmsteads, like the deserted cities, show that Britain's demographic cycle resembles at a slightly earlier date the pattern now familiar from numerous field surveys of Gaul, Italy and Spain (cf. Christie 2004b: 8-10). More recently, it seems to be the same for much of the Balkans, as recent surveys in Albania and Greece indicate. In short, the strange demise of Roman Europe illuminates as much the insubstantial foundations of its political, social and economic systems as the superficial embeddedness of its culture. In common with the ex-Soviet Union, much of which has dissolved in a decade, the Roman empire was an extraordinary but artificial apparatus, readily dismantled.

Finally, there is irrefutable evidence of environmental change. Around much of the Mediterranean harbours were deserted due to silting; great swathes of landscape, too, were abandoned as both the written sources and extensive field surveys now confirm. Once known as the Younger Fill, alluvial deposits characterise this era, bearing witness to the increasingly powerful discharge of rivers and, quite probably, to the widespread failure to maintain agricultural systems such as terracing. It is tempting, of course, to link the new conditions to climatic change, but this remains to be demonstrated. What is clear is that by the later tenth century there was a European-wide increase in temperatures that, in particular, facilitated the exploitation of uplands.

The rise of the North Sea region

Over the last sixty years, perhaps the greatest archaeological discoveries pertaining to early medieval Europe have been the sites of the first trading towns around the North Sea. These appear to take shape as the last archaeological hints of activities in the great Roman ports of the Mediterranean disappear. Notwithstanding the enduring focus of historians working with texts upon Italy and the Mediterranean, the motor of European activity seems to have passed in the seventh century to the regions around the North Sea. Archaeologists and historians of rural society have yet to come to terms with these places. Such sites challenge the otherwise readily measured character of a society conforming to readily comprehensible historical models (cf. Anderton 1999). Yet the discovery of these North Sea trading towns, as rich with material culture as the Mediterranean ones were at their Roman zenith, have certainly transformed the economic history of the age. Places such as Dorestad (Netherlands), Ribe (Denmark), Quentovic (France), and in England, Lundunwic (London), Hamwic (Southampton), Ipswich and Eoforwic (York) were precursors of Europe's medieval market towns.

No one now doubts that Roman town life had collapsed in north-west Europe by the sixth century. The rebirth of North Sea trade was largely promoted by the Franks and their intermediaries (such as the Frisians) in the later sixth century, and hugely expanded after *c.* 670 with the foundation of emporia at Dorestad and Quentovic. W.A. van Es's great excavations at the Rhine-delta town of Dorestad in the 1960s revealed a scale and complexity hitherto unimagined. Ribe in western Denmark, though smaller in scale, imitated the Dorestad model. Apparently founded by Ongendus, a Danish king at the beginning of the eighth century, it tellingly illustrates that whatever the later Christian chroniclers wrote of pagan primeval conditions in Denmark, the emerging kingdom could nevertheless sustain not only a regional market but also a growing international economy. Further north, the new campaign of excavations at Kaupang show the steady extension of the urban model and its adoption in south-east Norway at the limits of the North Sea world (Skre and Stylegar 2004). At the southernmost point of the trading zone, Hamwic – the emporium serving the West Saxon kings – still appears to have been the largest of the English emporia, with a grid of gravelled streets. Excavations like those at Six Dials in the 1970s, towards the northern end of the forty-hectare town, showed that a variety of crafts were practised in each timber hall.

The chronology of these new places is especially significant. The emporia conspicuously prospered in *c.* 670-725, suffered a recession in the period 725-750, experienced a boom as Charlemagne (the Carolingian king from 771 to 814) fused Europe's different regions together into a new Holy Roman empire, and mostly fell into terminal decline after the 820s. The well-preserved dendrochronological record of Dorestad, Haithabu and Ribe, like the ample coin sequences of Hamwic and Ipswich, reveals a boom-and-bust rhythm to the trade before the creation of new inland markets in the early to mid-ninth century eclipsed the importance of many of these monopolistic coastal towns (however, see Coupland 2002 on Quentovic). Ironically, most of these early towns, hitherto non-places in Marc Augé's sense (1995), like modern airports ignored in contemporary accounts (Hodges 2000: 70), are first recorded in the Viking age, as in their indifferent economic condition they suffered at the hands of pirates.

South of the Alps, Michael McCormick's encyclopaedic study of the Mediterranean region in this period invites speculation that the North Sea emporium was possibly emulated by the Venetians, and perhaps even at Commacchio at the Adriatic mouth of the river Po (Balzaretti 1996). Once Venice lay under Carolingian hegemony it undoubtedly grew fast, as several new excavations and a recent topographical survey have shown (Ammerman 2003). But was it a Dorestad, an entrepot with its merchants venturing out to Byzantium and Islam, the mirror-image of Dorestad's Frisian merchants in Scandinavia? Little is available to indicate this as yet, although distinctive objects such as Frankish swords and Venetian glass in ninth-century Croatian inhumation cemeteries offer a glimpse of the entrepot's immediate connections and perhaps its bid to engage with the Bulgars (cf. Milošević 2005) 2001: 733). Here is an intriguing archaeological riddle that compels us to ask whether for some centuries after *c.*

700, Italy was eclipsed by the engine of activity centred in the Rhineland. Certainly, on the face of it the Lombard aristocracy were investing in towns like Lucca and Pavia (and, seemingly, not in the countryside), yet to the archaeologist's eye eighth-century Lombardy itself appears wholly underdeveloped by comparison with the regions around the North Sea. Even by the ninth century the archaeological evidence is modest, if largely non-existent. Indeed, taking a wide-angled view of the Italian economy, the underdevelopment is most conspicuous in the case of coin-finds and hoards. A recent volume devoted to treasure in this period has attempted to explain the apparent poverty of treasures in comparison with, say, the Frankish regions, Anglo-Saxon England or, indeed, the North Sea littoral (Gelichi and La Rocca 2004). But the poverty of treasures is even more conspicuous given the negligible numbers of eighth- and ninth-century coins found in Italian archaeological excavations, compared to, say, England or France in the same period (Rovelli 2000; 2004). By the later eighth century Rome's churches were great consumers of imported luxury goods, as Delogu has shown (2000), but this wealth registered in the *Liber Pontificalis* has not yet been evident in the material culture found in recent excavations in the Crypta Balbi or the Forum of Nerva.

One explanation advanced to explain this situation is that southern Europe was more socially advanced that northern Europe. In the south investment was being made in social formations and amassing landed property, whereas gift-exchange was still a prominent instrument of relations in the north (thus accounting for the amounts of moveable wealth in circulation (and therefore lost and evident to the archaeologist) (Baldassarri and Favilla 2004: 172). Alessia Rovelli convincingly refutes this (2004), pointing out that Italian sites are not only materially poor in coins but also in imported goods such as ceramics or soapstone transported inter-regionally. In other words, the wealth of early medieval Italy may have been over-estimated. Indeed, following Rovelli it is tempting to conclude that the great European pre-eminence of classical Italy, repeated in an entirely different form in the High to Later Middle Ages, has clouded our view of its circumstances between *c.* 600 and 1000 when, with obvious exceptions such as Rome, the peninsula looked northwards and to the east for direction and development?

The origins of medieval villages and markets

Early medieval archaeology has made its mark over the past half-century by tracing origins: identifying the moment when farms, villages, towns, and monasteries first took shape. In England, the earliest Anglo-Saxon villages such as West Stow (Suffolk) occupied a settlement pattern determined in Roman times. But in the seventh century there was the so-called 'Middle Saxon shuffle' when new sites (with notably larger dwellings:

Hamerow 2004: 302-3) with richer farmlands were selected, most of which have remained until today. The same shuffle has been noted in the Merovingian territories (Louis 2004; Perin 2004). In Italy and much of southern Europe, on the other hand, new villages were not formally recorded until the tenth century (the process of village-formation known as *incastellamento*). For several decades archaeologists favoured the theory that the villages were created from dispersed homesteads belonging to the sixth to ninth centuries. However, numerous new excavations show that the origins of these tenth-century *castelli* lie in villages created by collectives of peasants as the fabric of the Roman provinces ceased to exist (Arthur 2004; Francovich and Hodges 2003). The same appears to be the case in the Balkans. The Middle Saxon shuffle, therefore, was not unique. It was part of an European response to the changing political and economic axes of the post-Roman world, pre-figuring what Pierre Toubert has recently described as the agricultural revolution and the formation of 'le grand domaine' of the Carolingian era (Toubert 2004).

This pattern is echoed to some extent in the foundation of Europe's market towns. The emporia, like the formative villages, denote monopolistic regional forms of the familiar medieval towns. The boom in town-building came in the wake of the ubiquitous ninth-century Arab and Viking attacks. Planned towns such as Winchester and York, to take two famous English examples, have been documented in great detail by teams of archaeologists. Their street grids, property tenements and craft operations all reveal an explosion of tenth-century civic activity – a new phenomenon widely repeated throughout Europe's regions.

Hundreds of town and village excavations throughout Europe over the past sixty years have charted the significant economic and social transformation launched in the later ninth century. What remains to be illuminated are the intermediary regional precursors of these market towns (as opposed to the international emporia such as Dorestad, Hamwic and Ribe, described above). In other words, how were major monopolistic centres, located in places to maximise long-distance trade, transformed into networks of markets familiar from the High Middle Ages onwards (through which taxes were levied), serving regions? The first archaeological illustrations are intriguing and invite us to look beyond the norms we might expect to special sites such as monasteries and palaces as the nodes around which these new markets were first administered. The particularly extensive and well-documented excavations at San Vincenzo al Volturno – a Benedictine monastic city – in central Italy are helpful in illustrating this theme.

Covering as much as ten hectares at its zenith, this ninth-century Carolingian Renaissance centre seems to have had not only a large abbey-church and hundreds of monks, but also workshops where craftsmen produced prestige goods for marketing throughout its region. It is the

1.3. Aerial view of San Vincenzo al Volturno, Italy, showing the location of the monastic city and its *borgo*.

nature of these workshops which galvanise our interest. Like the workshops in the emporia at Hamwic and Ribe, it is tempting to see them as the locus of artisans serving all sectors of the community. Yet closer inspection of the output from these shops – enamels, regalia and ivories, among other things – suggests that these were prestige goods designed for a specific economic purpose, for it is not at all clear that the objects were greatly used within the monastic city itself. San Vincenzo, like other great monastic cities of the Carolingian age, appears to have been as much a monopolistic centre, at the heart of its region, as the North Sea emporia were invariably at liminal locations. San Vincenzo's *borgo* beyond the monastic precinct appears to have covered an area as extensive as the ritual zone (Fig 1.3). As in the North Sea emporia, large numbers of artisans and peasants – serving the monkish community – were assembled. But as numerous historians have shown, the (well-documented) monastic city, best-known from the schematic Plan of St Gall dating to *c.* 820, was as short-lived a phenomenon as the emporium. San Vincenzo was no different. Its community was in transition by the mid-ninth century. Indeed, its economic character, as the excavations of its workshops show, was altering significantly, prefiguring the familiar feudal strategy of later centuries. Finally, it is perhaps no coincidence that it is monastic cities such as the emporia that are the most conspicuous victims of the Arab and Viking attacks. Again (in common with the emporia), it may be no coincidence that many of these monasteries were experiencing economic and political difficulties. This was certainly the case at San Vincenzo when its place on the European stage was summarily terminated on 10 October 881 by a warband of Arabs in league with the Bishop of Naples, who brutally sacked the settlement.

San Vincenzo al Volturno, like the short-lived and materially rich monastic settlement at Flixborough, Lincolnshire (Lovelock 2002), appears to belong to a growing number of elite sites, mostly identified by metal-detectorists, described as 'productive sites'. Thanks largely to the UK's 1997 Portable Antiquities Scheme, actively involving rather than alienating metal-detectorists, the volume of archaeological information about 'productive sites' is now quite astonishing. Of course the reporting has concentrated upon coin-finds and decorated (i.e. datable) metalwork; ceramics understandably receive scant treatment. Most of these 'productive sites' – places where coinage and prestige goods are lost – appear to belong to the increasing exercise of elite-controlled systems embedded in the hinterlands of coastal emporia such as Hamwic, London and even York. Further afield in Denmark, Lars Jørgensen (2003) has described the multi-period royal manor at Tissø as a similar category of site. Here the spectacular excavations give material character to Tina Thurston's (2001) anthropological geography of embryonic state-formation in south Scandinavia. The excavations also show how complex rural estate centres were in central Denmark at the zenith of the Carolingian era.

'Productive sites' are plainly not centres for production like, for example, the ninth-century workshops inside and, significantly, outside the early medieval monastic precinct at San Vincenzo al Volturno, but rather places of distribution or, more accurately, redistribution. As the coin histograms for Middle Saxon England compiled by the numismatist Mark Blackburn (2003) illustrate, these places were inland versions of extensively excavated early emporia such as Dorestad, Hamwic and Ribe. Given the absence of artisanal debris, in contrast to the emporia, there is good reason to suppose that the 'productive sites' were central-places of lesser importance – eighth- to ninth-century periodic fairs, perhaps, that served tribal sections, some way down the dendritically constructed chiefdom economies. These sites provide a measure of the substantial volume of coinage in circulation in Middle Saxon England on the eve of the Danish invasion (as the numismatist Michael Metcalf's (2003) trend model of coin-finds from England and Blackburn's coin histograms also illustrate). In addition, the conspicuous decorated metalwork lost in these places is a telling demonstration of the importance of jewellery in these societies, such that, with its abundance, silver pieces might be readily overlooked when clearing up the site of a fair or a feast. The comparative rarity of jewellery of later periods, by comparisons, makes such discard patterns appear to be an episodic phase of conspicuous consumption on the eve of new economic practices.

Re-reading early medieval history

As archaeologists, we no longer need to illuminate the margins of history. On the one hand, after sixty years of intensive research we have at our disposal sites that provide a new angle on the rhythms of the age. Places such as Mirandolo, Borg and Butrint, in common with Ribe and San Vincenzo al Volturno, cast light upon the early Middle Ages beyond the places controlled by those who wrote the familiar textual histories. More to the point, as Elizabeth Rio-Zadora has recently contended (2003), we are beginning to comprehend new forms of evidence from the archaeology that bear little resemblance to the many different terms employed by historians writing at the time. This is hardly surprising. These forms, such as villages founded in the seventh century outside elite control or even emporia which for the most part appear (unlike later towns) to be non-places resembling modern airports in contemporary chronicles, must now determine how we read the written perceptions of the age. No longer can the making of the Middle Ages be conceived without understanding how the medieval peasantry made villages and then surrendered their author-ity to an urban-based elite. No longer can any reading of the Carolingian Renaissance ignore the signal role of the excessively monopolistic charac-ter of the monastic cities. No longer can the dialectical relationship between the Carolingian Europe and the Arabs and Vikings be reduced to regarding the latter as simply 'the other', to use the late Edward Said's pejorative description. From the Arctic Circle to North Africa, the Carolin-gian impact – reduced so often to the symbolic image of the elephant given as a gift by the Abbasid caliphate to Charlemagne, was far more substan-tial, as Michael McCormick (2001), re-working the Pirenne thesis, has now shown. In many parts of western Europe, such as Borg, it gave rise to an aberrant moment of flourishing internationalism; in other places, such as Mirandolo, it favoured a platform for conspicuous political and economic development.

To re-phrase Hayden White's meta-historical approach, there are many different ways of writing history, each as plausible and even contradictory. Archaeology now helps us to re-read not only the familiar chronicles but also the secondary sources, and to construct a new paradigm. This is not a post-modern reading but rather an approach that brings together written records and objects, to formulate a textual history that, in the case of the early Middle Ages, permits us to comprehend how the Roman empire was transformed into what Henri Pirenne tellingly described as the scaffolding of modern Europe.

Pirenne and the question of demand in the sixth century

As I turn, however, to a new endeavour which is fraught with difficulty and is in fact extraordinarily hard to cope with, ... I find myself stammering and shrinking as far from it as possible, as I weigh the chances that such things are now to be written by me as will seem neither credible nor possible to men of a later generation; and especially when the mighty stream of time renders the story somewhat ancient (Procopius, *The Anecdota* or *Secret History* [Dewing 1935: i.4]).

Introduction

The European Science Foundation (ESF) project devoted to 'The Transformation of the Roman World' brought together more than a hundred scholars from all parts of Europe to re-examine a familiar problem. One theme which the project could not overlook was the question of production and distribution. The importance of economic history in the twentieth-century historiography of this period requires no introduction. The shadow of the Pirenne thesis is, if anything, as far-reaching today as it has ever been. A glance at recent studies in the field confirms this. Apart from historians of the transformation responding to this theme (McCormick 2001; Verhulst 1989), numismatists (Metcalf 1994; Noonan 1994) and archaeologists (Hodges and Whitehouse 1996) still find Pirenne's over-arching model seductive in parts. In some respects, Pirenne's theme, rather like Edward Gibbon's *Decline and Fall*, has stood the test of time despite its argument being conspicuously flawed, because it binds together antiquity and the Middle Ages, southern and northern Europe, history and material culture. It bridges historical and geographical divisions.

It is inappropriate to develop a critique of the durability of Pirenne's thesis here. It is evident that many other historians were engaged in equally ground-breaking research as Henri Pirenne fashioned his rather simplistic argument (Delogu 1998). This territory had already fascinated Werner Sombart and Max Weber, Alfons Dopsch and Geoffrey Dawson. At the same time, Pirenne made ineffective use of the available material evidence, disregarding, for example, the work of Rostovzeff in the Mediterranean and Holwerda in the Netherlands. But, paradoxically, these flaws have worked to Pirenne's advantage. *Mohammed and Charlemagne* is a sketch wherein each of us can find some fulfilment in its holistic scope.

But why does Pirenne's unfinished sketch continue to hold such fasci-

HENRI PIRENNE

2.1. Caricature of Henri Pirenne.

nation for us when its central tenets are so palpably flawed? The answer
has much to do with the present state of the historical sciences. In
comparison with the 1920s and 1930s, there is a much larger academic
community concerned with this period of European history. The social
dynamics of studying the period have changed. Academic demands have
altered as a result. We are all familiar with the individualised thrust of
our disciplines, and the response to increased student numbers as Europe
shifts from its emphasis upon manufacturing to service industries. This is
an age of deconstruction as well as the fragmentation and regrouping of
disciplines. The romance of Europe – as a historical theme and, simultaneously, an economic project – has been overshadowed in the post-war
years by preoccupation with dominance in some form or other. The individual's part in this romance is in jeopardy, or so the thesis goes. In
academic terms, the argument runs: no individual can master the source
material; look at the flaws in Pirenne's thesis. Not surprisingly, the
political trend in contemporary Europe is neither global nor nationalistic
in outlook, but regional. In every respect, our society has shunned the
empires of our immediate past, and the unedifying taint of colonialism.
Equally unsurprisingly, the trend in the historical sciences mirrors this,
albeit, paradoxically, at a time of increasing use of the World Wide Web.
In the strict sense, then, the European Science Foundation (ESF) is at
odds with our times: it aims to sustain the romance of European collaboration. It brings together scholars from different nationalities, who have a
multiplicity of specialisms. It aims to discover some common ground

beyond the parameters of the individual's nationalistic education and scholarly development. The barriers between disciplines, as between nations, are not easily broken down. In the humanities, in particular, such common ground is not easily identified, let alone acceptable to all. This is why Pirenne's thesis has such great status. It is a polyglot answer to the conception of our Europe.

Pirenne's thesis is a signpost for this group working within the framework of the ESF project on 'The Transformation of the Roman World'. We defined ourselves as seeking to devise a post-Pirenne paradigm. It is an impossible objective, which most participants considered inappropriate. Let us be quite clear: a post-Pirenne paradigm would need to define an entirely new sequence of historical relations to explain the transformation of Roman Europe. Re-interpretation on this scale is beyond us. Taking account of the present state of scientific knowledge in this field, we can realistically expect only to analyse new data and new interpretations of those data which cumulatively, in a generation or two, may make it possible to produce a new paradigm. In any case, by then 'the polyglot answer' will be anachronistic as the European Union propels greater trans-European collaboration in our research.

Having set our objective, we sought to define it more precisely by selecting time-slices where we might collaborate satisfactorily in interdisciplinary research. The first of these, in some respects the century Pirenne forgot or at least overlooked, is the sixth century. Recent archaeological excavations have transformed our understanding of this period, compelling historians with written and visual evidence to re-examine their sources.

The emphasis upon time-slices might seem anachronistic in an age concerned with processes in the past. Of course, there is a danger of overlooking *la longue durée*, as we examine transformation in such comparatively brief periods. Yet each of these time-slices serves as a framework for examining European change; for examining circumstances in northern as well as southern Europe. Examined on this geographical scale, extra-regional processes become the inevitable focus of our normal regional interests because these, as Pirenne comprehended, offer the means of explaining not only patterns, but also political action and, of course, transformations.

The sixth century

Almost by definition, colonial entanglement and struggle turn upon the difference between indigenous peoples and foreigners, natives and intruders, but recognition that this axis is fundamental should not obscure or marginalise the crucial fragmentation of knowledge and interests on both sides, the struggles which always take place within both the metropolitan project of colonialism and the indigenous project of appropriating or reacting to colonial intrusion (Thomas 1991: 205).

Pirenne forgot the sixth century. Late Roman patterns of production and distribution, in his view, had been set in the fourth or fifth centuries (Van Dam 1992). The seventh century, by contrast, witnessed the effective end of the imperial economy, and the effective reduction of imperial society to the courts of Constantinople, Ravenna and Rome (Angold 1985: 3-4). Pirenne's thesis concerned a super-power in transformation: an empire with colonies, unaffected by indigenous struggles. The reality, as we now know, was very different. The transformation of the economy of the Roman empire, in particular, is a complex history. To use the metaphor of Nicholas Thomas' provocative study of the anthropology of exchange in the Pacific between western colonial societies and indigenous peoples, this was a world of *entangled* exchanges (my italics), not one predicated upon the simple 'us/them' dichotomy between westerners and Pacific Islanders. Being a historian of the Age of Empire (Belgian, British, French, German and Russian), Pirenne, like the written sources of the later empire, favoured the 'us/them' transformation of the Roman world system. But then, in the absence of multidisciplinary sources, Pirenne possessed no grasp of the pattern of demand on the eve of this transformation. Objects of entangled exchange, understandably, were beyond the scope of his research. Using Thomas' theme as a point of reference, I will offer a few illustrations of the complex parameters of demand across the breadth of Europe in the course of this momentous century.

A glance at recent research on late antiquity confirms Bowersock's contention that 'the international revival of interest in Roman and Byzantine history between Constantine and the Arab conquest has transformed late antiquity from an exotic and neglected field into one of the most vigorous and exciting areas of current research' (Bowersock 1990: 244). This revival of interest bridges Europe. It concerns not only those, like Holy Men, who made history, but those who were, so to speak, denied it. The pattern of demand is no longer abstract, thanks to a wide range of historical and archaeological studies.

The centrifugal demands of the Byzantine court are now well-charted (cf. McCormick 1986). Likewise, the changing character of the later Roman aristocracy has attracted a good deal of attention in recent years (Marazzi 1991). Above all, there have been many studies dedicated to the power of the Church in late antiquity. Peter Brown, in particular, has championed the rise of Christianity and Holy Men in this age (Brown 1982; 1996), showing it (to cite one of his admirers) to be 'a period of extraordinary interest, which witnessed the extinction of traditional paganism, the perversion of Christianity, the introduction of ideology as a test of loyal citizenship, the spread of intolerance, institutionalised superstition and competitive asceticism' (Mango 1989). By the later fifth century the Church was embedded not only in metropolitan society but also in the countryside (Pietri 1986: 761-95). Its powerful role in economic strategies, especially in the field of reproduction strategies and inheritance, can no longer be doubted (Goody 1983). Yet, undeniably, by 500 the transformation of European society exceeded any project devised by the Church.

The sixth century is of particular interest because the imperial economy was still functioning despite the palpable collapse of imperial society. It was an age when, to quote Walter Pohl, 'the *gentes* could only define themselves *versus* the overwhelming reality of a polyethnic late Roman state' (1991: 40). Inevitably, in terms of demand as well as production and distribution, the reality was 'entangled' (Thomas 1991), more complicated than the unitary models proposed hitherto. This is most conspicuous in later Roman towns – centres of demand as well as of production-distribution, which were essentially alien to Germanic society. By 500, late Roman towns in the west had witnessed extraordinary changes, most notably the ruination of their great public monuments, while they inherited the roles of industrial *vici* as centres of production and distribution (Saguì 1993). As a result, in administrative terms, as Andrew Poulter put it 'the *poleis* of the sixth century bear little or no resemblance to the cities of the fourth, let alone the second century. They were essentially centres of imperial and ecclesiastical administration, and the civilian population appears to have been dependent upon, but largely excluded from, these Byzantine citadels. By the sixth century, it is doubtful if the urban population remembered or even understood the concept of urban self-government which had proved so attractive to the cities of the Early Empire' (Poulter 1992: 132; Ward-Perkins 1996). The emphasis was on fortification, great ecclesiastical monuments and, through investment in artisan activities, sustaining the economic umbilical cord with Constantinople.

More precisely, the late Roman town-house, with its apogee in the sixth century, embodied a hierarchy of access (Ellis 1988; 1991). Unlike the houses of the early Roman period, the late Roman aristocrat carefully defined the architectural context in which his public encounters occurred. Great effort was invested in displaying a concentration of wealth in order to underscore the aristocratic nature of patronage as well as, in Simon Ellis's view, to demonstrate overtly the ideology of the heroic host. The new taste and demands of late Roman society perplexed the excavators of San Giovanni di Ruoti in Basilicata, southern Italy (Small and Buck 1994). The plan of the Late Roman villa was altogether different in its morphology to its earlier imperial forebear. This quotation from the excavators' account explains these differences without any reference to the 'entangled' socio-economic circumstances of later antiquity:

> It is also possible that the plan of the villa points to new occupants with some un-Roman social customs. The clearest sign is the way they disposed of their garbage. The inhabitants of the previous villas followed the normal Roman practice of removing refuse from their buildings; but the occupants of the late villa at San Giovanni dumped their kitchen waste in the corridors and empty rooms, and immediately outside the entrances to the site. Most of the midden piles date to the last part of the fifth century and to the beginning of the

sixth, and belong to the second phase of this villa, but some go back to the beginning of its first phase, ca. AD 400. Even the dining customs may have changed, for if the long narrow room with a mosaic floor at the northeast end of the site is a dining-room, as seems likely, then the inhabitants must have eaten there seated beside a long table, as was the practice of Germanic barbarians, rather than reclining around a low table in traditional Roman fashion, for there is no room there for a *stibadium* (Small and Buck 1994: 4-5).

Changing attitudes to diet as well as to refuse disposal in late antiquity, tempting though it is to attribute these to ethnicity, are more reasonably the result of the changing nature of society itself (Hodges 1995b: 127-8). This has a resonance far beyond the Mediterranean regions. Ulf Näsman, for example, has cogently illustrated the close relations between Scandinavia and central Europe during this century (1998).

Concurrently, in southern Scandinavia, the relationship between the élite and the collective, as manifested in demand and taste, was also changing. Reviewing numerous excavations of timber dwellings from the later Iron Age, Frands Herschend showed that the long hall is a creation of the fourth to fifth centuries, and the norm by the sixth century as far north as central Sweden (Herschend 1994). Herschend contends that 'the hall was already the room of leadership, in an economic as well as a military sense, in the fifth century .... The interesting thing is that, centuries before we can talk of feudalism, the hall constitutes the room as a social space for the individual who in that room is the head of a nuclear family – a positive notion common to rich and poor – and not just one of a team that runs an estate .... Some time during the late Roman Iron Age, it became possible within the nuclear family to breed an individuality which acted for the collective and to make it a publicly accepted, social norm' (Herschend 1994: 195).

This individuality took other forms. The powerful, focused role of ideology in late antiquity, evident in the social ascendency of the Holy Man, reached its apogee in the politically-inspired monuments of Santa Sophia in Constantinople and San Vitale in Ravenna. It is no less evident at Gamla Uppsala in central Sweden where the putative timber temple has been found adjacent to the Vendel burial mounds. Whatever purpose this structure served, there is no doubting that it is a manifestation of its age. Equally, with time, it is highly probable that similar structures will come to light if excavations continue at Gudme on Funen – where a staggering quantity of goldwork associated with ritual practices has been found in the environs of a major hall (Nielsen, Randsborg and Thrane 1994). In her analyses of the patterns of gold hoards from Gudme, Charlotte Fabech concludes that the era of collective sacrifices of booty in bogs and wetlands ended in the fifth century: 'From about 400 religious manifestations both on dry land and wetland (gold bracteates) are related to the settlement with manorial dwelling (*sic*)' (Fabech 1994: 175).

24

2. Pirenne and the question of demand in the sixth century

This was an extraordinary period. Entangled ethnic tensions are evident in all the written sources. At the same time the place of the individual in society was becoming more prominent. Such changes encouraged a demand for prestige goods in particular. Not surprisingly then, craftsmen's quarters are as much the stuff of the archaeology of later Roman ports and towns as town houses and churches. A glassmaker occupied the grandiose latrines of the theatre of the Crypta Balbi (Saguì 1993). After identifying the wooden market stalls erected within the forum at Cherchel, Potter has tracked down the evidence for similar installations in many other North African cities of the period (Potter 1995; Ward-Perkins 1996: 11-15). Streets of shops serving the same purposes were erected in Sardis, Jerash and Palmyra, to name only a few examples (Crawford 1990; Walmsley 1996). Perhaps the most evocative discovery, illustrative of the complex economic transformation, occurred at Sardis where shop E13 was selling glass window panes on the eve of a devastating fire in *c.* 616 (Crawford 1990: 78-81). Over 350 window panes and 350 goblets were found in the ruins, indicating the capacity to produce ample capital in nearby workshops as well as the shop-owners' cash-flow capacity to purchase such a volume of merchandise. Finally, the illustration, one of many from the destruction of this extraordinary vignette of shop life in early seventh-century Sardis, reveals the nature of demand within the community, and the shopkeepers' ability to supply this demand. Citizens of Sardis had the means to purchase house-fittings and tableware.

Elsewhere in the Mediterranean the supply of commodities was by no means as buoyant, as Loseby (1998) in his studies of Marseilles has vividly illustrated. Production and distribution were inevitably affected by demand. Demand fluctuated as the aspirations of the farflung Byzantine élite were snuffed out by increasing state expenditure on the military, and the impossibly high taxation caused by this. By 600 the geopolitical implications for much of the old Roman empire were verging on the catastrophic. Traditional control was ceded in the mountains of Italy, most of the Balkans and the inland areas of North Africa. Ancient towns in these areas in the course of a generation were completely transformed. Populations dwindled dramatically, while social complexity was invariably reduced to a relic élite – local representatives of state power (Haldon 1993) – occupying the acropolis castle of a hitherto bustling urban centre. Not surprisingly, demand for commodities shrank dramatically as well. Indeed, in many areas the archaeology of consumption – notably household goods – is virtually invisible. The relic élite are scarcely a mystery to us, unlike the workforce occupying the shanty towns made within the ruined townscapes of the Mediterranean world (Haldon 1990; Ellis 1988; Ward-Perkins 1996). Invariably archaeologists have disregarded the latter as 'squatters', Slavs, Arabs and every other ethnic barbarian. But, given that in almost every case these poor quality structures – harbingers of Dark Age construction – are dated by occasional Byzantine coins and Byzantine amphorae and tableware, it is not farfetched to propose that these were the homes of the artisanal class who hung on in hope of a revival of Byzantine fortunes. The migrants, it appears, occupied new niches within the relic classical landscape, and, in keeping with these times, had recourse to minimal commodities. Such was the nature of indigenous, post-colonial demand in the entangled circumstances at the end of the sixth century in the Mediterranean basin.

A vignette of comparable misplaced aspirations has been highlighted by recent archaeological investigations in Dark Age Britain (cf. Chapter 3 below). In the early to mid-sixth century, the tribes of post-Roman western Britain entertained a short-lived contact with the Mediterranean. The objects in demand were North African and East Mediterranean (B-ware) amphorae, North African tablewares and some Mediterranean glassware. The small assemblages of amphorae and tablewares have received extraordinarily detailed attention because, being found at Tintagel and Cadbury-Camelot, they are associated with the legend of King Arthur. First, the majority of the imported wares derive from the East Mediterranean; only a small fraction emanated from North Africa (Alcock 1995: 141-3; Fulford 1989; Williams and Carreras 1995: 240-1; see now, though, Reynolds 2005: 426-9). This is consistent with the relative importance of East Mediterranean shipping vis-à-vis North African-based maritime activity by 500 (Panella 1993). Secondly, as all archaeologists have acknowledged, the quantities of sherds involved are tiny (e.g. 131 B-ware amphorae sherds from Cadbury Castle). In total the finds brought to light so far amount to no more than a few cargoes (Fulford 1989). Thirdly, just as these sherds belong to a western British culture zone, distinct in its material culture from the incipient 'Anglo-Saxon culture' of eastern England, so it is interesting to note the concurrent emergence of the hall house (Alcock 1995: 132-9) at a time when Anglo-Saxon settlements are noted for their absence of structural diversity manifested in dwellings for nuclear families (Hodges 1989: 65ff.; Hamerow 1991). In short, does the sixth-century world of King Arthur owe its lasting status to an incipient tension between the individual and the collective? Could it be a further illustration of the entangled circumstances in which demand for commodities played a part in the social transformation of the Roman world (cf. Chapter 3 below)?

These circumstances were short-lived. By the end of the century many of the 'Anglo-Saxon' tribes of southern and eastern England had entered into exchange relations with the Franks and other traders plying the Merovingian North Sea. The 'Anglo-Saxon' cemeteries after *c.* 550 were affluent with imported Byzantine, Frankish and Scandinavian gifts to the gods. Such is their number that Vera Evison argued for a Frankish invasion of England at this time (Evison 1965).

This invasion hypothesis has long since been rejected, but the presence of these objects begs an explanation. Simply put, Anglo-Saxon society was almost certainly responding to the strains of a demand for primitive valuables, as individuals sought to define themselves as late Roman aristocrats had, and as South Scandinavians were doing. From our standpoint the evidence remains largely speculative until the end of the sixth century when St Augustine arrived in Kent, introducing new, Mediterranean, temples which were placed at the disposal of the *parvenu* Anglo-Saxon élite for purposes in this life and for their privileged well-being, in common with Romano-Byzantine burial traditions, in death (Morris 1989; Deliyannis 1995). At the same time the élite responded by constructing hall houses, such as had existed for more than a century in South Scandinavia, and for some time in western Britain. Concurrently, the élite also designated type A emporia, such as Ipswich on the river Gipping, where they could administer periodic markets (Wade 1988).

The sixth century marks the moment of utmost confusion among the polyethnic cultures of Europe before the emergence of a new geopolitical order in which the Franks, Lombards and Visigoths play a pre-eminent part. Patterns of demand bear witness to the confusion. Mediterranean society embarked upon a transformation while traditional consumption and demand patterns outlived the first, dramatic episodes of transformation. These entangled circumstances touched northern and western Europe in improbable ways. South Scandinavia, as the investigations at Gudme have shown, was drawn into the complex orbit of Byzantium just as King Arthur's kingdom was. But it would be simplistic to attribute the ascendancy of the individual over the collective to such direct interactions. Rather, these touched the complex peer-polity interactions between the myriad tribes of the region (Renfrew 1986; cf. Hodges 1989).

Indeed, if there is any one conclusion to be drawn from these odd pieces taken from the geo-political jigsaw of Europe in 500-600, it is that the transformation of the Roman world triggered an astonishing diversity of responses. No doubt, instinctively aware of this as a result of his internment in a German prisoner-of-war camp in the turbulent multinational circumstances of 1916-18, Pirenne chose to overlook the sixth century in formulating his famous thesis.

King Arthur's Britain and the end of the western Roman empire[1]

British settlements of the fifth century either did not exist or they are archaeologically invisible; we cannot tell which, and therefore we cannot say whether Britain as a whole shut down, or only British *Romanitas*. But the latter's extinction is as certain as anything can be in archaeology (Faulkner 2002: 75).

Tintagel

In 1936 the Director-elect of the British School at Rome, C.A. Ralegh Radford, made his living from directing archaeological excavations for the government (cf. Hodges 1992a). The Ministry of Public Buildings and Works, as the government agency was called, was keen to create employment while making known archaeological sites accessible to the public. Radford, who had been a student of both the British Schools at Athens and Rome in the 1920s, was a leading circuit excavator. Being from the West Country, he had made a career excavating sites in Cornwall, Devon and south-west Scotland. So, when the Ministry acquired the prominent outcrop of Tintagel Head (Cornwall) with its castle erected in the 1230s by Richard, Duke of Cornwall, it fell to Ralegh Radford, the Ministry's man in the region, to investigate the earthworks on the outcrop itself (cf. Morris and Harry 1997). In the summer's dig, before he went to Rome, Radford excavated Building C on the exposed headland and there recognised a group of ceramics which were not high medieval but seemingly Roman in date. Being familiar with Mediterranean archaeology, Radford attempted to seek parallels for the 'red polished wares' and amphorae sherds – some 1,300 sherds in all. Although he published nothing on these discoveries until 1956 (Radford 1956), he quickly appreciated that these potsherds belonged to the post-Roman era and not to the Roman period in Cornwall. In short, he came to realise that he had discovered the material traces of King Arthur's age. Radford never published his excavations – his time as Director of the British School at Rome followed by wartime service disrupted this – but he interpreted the outcrop as a monastery which belonged to the world of King Arthur and benefited from trade with the Mediterranean.

[1]My thanks to Javier Arce for inviting me to the conference at Pisa where I delivered a version of this chapter. Thanks, too, to Paul Reynolds for his helpfulness regarding the Tintagel imported pottery.

3. King Arthur's Britain and the end of the western Roman empire

3.1. Portrait of C.A. Ralegh Radford by H.A. Freeth, *c.* 1936.

3.2. Aerial view of Tintagel Head, Cornwall.

New excavations by Professor Christopher Morris during the 1990s re-examined Radford's site C and excavated some of the undisturbed deposits left since 1936 (Morris and Harry 1997). In addition, Morris investigated other terraces. The excavations revealed a sequence of complex structures, mostly made in a traditional Iron Age or Romano-British form with stakes holding together turf walls. The buildings resemble similar western British secular sites, although it is still possible that it was a monastery. In a drain Christopher Morris's team discovered a broken inscription on a slate, reading COLIAVIFICIT ARTOGNOV. One reading of this is: 'Artognou, father of a descendent of Coll had this made'. The name ARTOGNOV is actually recorded in 882 from Brittany, western France, as a British name. The inscription, in Charles Thomas's opinion, is sixth-century in date, and the name, of course, has attracted comparison with Arthur (Charles Thomas, quoted in 'Tintagel', *Current Archaeology* 159 [1998]: 87). Associated with the inscription was a glass vessel, a jug, of which twelve pieces survived. This has been identified as a substantial glass flagon of a type not found elsewhere in Britain at this time with its closest parallels to vessels from Cadiz and Malaga in southern Spain (Morris and Harry 1997). The ceramics are no less interesting. According to Paul Reynolds, the most recent specialist to review them, they are dominated by Aegean Late Roman 2 (61%). However, a major component – *contra* the opinions of past scholars (cf. Alcock 1995; Fulford 1989; Thomas 1981; Williams and Carreras 1995) (cf. p. 26) – are thick-walled buff-coloured amphorae sherds in a fine fabric that would seem to be south Spanish in origin and reminiscent, he writes, of Cadiz fabrics. Previously these have been ascribed to Tunisia. Reynolds claims that there are no Tunisian imports. However, sherds of Samos Cistern amphorae types and the Ephesus region Late Roman Amphora 3 are also present. In short, Reynolds argues, two points emerge from a fresh reappraisal of the Tintagel collection (Reynolds 2005: 429-9):

1. Aegean Late Roman Amphora 1 are common – and indeed the type fossil on many western British sites, but these are rare in the west Mediterranean and the Iberian peninsula in particular.
2. Baetician imports that are comparatively scarce on Mediterranean and even eastern Tarraconensian sites, are present in notable numbers in Britain.

One further point merits careful consideration. Traditionally, the sherds from Radford's excavations have been dated to the late fifth or early sixth centuries (cf. Alcock 1971; Alcock 1995; Fulford 1989; Thomas 1981). The dates have been significant, causing historians and archaeologists to associate them with the loosely/imprecisely dated King Arthur called Ambrosius by the British chronicler Gildas a little later in the sixth century (Alcock 1971). Paul Reynolds, however, offers a wider span for these wares based upon the new excavations in Beirut and Butrint (Albania), in particular. He suggests the dates run from the late fifth to the mid-sixth century – in other words, to a period some 25-50 years later than the usual date for Ambrosius, closer to the time Gildas was writing, and more importantly, much closer to the time when the Anglo-Saxon communities were beginning to engage in what Ian Wood has called the Merovingian North Sea (Wood 1983;1993). This extended chronology is affirmed by Christopher Morris's careful excavations which have shown the alleged one-period occupation of Tintagel in fact to span at least three construction phases extending from the fifth to the seventh century (Morris and Harry 1997: 115, 120-1).

Morris and Harry, in concluding their excavation report, argue that Tintagel Head was a special site, the equivalent of a *villa regis*, 'a very major post-Roman royal citadel' (Morris and Harry 1997: 125). Smaller sites such as Dinas Powys in Wales, excavated by Leslie Alcock in the 1960s (1963), are defined as aristocratic. 'The discussion of the site's (Tintagel's) status is of course inseparable from the consideration of the implications of the rich material arriving at the site .... Pre-eminent amongst this material is, of course, the imported pottery.... Extraordinary concentrations such as this require extraordinary explanations and it is, therefore, not surprising that suggestions should be made of Tintagel being the primary point of entry for this material, with subsequent redistribution elsewhere .... Even if the question of return cargoes is to some extent speculative, being largely based on documentary sources, logical inferences, and attested occurrences of, for instance, Cornish tin or Mendip lead, it seems only logical to see the visible extent... as the tip of the iceberg .... [The] reality of north Cornwall being at the heart of this enterprise would seem undoubted' (Morris and Harry 1997: 124-5).

Of the numerous western British sites at which imported Mediterranean ceramics occur, two deserve brief mention in this context: the fortified hilltop site known as Cadbury-Camelot on the edge of the Mendips in central Somerset, and Bantham Bay, a beach site in southern Devon.

Cadbury-Camelot

The excavations made by Leslie Alcock during the 1960s for the Camelot Research Committee may have disappointed those in search of Disneyesque ruins (1971; 1995). Yet the results are intriguing. First, helped by the discovery of Mediterranean late Roman sherds, Alcock was able to show that at least one of the Iron Age ramparts was refurbished in the later fifth or early sixth centuries. Evidence was also discovered concerning the south-west gate. Four vertical timbers defined a nearly square area with sides 3.4 x 3.1 metres in area. These must have supported a heavy superstructure, though none was found. Next, in a large excavation Alcock discovered the remains of a substantial post-built hall about 19 metres long by 10 metres wide – a floor area of 190 square metres. The hall appears to have been divided by a partition into two compartments and in every respect is reminiscent of Romano-British proto-villas as well as the seventh-century Northumbrian palace at Doon Hill (Alcock 2003: 207ff.). Sherds of Bi and Bii amphorae (Late Roman 1) were found within the walls of the hall, dating it to *c.* 475-550. In all 12 sherds of ARS were found, 131 sherds of amphorae and 29 sherds of imported Spanish or Syrian glass from a minimum of 14 tableware vessels. The building, while not a palace in the medieval form, belongs to the group of halls known from the Baltic and North Sea regions in the Migration Period. This was a place for collective gatherings including feasting and the telling of epic stories such as Gildas's lament on the end of Britain (cf. Alcock 2003: 252-4).

Bantham Sands

Bantham Sands is a beach site on the south coast of Devon, close to Totnes where the twelfth-century chronicler Geoffrey of Monmouth begins his saga of Trojans creating the Arthurian court of Cornwall (May and Weddell 2001). Here well-made hearths were found associated with large quantities of animal bones and 570 pieces of imported Mediterranean potsherds with a few sherds of rare coarse local wares. Bantham is not unique. Beach sites are known from slightly later dates in Britain at places such as White Sands in Dumfriesshire (Griffith 2003), although the best investigated site of this kind is perhaps Lundenborg on the island of Funen in Denmark where the beach served as a market-place for the rich sixth-century royal centre at Gudme (Nielsen, Randsborg and Thrane 1994). Bantham, it would appear, like Lundenborg, was a periodic market-place, what I have previously described as a Type A emporium – often the proto-type for the planned permanent Type B emporia (Hodges 1982: 50-52; 67; cf. Verhulst 2002: 133).

These three major sites – Tintagel, South Cadbury and Bantham Sands – are not unique. Perhaps a dozen other settlements are known from this age with similar characteristics, including the presence of the diagnostic Mediterranean wares. They belong to a defining moment when, between *c.* 475 and 550, the Christian communities of western Britain were identifying themselves on Latin memorial stones (Thomas 1998). They belong to a distinctive cultural community that Charles Thomas has provocatively termed 'Fortress Britain' – a sub-Roman Christian community that was defined by its Latin culture and its connections to the West Mediterranean, if Reynolds's identifications are correct.

3. King Arthur's Britain and the end of the western Roman empire

The Anglo-Saxon threat

Who were the aristocrats of Tintagel and Cadbury-Camelot distinguishing themselves from? The archaeology is quite clear about this (cf. Hines 1997). The eastern border of western England was defined by the forest of Selwood. Beyond this lay the Anglo-Saxon territories. The political structure of these areas, like western Britain, appears to have been highly fragmented. Judging from the seventh-century Tribal Hidage, which depicts 30 Anglo-Saxon tribal units, it is evident that much of Roman Britain broke up into numerous tribes in the fifth century. Indeed, it is possible that as many as 50 to 100 tribal groups existed between c. 475 and 550, some coalescing into larger entities from c. 550 onwards and emerging as kingdoms – the *Angli,* as Pope Gregory the Great defined them – at the end of the sixth century (Hodges 1989: 64-5; Wormald 1994). Sub-Roman Britain, in other words, was a patchwork of differing tribal communities. The archaeology of these communities shows the steady migration into the traditional sub-Roman areas – westwards along the Thames valley and from Hampshire, eventually into Dorset and northwards into Northumbria. Southern Britain, however, is particularly interesting, not least because it is defined by two groups – those west of Selwood distinguished by the Mediterranean pottery found at Tintagel and so forth, and those east of Selwood with the so-called Anglo-Saxon cultural traits.

Anglo-Saxon communities were settling around the edge of Selwood from c. 500, no more than a day's walk from South Cadbury. Here, it would seem, was the point of tension. But who were these people? It is not at all clear that they were Anglo-Saxons, although by c. 600 they began to regard themselves as descendents of immigrants. Small amounts of their material culture – their funerary equipment and some dress features – belonged to the North Sea Migration Period culture, but then, on the face of it, the material culture of western Britain – the amphorae, the African Redslip tablewares and glass, would point to these people as being Romans from Spain and western Turkey! The so-called Anglo-Saxons lived in small communities of 3-5 timber houses (such as Charlton Down (Hampshire) and West Stow (Suffolk)) (cf. Hamerow 1991) – essentially small versions of Romano-British peasant dwellings – which were unfortified (Hodges 1989: 34-8; see, however, Hamerow 2002: 46-50). In striking contrast to western Britain, no defended Anglo-Saxon sites exist. In addition, the Anglo-Saxons had a conspicuous North Sea burial rite – either cremating or inhuming their dead with a range of dress and other accoutrements. Around 550, however, the Anglo-Saxon communities began to change significantly. The Kentish king Ethelberht took a Frankish wife, Bertha, who brought a Christian priest in her entourage. It is a small glimpse of the new cultural pattern that included Frankish prestige goods (swords, dress jewellery and so forth) as well as a range of east Mediterranean objects ranging from glasses and silverware to Coptic bowls (cf. Harris

2003: 161-88). A Byzantine lead seal from London has suggested that Byzantine traders might have been present, not least because the Justinianic chronicler, Procopius, provides us with an imprecise record of cross-Channel trade at this time (Harris 2003: 176). Most archaeologists, however, now agree that the traded goods, mostly used in feasting and burial practice, formed part of trade connections with either northern France (via the Seine) or the Rhineland. The goods were given as gifts in a chain of directed relations rather than traded as cargoes, such as was the case with the Late Roman amphorae. The pattern of gift-giving, concentrated in south-east and eastern England after *c.* 550, looks to form part of the so-called Merovingian North Sea zone identified by Ian Wood (1983). In short, the Frankish community was renovating earlier Roman-period trade connections that reached not only across the English Channel but also embraced northern Germany and the western Baltic. Meanwhile, as is now clear, the western Baltic was in receipt of traded Byzantine gold that was entering this region either from the east Baltic (by way of eastern Europe) or through down the line directed gift-giving affecting the tribes of central Europe (Näsman 1998; Randsborg 1998).

From this moment, when the tensions within the patchwork quilt of kingdoms gathered speed, not surprisingly competition for resources grew. Competition to appear Continental grew as well (Harris 2003: 182-7). There were two outcomes: first, a dramatic attempt to conquer the rich farmlands of western Britain, and secondly, the coalescing of the many small tribes into a few large tribes (Kent, Wessex, Mercia etc.) to a greater or lesser degree adopting the political apparatus of the Merovingian courts (cf. Hodges 1989: 43-53). By 600 with Merovingian culture came such tools as writing (invoking Latin legal instruments including property charters) and the Church accelerating the tensions between the competing Anglo-Saxon tribes, as the Venerable Bede's colourful eighth-century chronicle of these years illustrates (cf. Hodges 1989: 44-5; Wormald 1994). In archaeological terms the tension is best shown by the Sutton Hoo ship burial, excavated in 1939. Here in *c.* 625 a king, possibly Redwald of East Anglia, adopted a mixed Christian and pagan rite and in his large ship created a funerary mausoleum of Vendel and Frankish proportions with Byzantine silverware, Coptic vessels, Celtic vessels, Anglian jewellery and Merovingian gold to recompense the celestial oarsmen (cf. Carver 1998). The destruction of such wealth marks the final moment of a burial culture which within a generation had been superseded by the Christian practice of measuring inheritance principally in terms of landed property rather than moveable prestige goods.

It is tempting to attribute the great objects from the Sutton Hoo ship to direct relations with the Baltic and Mediterranean Seas, but this would be misleading. East Anglian England, even at the apogee of the Anglian burial rite, never belonged to the Byzantine commonwealth (*contra* Harris 2003). Far from it, these goods mark it out as part of the Merovingian

North Sea and, more specifically, with a set of explicit relations with royal households around the Rhine-Seine basin. In its moment of expansion, the Rhine-Seine basin attracted wealth from the south. Hence the rise of Anglo-Saxon England is linked to the rise of the Frankish territory and its attendant connections with the tribes of the western Baltic. The source of Byzantine goods from the south, though, merits a brief word.

When the Romans lost the Danube, the river corridor to the east closed down. On the other hand, Merovingian colonisation eastward transformed the Rhineland's geopolitical role. Now the former frontier became the backbone of a new kingdom, which greatly enhanced the river's importance as an artery. However, as a direct route the value of the Rhine depended on who controlled the southern exits of the Alpine passes and who was in control in the Po valley. Power in the Po basin changed twice in the sixth century, as first the Byzantines drove out the Ostrogoths and then the Lombards evicted the Byzantines. These disruptions greatly affected the Alpine-Rhine corridor and left the Rhone with its great entrepot, Marseilles, as a crucial connection between the Mediterranean and the Franks. The Rhone corridor, however, declined in importance as the commercial vitality of the western Mediterranean declined. In other words, by *c.* 625 – the era of the Neustrian Mayor of the Palace, Dagobert, judging from the study of coin hoards, the volume of traffic began to drop and with the threat posed by the Arabs in the later seventh and early eighth centuries, Rhone traffic became minimal as the old trans-alpine routes were once again considered the best passage to Italy (cf. McCormick 2001: 78-9).

To summarise:

1. Competition between the Anglo-Saxon tribes – peer polity interaction – was fuelled and accelerated dramatically as the Franks, rich with Byzantine goods by way of the Rhone river connection, entered into specific alliances in south-eastern England. This began around 550 if not as early as 500-525.

2. The Anglo-Saxon tribes, defined by a common North Sea culture, although essentially structured around small villages rather than palaces or fortresses, appear to have pushed westwards into the rich farmlands of Somerset as early as the mid-sixth century.

3. Fortress Britain, as Thomas described the communities west of Selwood forest, distinguished by direct access to small amounts of Spanish and Aegean feasting goods, responded by fortifying their strongholds, such as Cadbury-Camelot and Cadbury Congresbury (Somerset). The resistance associated with the legend of King Arthur, in sum, was a response to a growing sense of identity provided by Mediterranean-based economic connections and the common threat posed by Anglo-Saxon pioneers penetrating the region from the east, armed and dressed in Frankish fashion.

The end of the Mediterranean world

Let us take a wide-angled geopolitical view of this situation. The superpower of the time was Byzantium, so it is from its immediate sphere of influence that we must examine the contexts for the rise of Fortress Britain and the concomitant circumstances in the Anglo-Saxon tribal areas.

As Hayes (1971; cf. Panella 1993; Saguì 1998) and many other specialists, including Reynolds (2005) have shown, the Later Roman ceramic industries permit us to measure the changing axes of Mediterranean commerce and regional conditions in the fifth to seventh centuries (cf. Saguì 1998). In the past twenty-five years archaeological investigations have revolutionised our understanding of the Mediterranean in late antiquity. The patterns of maritime trade were most definitely not static. First, the even mixing of western and eastern Mediterranean commerce during the fifth century was seriously disrupted by *c.* 475-500, leading to the growing importance of eastern pottery centres and indeed, eastern commercial activity as the dominant distributors in the Mediterranean. Even with the powerful military re-conquest of much of the central Mediterranean by Justinian's armies in the 530s, there is little doubt that the motor of production was diminishing in the western and central parts of the Mediterranean basin and only sustained on any scale after *c.* 550 in the Aegean and areas such as Asia Minor, Egypt and Palestine to the east. Hence, Italian ports such as Naples and Rome were in decline, while inland Italian towns were in ruins and in the countryside, the Roman estate system barely existed (Christie 2000). Perhaps the most telling example is provided by Michael McCormick: 'if the population of Rome dropped (he writes), roughly, from 800,000 to 60,000 souls between AD 300 and 530, how can this not have curtailed the volume of goods and people travelling toward that point on the Tiber river? Change of such calibre will have made waves across the entire system of late Roman communications' (McCormick 2001: 66). Further, with the sixth-century struggles over Italy, the management of the classical landscape came to an abrupt end (Francovich and Hodges 2003). Great rural centres like the bishop's estate centre at San Giusto (Apulia) and the elegant villa at San Giovanni di Ruoti (Basilicata) were deserted; small hilltop villages such as Montarrenti and Poggibonsi (Tuscany), similar in character to the Anglo-Saxon communities, now inherited these landscapes, building a new medieval personality that was given real identity in the Carolingian age and after with villages denoted in land charters as *castelli* (Francovich and Hodges 2003; Valenti 2004).

Similarly, from my excavations at Butrint in southern Albania, on the sea routes connecting east and west, *c.* 475 marks a moment of severe disruption, while *c.* 550 marks a moment of virtual economic extinction (Hodges, Bowden and Lako 2004). In other words, the central Mediterranean was in headlong decline from *c.* 550 onwards and virtually an economic shadow of its fifth-century form by *c.* 600.

To summarise an immense body of data, mostly assembled over the last twenty years:

1. Around 475, coinciding with the fall of the last western Roman emperor, the economic motor of the Mediterranean commerce changed gear. To take one illustration: Vandal raids on the Balkans succeeded Vandal traders from the previous era (Bowden 2003). Economic tension was intense, giving rise to immense expenditure by communities upon urban defences and then, worse still, taxation to create the military means to reconquer territories taken by the Ostrogoths and others.

2. The next point of change occurred in *c.* 550, at the height of the Byzantine attempt to re-conquer the empire. The economic motor was plainly beginning to lose impetus as ports declined in size and as the countryside no longer functioned in integrated regional economies in much of the central Mediterranean. Spain, like Provence, was not spared from this disruption.

This is the geo-economic context for, first, a modest but distinctive attempt to find a new market in western Britain around *c.* 475-550. Perhaps it was composed of a few cargoes, beached, for example, at Bantham Bay as well as in the royal harbour at Tintagel. Yet while this was an insignificant commerce for the future of the Mediterranean, it was immensely important for Britain. As we have seen, it provided a palpable connection to the western Roman world in material matters that played a great part in the social activities of this much reduced tribal world (cf. Alcock 2003). Secondly, the further downturn in Mediterranean economic affairs, exacerbated by Justinian's expensive military campaigns, led to the search for new markets in central Europe. Aspiring barbarian courts were obvious commercial targets. With the Alpine passes partly closed, this gave rise to the ascendancy of Marseilles and the river-borne route to the Frankish kingdoms of Austrasia and Neustria that, in turn, fostered their ambitions in the courts of southern England, north Germany and western Denmark. This southerly thrust, we may note, came just as the western Atlantic route appears to have closed. Were the two events connected? It is perhaps too soon to tell. But in southern England there can be little doubt that as the Anglo-Saxons aspired to Frankish and Byzantine cultural habits, so the British lost their last link with the Mediterranean. The descendants of the age of the legendary King Arthur cannot have been happy or passive about this. Subsequent connections with Aquitaine in the seventh century bringing E ware tablewares in small quantities were no compensation for the overtly prestigious feasting potential of Aegean oils and wines alongside those from Spain (Campbell 1996).

Conclusions

My contention is that the changing rhythms of the later Mediterranean economy had unexpected and, in Anglo-Saxon England, lasting implications for its cultural character. I am reminded of the anthropologist Marshall Sahlins's description of the immense competition created following the momentous visits of the imperialist adventurer, James Cook, in Hawaii. Among the Hawaiian élite, Sahlins recounts, there was a fascination with British and American names as well as British dress codes. So, for example, at one tribal assembly in 1812, an American chronicler noted chiefs named Billy Pitts, George Washington, Billy Cobbett, Charley Fox, Thomas Jefferson, Bonapart and Tom Paine. Even though the leaders of Hawaiian society were on the periphery of the Industrial Revolution, they were powerfully manipulated or seduced by the prevailing world order and in particular by the images of those ruling its leading societies (Sahlins 1985). In a similar way, we may project how in western Britain, thanks to Atlantic sea traders, and then in southern England, in response to the rise of the western aristocracy and the counterforce of Merovingian relations, there was a similar unwitting manipulation by Mediterranean forces. The legendary King Arthur and the Anglian king buried in the great warship at Sutton Hoo were not direct products of the Byzantine commonwealth, but of traumatic and ultimately fatal economic tensions within that commonwealth. Further, we might add, the individual responsible for the aristocratic sites at either Cadbury Camelot or Tintagel is a heroic figure in Marshall Sahlins's terms: someone who lived the life of a whole tribe, shaping an identity that, as the sixth-century chronicler Gildas recognised, has left a curious epilogue of Roman Britain that is paradoxically also a beginning for English history.

Finally, since Ralegh Radford identified the sub-Roman sherds from Tintagel Head, our understanding of the archaeology of the Roman empire has been transformed. But of all the many elements that we now understand, few measure up to the extraordinary collapse of the empire and the many dramatic and far-reaching implications of that collapse – a seismic event no less extraordinary than the demise of the Communist Eastern Bloc over the past decade. In measuring this transformation, generation by generation, as McCormick indicates (2001), we now have tools to show what documentary sources do not show us: namely a drama so profound that it changed Europe forever and fashioned the conditions for the creation of an island community, the English, who until this happened were mostly a patchwork of tribes with their cultural roots not in Germany but in Roman Britain.

4

Balkan Ghosts? Nationalism and the question of rural continuity in Albania[1]

Why this sudden bewilderment, this confusion?
(How serious people's faces have become.)
Why are the streets and squares emptying so rapidly,
everyone going home lost in thought?

Because night has fallen and the barbarians haven't come.
And some of our men just in from the border say
there are no barbarians any longer.
Now what's going to happen to us without barbarians?
Those people were a kind of solution.

C.P. Cavafy, 'Waiting for the Barbarians', 1904
trans. Keeley & Sherrard 1975: 15

Introduction

Albania was formally defined as a country by the Treaty of London in 1913. Its inter-war history was marked by desperate poverty and eventual invasion by Italy in 1939. In 1944, Albanian partisans, led by the Marxist Enver Hoxha, succeeded in expelling the occupying German forces and, initially in collaboration with the Yugoslavians, set out to build a new country. In 1947, as tensions with neighbouring Yugoslavia developed, Hoxha boldly instigated a nationalist archaeological programme, run by a branch of the Academy of Sciences' Institute of Geography. A series of excavations began and promising young students were despatched to study in the Soviet Union, adding to a small, older generation of scholars who had been trained in the classical tradition in pre-war western Europe with its emphasis upon monuments and art history. The 1960s, marked by Albania's switch from an affiliation to the Soviet Union to one with the Chinese, was a period of intense activity for its small band of archaeologists, which culminated in the establishment of the Institute of Archaeology as a branch of the Academy of Sciences in 1970. Locked into the rationale for its existence was an explicit nationalist model evolved over the previous two decades of archaeological research.

This chapter examines the problems this model created with regard particularly to the late antique and early medieval periods of modern

[1]This paper was written with William Bowden, to whom I am very grateful for permitting it to be re-published here.

39

Albania. What role did 'barbarians' play in this? Were they a 'solution' for the Academy of Sciences? And how has this model been allowed to evolve?

'Our archaeologists have proved the Albanian-Illyrian continuity'
(*Handbook of English-Albanian Conversation*, 1972)

One of the principal problems faced by Albania during the communist period was the organisation of efficient control mechanisms for all human sciences in order to provide the country with a distinctive identity. The task of historians and archaeologists was to construct a systematic and well-documented Albanian past. To counter the territorial claims of surrounding powers (notably Greece, Italy and Yugoslavia), the issue was to prove that the Albanians had inhabited their country from the most ancient of times. To this end, the main line of research supported by the authorities was the study of the Illyrians, with particular emphasis on their ethnogenesis and their ethnic and cultural links with the modern Albanian population. Signal importance was attached to their social structures, especially with relation to a Marxist view of historical development.

The question of continuity with the country's Illyrian past has therefore been a constant theme in post-war Albanian archaeology. Enver Hoxha (1985: 40) adopted an explicit view of the past which he described in a speech at Shkodër in 1979:

> Ne jemi pasardhësit e fiseve ilire. Në këto troje të lashta të të parëve tanë kanë vërshuar grekët, romakët, normandët, sllavët, anshuinët, bizantinët, venedikasit, osmanët e shumë e shumë pushtues të tjerë, por ata nuk izhdukën dot as popullin shqiptar, as kulturën e vjetër ilire, as vazhdimësinë e saj shqiptare.

> (We are the descendants of the Illyrian tribes. Into the land of our ancestors have come Greeks, Romans, Normans, Slavs, Angevins, Byzantines, Venetians, Ottomans and numerous other invaders, without having been able to destroy the Albanian people, the ancient Illyrian civilisation and later the Albanians.)

Hoxha's need to demonstrate the social integrity and homogeneity of Albania and its people was of course directly related to the fragile country's increasing isolation from the rest of the world. Under the policy of self-reliance, following the split with China in 1975, the purity of Illyrian ethnicity was essential to the nationalist government's political ideology.

The broad thrust of the Albanian historical narrative in this sense was that the Illyrians occupied the entire area of modern Albania throughout antiquity and maintained a cultural identity distinct from that of interlopers such as the Greeks and Romans. Greek colonists in Epirus were thus a minority among an Illyrian majority. All the major antique settlements

were considered to be Illyrian foundations, showing little Hellenic influence. The Roman period was identified as a period of occupation, implicitly
compared to the Italian occupation of 1939-43, while the slave-owning
Romans themselves were co-opted into a rather crude evolutionary Marxist framework (Anamali and Korkuti 1971). According to this model,
although the Illyrians participated in the economic life of the Roman
empire and adopted Latin as the language of commerce, their identity as
Illyrians remained unchanged. Indeed, Illyrian remained the language of
the common people who moreover retained their customs and their traditional material culture (for example, coarse ware ceramics). However, in
the immediate post-Roman period the Illyrian identity was reasserted and
restored; accordingly, this period formed one of the main areas of research
for Albanian archaeologists.

As in Greece, the presence of barbarian invaders in the early medieval
period remained a constant obstacle to an ethnic history that flowed in a
seamless continuum from prehistory to the present day. But, unlike
Greece, where archaeology has largely side-stepped the issue, Albania's
archaeologists confronted the problem head-on, creating what John
Wilkes has referred to as 'a highly improbable reconstruction of Albanian
history' for the post-Roman period (1992: 278). This reconstruction saw the
'southern Illyrians' (the Albanians) as unaffected by the migrations of
Avars, Slavs and others, even though the northern Illyrians (who inhabited the area occupied by the former Yugoslavia) were overwhelmed by
Slavs. This was intended to counter the claims of Yugoslavian archaeologists to an Illyrian heritage. The strong organisation of southern Illyrian
society, however, and the mountainous geography of the area were held to
have ensured the continued ethnic integrity of the Albanians.

'We have built a wall around Butrint'
(Handbook of English-Albanian Conversation, 1972)

Albanian archaeologists therefore painted a rather simplistic picture of
the early medieval history of their country, in which archaeological material was used to illustrate a pre-determined historical narrative. Like the
borders of modern Albania, the walled towns and *castra* of late antiquity
provided a definable context with clear boundaries and limits separating
the indigenous population from the barbarian Other. Slavic settlements
were considered to be 'islands in an Albanian sea' (Frashëri 1982: 104-6).
Approaches to the landscape within this model took two basic forms. One
of the earliest projects of Albania's archaeologists was the creation of an
archaeological map, with the intention of documenting all the country's
archaeological remains on a region by region basis. This topographic
approach has remained a central part of archaeological methodology in the
country, resulting in a number of useful synthetic surveys (e.g. Budina
1971; 1975; Mucaj 1980; Bela and Përzhita 1990). The surveys took the

form of descriptive gazetteers of known sites and monuments, usually of all periods until the end of late antiquity. The role of archaeology, however, remained passive, and archaeologists limited themselves to empirical observation and description. This was compatible with a second approach which viewed the countryside within an evolutionary Marxist framework (see also Bejko 1998). In this parallel approach the rural landscape remained a hypothetical environment inhabited by an indomitable peasantry, who moved from Roman-dominated slavery towards medieval feudalism in their inexorable progress towards the communist ideal. Damian Komata summarised the position in his 1976 synthetic treatment of the archaeological investigation of early medieval fortresses (1976: 183):

> Pour mieux comprendre la réalité de l'époque quand au développement de l'artisanat et de l'agriculture, référons-nous à Engels qui, parlant de moyen âge, observe: 'Il existait partout une petite production basée sur la propriété à partielle des travailleurs sur les moyens de production; dans les campagnes dominait l'agriculture des petits paysans, libres ou serfs, dans les villes, l'artisanat.

However, Marxism and the actual results of archaeological investigations were never fully reconciled with one another. As Bejko (1998) points out, the dominant ethos of Albanian archaeology remained that of nationalist-driven culture history that precluded a more sophisticated application of Marxist theory.

Any in-depth consideration of the landscape was also limited by the desire for a sophisticated urban Illyrian society. Urbanisation was a constant theme for Albanian archaeology, and a typology of settlement was constructed in which Illyrian settlements went through a proto-urban phase before attaining their fully evolved urban form (e.g. Ceka 1998). Moreover, evidence of autochthonous urban development was a crucial factor in playing down the influence of Greece and Rome, although ironically this involved an acceptance of some of the basic tenets of classical history, such as, for example, the cultural superiority of urban life. This focus on urban settlement is a defining feature of late antique and early medieval archaeology in Albania, in which urban continuity was viewed as of paramount importance. This was particularly true in the cases of settlements such as Butrint, which were clearly occupied in both the late antique and later medieval periods, thereby allowing archaeologists to demonstrate occupation in the intervening period (e.g. Anamali 1989).

We are therefore left with a situation in which the countryside became ideologically questionable. Its perceived lack of sophistication had little role in an historical narrative that stressed Illyrian society as advanced and urbanised in a way that owed little to Hellenic influence. Furthermore, the early medieval countryside became the realm of the barbarian 'Other', the culturally backward Slavs who were divided from the Albanians by the walls of the cities and fortresses.

However, notwithstanding these problems, concentration on the early medieval period during several decades of well-funded research has created an wide and interesting body of archaeological material that sheds a certain light on the transformation of the landscape between *c.* 400 and 800.

'The Albanians built castles ... to defend themselves from the attacks which came from all directions'
(Korkuti 1971: 1)

Of particular importance to Albanian archaeologists was a group of *castra* excavated in central and northern Albania, seemingly associated with a number of remarkable, furnished inhumation cemeteries, which were held to represent the early medieval Albanian population, known as the Koman, Arbër or proto-Albanian culture (see Popovic 1984; Wilkes 1992: 273-8; Bowden 2003). The objects within the graves are characteristic of grave assemblages from contexts throughout migration period Europe, and include objects imported from the Byzantine world, together with dress items and weapons which are paralleled in Lombard, Merovingian and Avar contexts. These objects suggest that the cemeteries were in use between the late sixth and late eighth or early ninth centuries. Despite the presence of grave goods, both Albanian and non-Albanian scholars contend that the occupants of these graves were Christian and represent a surviving post-Roman population. This is based partly on the concentration of Latin toponyms in the area of the cemeteries and a corresponding absence of the Slavic place names that are common elsewhere, and partly on the presence of Christian objects within the grave assemblages themselves.

These cemeteries have often been used to provide comparative dates for the fortified sites that sometimes lie in the vicinity. This tactic is by no means unproblematic: the distribution of the fortified sites is far wider than that of the cemeteries, suggesting that the cemeteries reflect a more localised phenomenon. The relationship between cemeteries and *castra* is therefore almost certainly far more complex than has previously been allowed. Furthermore, later occupation of these sites recommends that the dates given for the occupation phases of the *castra* should be treated with some degree of caution.

The appearance of these sites is part of a widespread phenomenon in the Balkans whereby populations transferred periodically, temporarily, or permanently to more defensive positions on fortified hilltops. This can be observed in FYROM/Macedonia, Bulgaria and northern and central Greece (Dunn 1994; 1997). Komata (1976) counts around seventy of these late antique and early medieval fortresses and citadels in Albania, although even at the most extensively excavated sites the results remain ambiguous (Fig. 4.1). These sites are frequently located along river valleys and lines of communication. It is unclear as to whether this is indicative

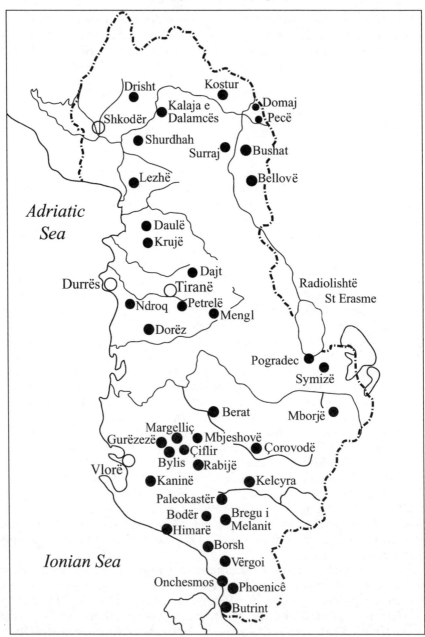

4.1. Albania: distribution of known and presumed late antique and early medieval hilltop and fortress sites.

of a co-ordinated defensive policy on the part of the emperor, or merely a reflection of the location of the earlier settlements that required these fortifications. Procopius' *Buildings* suggests the former, but this remains a highly ambiguous source (see below and Bowden 2003). Some of these fortresses lie in proximity to the early medieval cemeteries such as Shurd-hah. We shall briefly note the results of the excavations of various sites and outline some of the problems associated with their interpretation. In general, the fortresses present a picture of remarkable uniformity, al-though the methodologies employed and the ideological background of the excavations make this result unsurprising.

The fortress of Shurdhah (Sarda) is situated in northern Albania on a promontory above the Drin valley and close to Koman itself. Excavations during the early 1970s failed to produce conclusive evidence of its early medieval occupation, although a number of objects were found that are paralleled in the early medieval cemeteries (Spahiu and Komata 1975; Komata 1980). However, the excavation report implies that no early medieval contexts were found within the fortress itself, which seems to date mainly from the late eleventh century. Nonetheless, the presence of early medieval objects and the cemetery are suggestive of earlier occupation.

The fortress of Symizë is also interesting in this context. Symizë occu-pies a steep-sided pyramidal hill to the north of Maliq in central eastern Albania. It was excavated from 1973 to 1975 by Gjerak Karaiskaj, who concluded that the site had been settled without interruption from late antiquity until the start of the Ottoman period (Karaiskaj 1980). Like many of the late antique hilltop sites, Symizë was constructed within an earlier pre-Roman fortification, which at some point was augmented with a poorly-constructed masonry wall. Excavations focussed on two cisterns, one of which was dated to the late antique period although its contents suggest that by this period it was used for the rubbish disposal rather than for water storage. A single burial was also discovered within this. Ceram-ics recovered from the cistern, dated by Karaiskaj to the fifth and sixth centuries, are dominated by coarse wares and great storage jars or *pythoi*. The coarse wares resemble those found in other late antique contexts in Albania. These are frequently thin-walled globular jars with flat bases and flaring rims, with two handles joined directly to the rim. Possible examples of eastern Mediterranean cooking wares have also been noted from the published assemblages (cf. Arthur et al. 1992: 110-11). In addition, coins of Anastasius and Justinian as well as unidentified late Roman issues were recorded, but without clarity as to exact provenance on the site. The coin sequence from the site recommences in the twelfth century. Fourth-century occupation of the site was ascribed to a small group of Goths who, it was suggested, were assimilated into the dominant Albanian culture.

A broadly similar sequence can be observed at other sites in central and northern Albania. A series of fortifications were investigated in the area

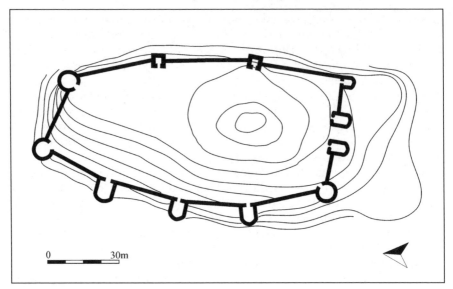

4.2. Plan of the fortified site of Bushat near Kukës.

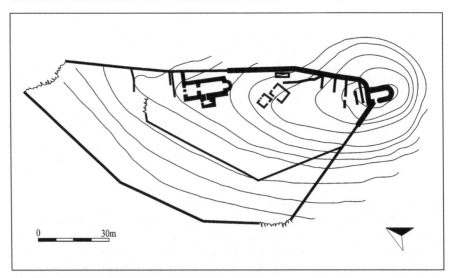

4.3. Plan of the small fortified site of Pecë.

of Kukës, close to the border with Kosovo. These include Bushat (Fig. 4.2) and Pecë (Fig. 4.3), which, like Symizë, were active between the fourth and sixth centuries with a second phase of occupation attested in the later medieval period (Përzhita 1986; 1990). The excavator postulated continued usage in the intervening period. Both sites occupied precipitous positions on hills and were surrounded by substantial mortared fortifica-

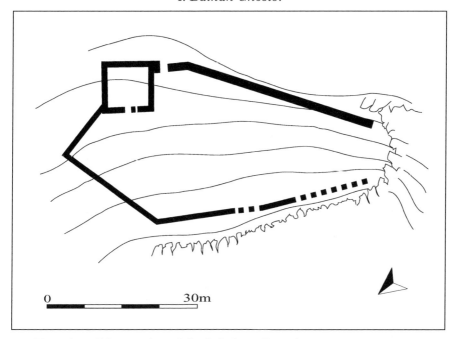

4.4. Plan of small late antique defended site at Domaj.

tions. Bushat (0.70 hectares) in particular was a major defensive work, ringed with towers of varying forms; Pecë's walls enclosed an area of 0.13 hectares. A smaller castle at Domaj (Fig. 4.4), with a surface area of only 325 square metres, was also investigated, although in this case only one phase of occupation was noted, dated by a single coin of Justinian (Përzhita 1995).

In central Albania, fortified sites were recorded in the region of Mallakastra (Muçaj 1980). Apart from the major city of Bylis, with its large fortifications dated by a series of inscriptions to the reign of Justinian, five further fortresses were noted (Rabijë, Margelliç, Çiflik, Gurëzezë and Mbjeshovë), together with a number of basilicas spread along the valley of the Gjanice river. Four of the fortresses produced evidence of late antique occupation including quantities of *pythoi* of a type characteristic of late antique contexts at Bylis. The fortresses were interpreted as military centres used by the Byzantine administration to oversee/subdue the autochthonous population. The wealth of the basilicas, however, was viewed as indicative of the economic development of the rural areas. The apparently quite dense occupation of the area covered by Muçaj is in marked contrast to the results of the Mallakastra survey, where field survey in two areas a few kilometres to the west failed to produce any late antique traces (Korkuti et al. 1998: 262).

A final site of particular interest is that of Paleokastër in the Drinos

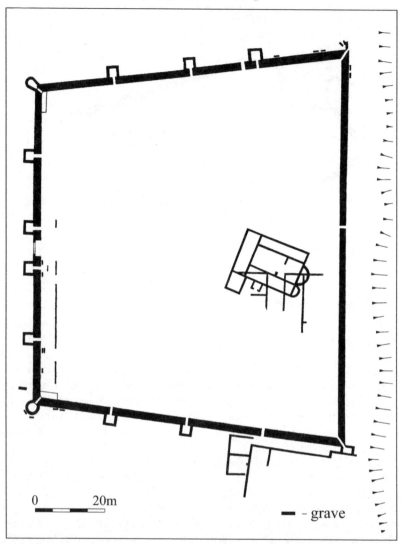

0 _____ 20m

▬ - grave

4.5. Paleokastër: late cavalry (?) fortress and fortified complex.

valley close to the town of Gjirokastra (Baçe 1981) (Fig. 4.5). Paleokastër differs from the other sites in that it occupies a low-lying position at the confluence of the Drinos and Kardhiq rivers. The fortress is of a regular, trapezoidal plan, covering an area of 0.915 hectares. Its excavator, Apollon Baçe, suggested that it was originally a base for a cavalry cohort of 500 men, constructed in the early fourth century. This date is proposed on the basis of a fourth-century grave *stele* incorporated into a later phase of construction. Excavations also revealed traces of regular barrack blocks.

4. Balkan Ghosts?

Twelve coins of the third and fourth centuries were found, with the latest dating to the reign of Constantius II (AD 335-361). An inscription from the reign of Licinius, overwritten during the reign of Constantius II, also points to a significant fourth-century presence at the site.

During the sixth century, a civilian population apparently reoccupied the walled enclosure. Two basilicas were erected: one inside the enclosure and a second c. 100 metres to the south. The church within the wall circuit overlay the earlier barracks but followed a completely different alignment, suggesting that these were no longer standing at the time the fortress was reoccupied. Substantial quantities of ceramics were recovered relating to both periods of occupation. The published drawings suggest that these included LR 1 and LR 2 amphorae, Late Roman C ware and African Red Slip ware. As at Symizë, eastern Mediterranean cooking wares are noted in the published assemblages (Arthur et al. 1992).

Within their socio-political context these excavations were highly successful, providing material with which to illustrate an accepted cultural history. Archaeologists played a largely passive role in maintaining and augmenting a pre-existing historical model, with the result that there was little requirement to demonstrate the veracity of their findings, which, publicly at least, were accepted without question by their colleagues. This presents significant problems in approaching the results of these excavations, in which the claims are seldom substantiated by more detailed explanations. Ceramics in particular were interpreted within the context of a model that assumed cultural continuity between late antiquity and the later medieval period, with the result that coarse wares were often assigned uncritically to the intervening period. Nonetheless, despite the problems associated with these excavation results, they provide some interesting indications as to the changing patterns of life outside the walled towns during late antiquity, or at least some indication as to directions for future research.

The finds on many of these sites suggest that they were occupied permanently or semi-permanently, rather than functioning solely as refuge sites. In the absence of evidence from outside the fortresses this must remain largely supposition. Andrew Poulter, for example, argues the opposite for the hilltop sites of Moesia Inferior, basing his conclusions on survey data which suggest continued use lowland settlements and villa sites (1983: 97-100). Similarly, the large number of churches noted by Skender Muçaj in the Mallakastra region would indicate continued occupation of unprotected lowland sites, although the general absence of late antique material noted nearby in the Mallakastra Survey denotes a complex situation with very localised variations. Equally, while we may note that the occupation of certain sites is broadly contemporaneous, the available information does not allow us to detect whether a site was occupied for two years or two centuries. However, the frequent occurrence of the large *pythoi* or storage jars at the sites, and indeed the quantities of other material present, could signify quite lengthy periods of occupation.

The apparent lack of fine wares or amphorae in any quantity is notable on the more remote sites such as in the region of Kukës, although in the absence of quantitative data this can remain no more than a general impression. The seemingly wider range of imported material at Paleo-kastër, situated on one of the main north-south routes through Albania, and indeed much closer to the coast, could suggest that imported material seldom strayed far from the coastal littoral.

The question of continuity remains unanswered. It is certainly possible and indeed likely that these sites remained occupied into the seventh century and beyond. The presence of the early medieval Komani cemeteries mentioned above shows that the landscape continued to be utilised in some form, and it seems not unreasonable to suggest that the Komani population were using the same sites as had been used in the sixth century. However, this question needs to be tackled rigorously and removed from the ideological constraints that have previously prevented this from happening. Perhaps most importantly the hilltop sites need to be examined in relation to earlier Roman settlement and land use patterns, from which they appear such a radical departure.

'May we see a cow shed?'
(*Handbook of English-Albanian Conversation*, 1972)

Our knowledge of the Roman countryside is thus far very limited. This is particularly true of Albania, where, with the exception of the Diaporit villa and the site of Malathrea (see below), no excavations of villas or other rural Roman sites have ever been conducted. There is a similar absence of systematic villa excavations in Greece. Although a number of villas have been investigated here, published results are limited to partial building plans and mosaics, with little consideration of associated land use and material culture. This is partially alleviated by the wealth of field survey evidence. Greece, for reasons not unconnected with the difficulties of obtaining excavation permits, is probably the most intensively surveyed area of the Mediterranean, providing a remarkable, if problematic, database of material (see, in general, Alcock 1993). Surface survey, however, is inevitably a broad-brush approach that cannot easily detect important nuances of site history. Equally, although they are ostensibly diachronic, many of the surveys were carried out by archaeologists whose research interests lay in the pre-Roman period and who correspondingly paid less attention to Roman and post-Roman sequences.

Related to the above, there is a general absence of published ceramic sequences resulting from detailed stratigraphic excavation. This is wholly the case in Albania and partly true for Greece, meaning that with the exception of a handful of sites (notably the agora in Athens, Corinth,

4. Balkan Ghosts?

Knossos, Argos and Gortyna) almost nothing is known of locally-produced Roman and late antique coarse wares. Survey results have been entirely dependent on analysis of fine wares and amphorae, with the potential for distortion that this entails – a fact acknowledged by many of the archaeologists in question (Alcock 1993: 49-53). This absence of stratified sequences has meant that field survey has been unable to meet its full potential as a research tool with relation to the Roman and post-Roman periods.

The absence of rural excavations also means that our knowledge of agricultural practice is largely dependent on documentary sources. There is a corresponding need for the application of zooarchaeology and archaeobotany in both urban and rural contexts; equally, we need to examine the relationship between urban centres and their rural hinterlands. Is it indeed possible to detect a pattern in the changing fortunes of the towns and the sites in their vicinity?

The Roman and late antique landscape: Butrint and its hinterland

The Butrint Project is an attempt to answer some of the questions outlined above. Butrint (ancient *Bouthrotos* or *Buthrotum*) is situated on the Ionian coast of Albania immediately opposite the island of Corfu and within the former Roman province of *Epirus* (later *Epirus Vetus* following the provincial reforms of Diocletian). The site and its hinterland have been the subject of a multi-disciplinary research project since 1994, which started with the aim of charting the history of the city and its relationship with its environment during the late antique and medieval periods (Hodges et al. 1997; 2000; Hodges, Bowden and Lako 2004). The project has subsequently expanded to take account of all periods of the site's history.

The central area of Butrint occupies a small peninsula that extends into a large inland lake, connected to the sea by the Vivari Channel (Figs 4.6 and 4.7). This geographical position aided the construction of a topographic model that saw Butrint as constituted by only the walled area that occupied the peninsula. The walled city became the focus of research, despite the presence of significant standing remains beyond the intramural area. This topographic model of Butrint that remained in place until the start of the present project was therefore entirely a cultural construct that emphasised the division between urban and non-urban in accordance with the ideology outlined above.

The site was first settled around the eighth century BC and quickly thrived, aided by the presence of a popular (and doubtless lucrative) cult dedicated to Asclepios. It was not one of the cities that sided against Rome during the Third Macedonian War and consequently it escaped the ravages of Aemilius Paullus in 167 BC, in which seventy other Epirote cities were razed to the ground and 150,000 people reportedly taken captive.

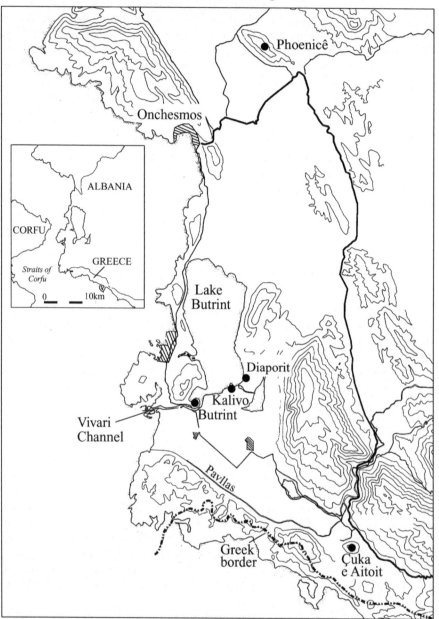

4.6. Butrint and its region.

In the first century BC members of the Roman aristocracy began to acquire land holdings in Epirus. This availability of land possibly resulted from the depredations of Aemilius Paullus, although it may also have been

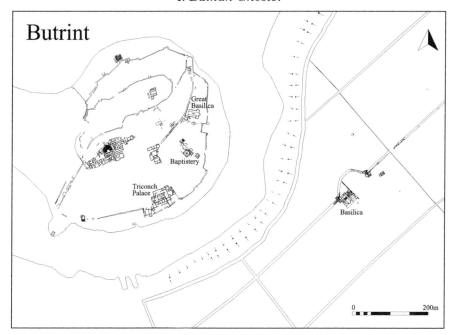

4.7. Butrint: plan of the city and its main excavated and monumental sites.

part of an ongoing process by which land and wealth became concentrated in fewer hands during the late Hellenistic period. This process of social change is documented in a set of manumission inscriptions inscribed on the *parados* of the theatre at Butrint which reveal, during the last two centuries BC, a reduction in the number of group manumittors and a concomitant increase in individual slave owners, who appear to derive exclusively from certain important families (Cabanes 1976; 1997). What-ever the timing of the process, it is clear that members of the Roman senatorial aristocracy acquired large estates in Epirus. These landowners, described by Varro in the second book of *De Re Rustica*, included Cicero's correspondent, T. Pomponius Atticus, who owned an estate in the vicinity of Butrint.

In 44 BC Caesar attempted to establish a veteran colony at Butrint, in part in retaliation for the Buthrotians' failure to pay a certain tax, the nature of which is unknown. This plan was met with stiff resistance on the part of Atticus, who asked Cicero to intervene on the town's behalf in order to avoid the loss of lands that would result from the arrival of the colonists. Atticus eventually avoided the imposition of veterans by himself paying off the town's debt. The respite was short-lived, however, as the colony was eventually established by Augustus sometime after his victory at Actium in 31 BC (Deniaux 1987; 1998). The physical effect of the colonists' arrival on land-holding patterns is unknown but the territory of Butrint should probably have undergone a process of centuriation as occurred in the landscape surrounding the contemporary foundation of Nikopolis (Doukellis 1988) and slightly earlier at Corinth (Romano 2000). Indeed, aerial photographs of the Butrint region, taken prior to the communist period programme of land drainage, show traces of field patterns that are aligned with structures associated with the city's colonial expansion, notably the aqueduct and the orthogonal street grid of the south-eastern suburb of Butrint, as inferred from geophysical evidence.

Field survey has demonstrated that the plain south of Butrint, on which the new suburb emerged, was quite densely occupied during the imperial period and continued thus into late antiquity (Hodges et al. 2000; Pluciennik et al. 2004). This apparent continuity is closely paralleled by the evidence from the Nikopolis Survey which showed only a slight drop in site numbers (from 36 to 30) between the Roman and late antique periods (Wiseman 2001). There is, however, a sharp contrast between the evidence from Butrint and Nikopolis and that from surveys elsewhere in Greece, where a dramatic drop in site numbers can be observed during the late Hellenistic period and a low density of occupation is sustained until the late Roman period after which a significant increase in sites occurs (Alcock 1993: 48). By contrast, as mentioned above, the Mallakastra Survey in central Albania detected very little late antique activity (Korkuti et al. 1998: 262).

Sources indicate the continued presence of substantial estates in Epirus Vetus during the late Roman period. Paula of Rome is noted by Jerome in 384 as owning land at Nikopolis, 'which is located on the coast near Aktion and constitutes a large part of your property', while Paulinus of Pella inherited estates in Achaea, Epirus Vetus and Epirus Nova, which provided sufficient income 'to cover the most ambitious pretensions of an aristocrat' (Chrysos 1981: 91-3). Like Atticus and his contemporaries four centuries earlier, these landowners were both members of the western senatorial aristocracy.

Roman Butrint itself in fact emerges as a small and fairly unremarkable maritime town. During late antiquity it underwent changes of the type widely recognised in towns elsewhere in the Mediterranean: a possible contraction of public space and the construction of palatial *domus* – the so-called triconch palace (Hodges, Bowden and Lako 2004), one of which extended across a series of building plots on the waterfront; during the later fifth century a new city wall was erected, limiting the defended area to the peninsula and excluding the suburb on the side of the Vivari Channel; and in the first half of the sixth century Christian buildings were erected, including a substantial basilica and a large and elaborately decorated baptistery. By the early seventh century, however, most areas of the lower part of the town appear to have been largely abandoned, although limited occupation continued on the acropolis. The latest Roman coin from the site dates to the reign of Constans II (641-668). Butrint reappears in historical sources at the end of the ninth century, when a coin sequence also recommences indicating it was a periodic fair or *emboropanegyri* (Hodges, Bowden and Lako 2004: 324).

The agricultural economy of the Roman town was probably not dissimilar to that practised in the Butrint region today, which is based largely on pastoralism and fishing. Midden assemblages recovered from late antique contexts in the palatial *domus* indicated that sheep/goat and pig formed a high proportion of animals used for domestic consumption, with cattle and horse appearing less frequently. Not surprisingly, fish played a major role in the diet of Butrint's inhabitants, which was supplemented with game, including hare, boar and wild fowl (Powell 2004).

Recent excavations have also begun to shed some light on the relationship between Butrint and the sites within its hinterland. A substantial villa and Christian basilica have been located at Diaporit on the south-east corner of Lake Butrint (Figs 4.8 and 4.9), marked by standing remains and by surface ceramics (recovered by the field survey team) which suggested that the site was occupied from the late republican period until the mid-sixth century. The site features a series of terraces that slope down towards Lake Butrint, while walls in fact run under the surface of the lake, providing further indication that the water level has risen since the Roman period. The excavations revealed that the earliest villa belongs to the third century BC and is dated by coins of King Pyrrhus. The presence of republican ceramics raises the possibility that Diaporit could be the site of the villa of Atticus or one of his contemporaries, although the exact chronology is still being evaluated (Bowden and Përzhita 2004). After various modifications, the buildings seem to have been abandoned around the start of the third century. Nearby Malathrea too has been suggested as a contender for the villa of Atticus. Malathrea was a fortified farm dating mainly to the Hellenistic period, but in use or re-used during the Roman period. The excavator dated the latest occupation of the site to the early fourth century, indicated by coins of Diocletian (Çondi 1984).

Diaporit was reoccupied around *c.* 490, focussed around a three-aisled Christian basilica, built on the northern side of the site and probably involving partial re-use of some of the buildings of the bath complex. The complex of associated rooms includes a two-storey building, an accompanying chapel, a small bath-house and a tower. The ensemble has been interpreted as either as a monastery or pilgrimage centre. However, in the context of this chapter it is important to note that the late antique use of the site appears to differ significantly from its early imperial occupation, with no sign of grandiose residential structures and with a predominantly religious role. Equally, the suggestion of a period of abandonment lasting for up to 250 years is a further indication of the dangers inherent in assuming continuity of occupation derived from field survey data that indicate activity in both the Roman and late antique periods. As at Butrint, the sequence of occupation at Diaporit extends into the second half of the sixth century.

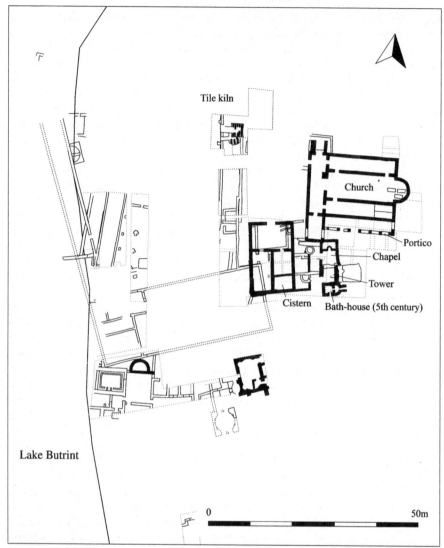

4.8. Diaporit: plan of the late antique monastery (black) and earlier villa.

The excavations overall raise questions regarding the relationship between Diaporit and the town of Butrint. There are certainly significant
differences between the pottery assemblages from the two sites (Reynolds,
in Hodges, Bowden and Lako 2004). For the earlier period of the villa's life
(*c.* mid-first century AD), the ceramics assemblage contains (as might be
expected) significant quantities of fine wares. However, the later first- to
third-century levels, although ceramic-rich, produced almost no fine wares
at all, in marked contrast to Butrint. Differences likewise emerge in the

4.9. Diaporit: reconstruction of the sixth-century monastery.

coarse wares from the two sites: although a similar range of imported kitchen wares is present at each, the local coarse wares at Diaporit appear to derive from a different source to those from Butrint. And yet these two sites are inter-visible and separated by only forty minutes on foot or by rowing boat. Clearly additional studies at Diaporit and at other comparable sites in the vicinity are required to clarify these somewhat surprising economic discrepancies.

'We must live and work as in a state of siege'
(Handbook of English-Albanian Conversation, 1972)

The continued use of the basilica at Diaporit into the later seventh century and beyond is also of significance in relation to the use and occupation of the landscape in the early medieval period. Albania, as we have already seen, is dotted with late antique fortified sites including both newly established hilltop defences and reoccupied prehistoric and classical sites. The Butrint region is no exception to this. The town of Phoenicê (to the north of Lake Butrint) retreated to the eastern end of its fortified acropolis, probably during the sixth century (Bowden 2003) (Fig. 4.10). Phoenicê is of particular note owing to the quite lengthy description provided by Procopius (*Buildings* IV.i, 36-8):

> These two towns, namely Photicê and Phoenicê, stood on low-lying ground and were surrounded by stagnant water which collected there. Consequently the Emperor Justinian, reasoning that it was impossible for walls to be built

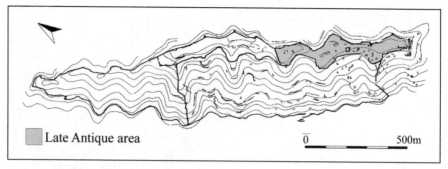

Late Antique area

0   500m

4.10. Plan of Phoenicê showing the city defences.

> about them on foundations of solid construction, left them just as they were,
> but close to them he built forts on rising ground which is exceedingly steep.

Despite the problems of interpretation associated with Procopius and the *Buildings*, it is tempting to see a correlation between his description and the remains of late antique Phoenicê (cf. Karagiorgou 2001: 214-15 for comparable shifts in Thessaly). Much of the Roman town appears to have been built on the lower slopes of the long saddle-backed hill on which the classical and Hellenistic settlement was situated, and on the plain immediately to the south-west. Substantial Roman remains can still be seen, interspersed among the houses of the present village (Ugolini 1932: 14). Environmental data indicate that the Butrint lake originally extended as far as Phoenicê and it is possible that marshy conditions did prevail in some areas of the plain (much as they do today). Certainly, late antique occupation is concentrated on the summit of the steep-sided acropolis, where a basilica was excavated in the 1920s (ibid.: 124-33). A few traces remain visible of a poorly constructed fortification, which follows the line of the classical or Hellenistic city wall for much of its length, although the association of this circuit with Justinian is yet to be proven (see Bowden 2003).

Finds from the summit include the *pythoi* that are characteristic of late antique contexts at Butrint and Diaporit (Ugolini 1932: 189). Coins from the basilica excavations included a number of small Ostrogothic coins with a monogram of Baduila, plus three from the reign of Justinian and a single coin of Heraclius. The baptistery associated with the basilica, erected within a former Hellenistic 'treasury', showed signs of having been destroyed by fire (Ugolini: 107-8).

The classical and Hellenistic site of Çuka e Aitoit, some 12 kilometres south-east of Butrint, was also occupied in late antiquity (Fig. 4.11). Çuka e Aitoit (literally 'Eagle Mountain') is a steep-sided pyramid-shaped hill that dominates the surrounding area of the flood plain of the Pavlas river, at the point where the Pavlas emerges onto the plain. The site therefore controls one of the main north-south land routes. The hill is also clearly

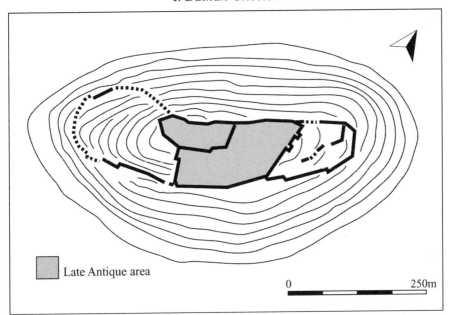

4.11. Çuka e Aitoit: plan of the city defences and later *castrum*.

visible from Corfu. The Hellenistic fortified area of *c.* 4.5 hectares (probably ancient Kestrine), enclosed by three substantial circuit walls of
polygonal and isodomic masonry, was reduced to 1.3 hectares by a later
wall circuit, thought to date to between the fourth and sixth centuries AD
(Lako 1982: 214). The later fortress or *castrum*, built of mortared masonry,
was trapezoidal in shape with at least three towers of triangular, semi-
circular and rectangular plan. Parts of the earlier lower circuit show signs
of reinforcement which are probably contemporary with the construction
of the fortress. Excavations at Çuka e Aitoit in 1959 recovered material
dating from the first to fourth centuries AD, suggesting that these sites
were not necessarily occupied *ex novo* in the later period (Lako 1982: 214).

The hill of Kalivo, lying between Butrint and Diaporit, with its massive
polygonal wall, was also utilised during late antiquity, although surface
finds also indicate Roman-period activity as at Çuka e Aitoit (Budina 1971:
317). Kalivo is in fact a much larger site than nearby Butrint, and appears
to have been densely occupied in certain periods, but it so far lacks trace
of a late antique fortification; it is likely that the combination of the lake
and surrounding marshland afforded considerable protection.

Butrint itself, as stated, may have been confined to its acropolis from
the seventh to ninth centuries, in way similar to that postulated by Haldon
(1999) for the cities of Asia Minor, although this remains to be confirmed.
Those areas excavated in the lower city thus far show no sign of activity
between the early seventh and later ninth century. However, grave finds

59

published by Ugolini, from the cemetery area to the west of the city, indicate that the cemetery remained in use, or was re-used, during the early medieval period (1942: 157).

The initial impression given by this agglomeration of fortified sites is of a population forced to take refuge behind strong walls and only able to survive, as Timothy Gregory puts it in relation to Greece, 'as islands of Hellenism in an increasing tide of barbarism' (1992: 233). While Gregory's ethnic emphasis is different to that of Frashëri cited above, who saw the islands as Slavic and the sea as Albanian, the essential idea is the same, suggesting a population divided along bipartisan lines and existing in a more or less permanent state of hostility and siege. This model of a society polarised on ethnic lines is of course highly compatible with Albania's image of itself during the communist period.

The presence of fortified settlements throughout the Butrint region is certainly indicative of local insecurity. Çuka e Aitoit, Kalivo and the acropolis of Phoenicê are inhospitable sites – steep and rocky and poorly supplied with water, with little to recommend them apart from their defensive properties. Indeed, their locations suggest a dependence on territory beyond their walls in terms of pasture and arable land, although a number of sites such as Çuka e Aitoit include sufficient space for storage of animals within the late antique walled enclosure. A similar question is raised by the intensive late antique occupation of the tiny island of Kephalos in the Ambracian Gulf some 100 kilometres to the south, which must have been dependant on the mainland for grazing and arable farming (see Bowden 2003).

The nature of the Slav incursions into Epirus is a contentious issue, but leaving aside their effect on the region's gene pool, the documentary and archaeological evidence indicate that the impact on social and economic patterns was significant (Chrysos 1981: 68-80; Bowden 2003). While the contraction and abandonment of sites in the early seventh century and the contemporaneous decline in the use of coinage and imported ceramics should not be wholly ascribed to the reportedly devastating raids of the late sixth and early seventh centuries, it would be foolhardy to dismiss a possible connection.

Yet, as we have seen, at Diaporit excavations indicate that activity, including modifications to the church, continued into the late seventh century and possibly beyond, thus demonstrating a Christian presence on an undefended lowland site some sixty years or more after the purported arrival of Slavic settlers. Its relationship with the hilltop site of Kalivo, which lies a few hundred metres to the west, is obviously important in this context. It is unclear if Kalivo was permanently occupied or whether it functioned as a temporary refuge in times of insecurity. Nor can we determine if occupation at Diaporit was continuous or extended beyond pilgrimage, occasional festivals or similar. However, the evidence does suggest that a bipolar model in which *castrum*-dwelling autochthones and

barbarians exist continually separated by physical barriers is overly simplistic. Equally, we can envisage a situation in which the local settlement
hierarchy – Butrint and Phoenicê surrounded by a constellation of satellite
sites – had entirely changed. Although sixth-century Phoenicê is listed as
a *polis* by Hierocles, there seems to be little to distinguish it physically
from numerous other sites, in terms of the strength of its fortifications and
the size of the defended area. By the mid-seventh century, Butrint may
have been little different from the settlements in its hinterland. However,
our present state of knowledge dictates that this must remain a working
hypothesis, as we know very little of the extent of occupation and the
differential nature of material culture at any of these sites.

Conclusion

Numerous questions thus remain unanswered regarding the nature of
land use and occupation in the early medieval Balkans. In Albania, the
later seventh to ninth centuries are largely unknown in many important
respects, yet this basic fact has been obscured by a nationalist historical
model that stresses continuity. This model, which was an entirely political
construct, created a division between the Roman/autochthonous population and the semi-mythical barbarian 'Other'. While this served the purposes of an isolationist regime that needed to stress the unity and
homogeneity of its people and their difference from the world beyond
Albania's borders, the results are at best questionable and at worst
entirely unsustainable. Nonetheless, more than four decades of archaeological activity have resulted in a remarkable body of archaeological
material, at least some of which dates to the period in question. The revival
of a furnished burial rite, represented by the Komani cemeteries, is
indicative of the dramatic changes in social structures that occurred
during the seventh century. This apparent transformation is also indicated by the archaeology of towns such as Butrint, which, despite considerable efforts of archaeologists to demonstrate cultural continuity, cease
functioning as true urban centres in the late sixth or early seventh
century. Whether a consistent population remained within their walls has
yet to be demonstrated archaeologically.

The development of the hilltop fortresses remains equally obscure.
Some sites may have been occupied by the fourth century (if not before),
while others may date to the later fifth and sixth centuries, as was
happening in Italy (cf. Francovich and Hodges 2003). It is likely that we
are looking at a multi-faceted process involving a combination of local
initiatives and possible interventions on the part of the provincial or
imperial administration. The appearance of the *castra* accompanies a
blurring of the distinctions between the urban and rural spheres. By the
later sixth century areas within the city walls of Butrint may have been
undergoing a process of ruralisation, which saw the abandonment of areas

such as that formerly occupied by the triconch palace – symbolic of a rich urban élite.

Nothing can yet be said of settlement patterns in Albania during the eighth and early ninth centuries. Despite the sustained excavation campaigns of the communist decades, no occupation horizons or structures dating to this period have been recovered. An analogous situation exists for the Greek countryside, where recent field surveys have failed to shed light on this period, other than emphasising its apparent invisibility. In Albania, and to some extent in Greece, these lacunae can only be filled by systematic and detailed stratigraphic excavation on a variety of sites, as has occurred in Italy where vast strides have been made in recent years. At Butrint, excavations within the city are allowing the creation of an increasingly coherent local ceramic typology for the fourth to sixth centuries, which can now be applied to sites within the region with the intention of charting changing relationships between the urban and rural spheres. A decade of excavations at Butrint has raised more questions than it has answered, but we are now in a position to take the first tentative steps towards an understanding of the complex interaction between sites in the Butrint region.

Thus, night fell in Albania and the barbarians didn't come. Communism as it was in Albania is over, and its historical platitudes cannot be maintained. For nearly fifty years the barbarians have been 'a kind of solution' in both Albania and Greece, where the creation of a non-Albanian or non-Greek 'Other', both in antiquity and in the present, has sustained a unified national identity. Archaeology has often participated in this construction, which has precluded detailed research on the early medieval period in both countries. Archaeologists from across the political and ideological spectrum (from which we clearly cannot exclude ourselves) must therefore continually question and deconstruct their own preconceived ideas of what the early medieval landscape was, how it was used, and who lived and worked within it.

5

Dark Age Economics revisited

W.A. van Es and the end of the mercantile model in early medieval Europe[1]

W.A. van Es has played a historic role in the study of Dark Age economics. His most important contribution, of course, has been the effective discovery of Dorestad, a critical place in the economic history of early medieval Europe. Before van Es launched his huge excavations at Dorestad, the history of urbanism in post-Roman Europe was determined by the long-distance trade or mercantile model (Hodges 2000: 75-6). At that point, drawing upon a combination of written, archaeological and numismatic sources, historians favoured a paradigm that lent emphasis to the pioneering endeavours of merchants after the end of the migrations. It is hard not to associate the model with the free-market spirit of later nineteenth- and early twentieth-century Europe, coming hard on the heels of Europe's great nineteenth-century migrations to America and Australasia.

The bases of this mercantile model are easily identified. The early medieval written sources mostly address issues of merchants or pilgrims moving between places. Dorestad and Hamwic (Anglo-Saxon Southampton) are typical examples, each known between the later seventh and mid-ninth centuries as a result of references to individuals arriving or leaving the port. Archaeologists, not surprisingly, were greatly influenced by these sources. As a result, in the 1930s and 1940s, Holgar Arbman and Herbert Jankuhn, for example, developed models of long-distance trade between Latin Christendom and southern Scandinavia which modestly echoed Maurice Lombard's global picture of routes joining places (Lombard 1972). Lombard's maps resemble early versions of those airline routes illustrated in the back of airline magazines. The long-distance trade model placed emphasis upon mercantilism rather than the evolution of urbanism. It encouraged an archaeology that concerned itself with the chronology of trade relations rather than how towns and trade played a critical role in the political formation of post-Roman Europe. The history of this model can be readily explained. Resources to excavate large tracts of early medieval urban sites were not available before the late 1960s.

[1] I owe the theme of this chapter to Peter Addyman's remarks in an undergraduate tutorial at Southampton in the spring of 1972 when he had returned from the Göttingen conference. He had been awestruck and possibly a little shocked by W.A. van Es's audacity in excavating large tracts of Dorestad, albeit in advance of imminent development. He recognised, though, that van Es's method offered a topographical interpretation of Dorestad which was impossible at Hamwic, Anglo-Saxon Southampton, where Peter was then digging.

Archaeology, therefore, tended to offer a rather primitive perspective of early medieval urban society. It was tempting to conclude that early medieval urban man was involved in modest operations which, not surprisingly, barely attracting the attention of chroniclers writing in monastic scriptoria. Nevertheless, since the 1930s there had been a tradition of excavating rural settlements on a large scale in Denmark, the Netherlands and Germany. But this archaeological tradition, developed, for example, by J.J. Hatt and A.E. van Giffen, focussed upon a peasant world well outside the remit of early medieval authors, and therefore the results from these large excavations were not related to those from urban sites such as Birka, Dorestad or Haithabu.

When the opportunity to investigate Dorestad arose in the 1960s, van Es approached the excavations in the manner of a Dutch classical archaeologist. He set out to examine the settlement as a regional entity, rooted in a locality. As in his earlier excavations at Wijster, the Roman and Migration-period village, he was interested in a 'native' settlement 'beyond the Imperial frontier' (van Es 1967). The concept, perhaps, involved grafting together two very different historical investigations: the so-called long-distance trade model advanced by Arbman and Jankuhn with the established approach to rural settlements developed by van Giffen and Hatt. Van Es, with the support of the Dutch State Archaeological Service (ROB) behind him, possessed sufficient resources to do this, but inevitably it meant developing a strategy that was controversial at the time (van Es 1973). The implications of van Es's strategy have not been fully appreciated, perhaps because we still await some of the rich body of data unearthed by the project. Nevertheless, after nearly thirty years the mercantile trade model still fascinates archaeologists and historians alike, while van Es's approach to the subject, treating Dorestad as a regional urban entity, has yet to be fully grasped.

My book *Dark Age Economics* (Hodges 1982) (hereafter *DAE*) reified the mercantile model, although it called for regional approaches to the interpretation of urban evolution in the early Middle Ages. It owed much to van Es. He showed great interest in my research on the imported ceramics of Hamwic, Anglo-Saxon Southampton, and served as the external examiner for my doctoral thesis on that subject. Not unnaturally, I was influenced by his innovative and thoughtful research at Dorestad. However, in the wake of the publication of *DAE*, I had the opportunity to reassess the model (see Astill 1985; Moreland 2000: 72-6; Whyman 2002). In *The Anglo-Saxon Achievement* emphasis was given to urban evolution with a diachronic regional framework (Hodges 1989; for an elegant critique see, for example, Moreland 2000: 72-3). This new approach owed much to the discoveries made at the Benedictine monastic site of San Vincenzo al Volturno, a Carolingian-period monastic city.

In the remainder of this chapter, I shall offer a few reflections on *DAE*, taking into account the changing nature of research in this field,

5. Dark Age Economics *revisited*

while paying particular heed to van Es's contribution to one of the formative debates about European history which, with time, only grows in importance.

*

In *Dark Age Economics* I proposed an evolutionary scheme for regional urban development in early medieval Europe based upon Carol A. Smith's model of the spatial arrangements of centres and their satellites. In the 1970s, when Smith formulated her model, it seemed a far more pertinent method for approaching urbanism than the attempts by archaeologists and historians to define urbanism in terms of whether a place conformed to certain specific criteria (Smith 1976). This anthropological and geographical approach to the past seemed an apposite means of moving beyond the long shadow cast by historians like Henri Pirenne because it placed emphasis upon the regional integration of Europe rather than on the casual recording of places and people by monkish chroniclers. Taking this ambitious framework, I attempted to chart the rise of the North Sea mercantile system as trade around the Mediterranean 'pond' collapsed. In particular, emphasis was given to an Austrasian-driven system in the North Sea, influenced, it must be admitted, by the discoveries made at Dorestad, and in competition with a Neustrian-driven trade system, emanating from Quentovic (cf. Lebecq 1991). Within this context, I attempted to define a typology for the principal urban centres linked to this trade: class A emporia being periodic fairs; class B emporia being large monopolistic centres; class C emporia being solar central-places – regional centres (see now Verhulst 2002: 133-4). Much of the study was then given over to a gazetteer of such sites, the traders, their ships and the objects of their trade. With a small excursus on the subsistence strategies of these places, I then focussed upon how class B emporia like Dorestad were eclipsed, and replaced by regionally-oriented markets, and, as such, this was an expression of the transformation of much of Europe from kin-based political structures towards the creation of state systems.

    DAE was described by one historian in a review as catatonically obscure. Another recently commented that it 'provides a rather peculiar view of North Sea and Baltic trade' (Bachrach 1998: 223 n. 46). In retrospect, its originality lay in its use of archaeology to investigate a major historical problem – the origins of towns and trade. It was an anthropologically-oriented predecessor of Stéphane Lebecq's detailed historical analysis of the same theme (Lebecq 1983; 1986; 1991). However, while the archaeology and anthropology of *DAE* owed much to Colin Renfrew's provocative writings on European prehistory in the 1970s, the axiomatic basis of its archaeological argument drew upon my research at Hamwic and inevitable comparisons with Dorestad.

    The fundamental concept of *DAE*, as I have already noted, was Carol A.

Smith's model for the evolution of production-distribution systems. The model draws upon Smith's research in Middle America where, as an anthropologist and geographer, she recorded peasant marketing (Hodges 1988: 16-25). The attraction of her model is that it emphasises spatial arrangements, and in particular the relationship between central-places and their regions. As I have pointed out elsewhere (Hodges 1988: 16-25), if there is a flaw in Smith's work, it is the (understandable) tendency to present her typology of regional systems as a series of static phenomena (or anthropological/historical time slices). In practice, the evidence from Dark Age Europe, first explored in *DAE*, illustrates the evolution of each one of these regional systems. For example, in *DAE* some emphasis was placed on the evolution of monopolistic dendritic central-places (gateway communities) from places of periodic exchange (class A emporia) to planned urban communities (class B emporia).

It is likely that the future of regional models such as Smith's will be contingent upon models drawn from a multi-disciplinary data base including archaeological and written sources. These sources, used together, offer the time-depth wide-angled view of regional development that is effectively concealed from the anthropologist or geographer.

The second theme of *DAE* was a preliminary approach to examining Pirenne's thesis on the relationship between the collapse of Mediterranean trade in later Roman times and the rise of the Carolingian empire with its concomitant implications for the origins and growth of long-distance trade and urban communities around the North Sea area. The main objective was to use archaeological evidence to shed new light on the debate. Twenty-five years later there can be no doubt that *only* archaeological evidence will permit us to move beyond the shadow cast by Pirenne's seminal essays on both the origins of medieval cities and the rise of Carolingian Europe. The complex chronology of change in the Mediterranean is well documented by archaeological means, and wholly challenges Pirenne's thesis. On the other hand, the new data for the evolution of trading systems around the North Sea, largely on the basis of excavations at emporia such as Dorestad, tend to confirm and flesh out the skeletal lines of Pirenne's far-reaching studies. Pirenne's model is still valuable because it serves to articulate a history of European regional development. Born of his multinational experience in a German concentration camp, Pirenne's central tenet is that post-Roman Europe cannot be viewed as a collection of discrete regional units. Instead, it was linked by a common past to Rome that embraced not only the only Roman provinces but, in Mortimer Wheeler's phrase, the regions beyond the Roman frontiers.

As to the details of *DAE*, much has changed. Numerous excavations during the 1980s have enlarged our understanding of the chronology of the trading systems. For example, it is now evident that the roots of the seventh-century North Sea system lie in the sixth century and owe much to Frankish mercantile incursions into the region (cf. Näsman 1998).

Indeed, by *c.* 600, as the Roman pond, as Pirenne described the Mediterranean, was reduced to a core of mercantile activity largely focussed upon the Levant, the North Sea was evolving as an integrated system embracing not only the littoral between the Rhine and Seine estuaries, but also the tribes of Wessex, Kent, East Anglia and, significantly, western Denmark. These long-running connections, almost certainly founded upon personalised trading treaties, were the basis for the significant changes of the last quarter of the seventh century.

The creation of Dorestad as an urban centre effectively belongs to the late seventh century when, in conflict with the neighbouring Austrasians, the Frisian king established an urban community. Quentovic and Hamwic belong to the same moment in time (Hodges 1989: 71-114; Lebecq 1991). Ian Wood has cogently described the peer-polity interaction – the tensions between the Franks and their coastal neighbours – which provided the stimulus for investing enormous resources in these permanent gateway communities (Wood 1983; 1993). The result was to increase the scale of North Sea interchange, while giving it an institutional status that the periodic activities of the sixth and first three-quarters of the seventh century did not possess. This was the moment of transformation of the Migration-period economies. The next critical moment arrived when the emporia were eclipsed in the first quarter of the ninth century by the establishment of dispersed regional markets – the so-called *portus*, or regional market-place – in line with Charlemagne's economic strategy to integrate and enlarge his underdeveloped economy.

Chapter 3 of *DAE* contended that there were three types of emporia: class A, periodic trading places; class B, urban communities with a pronounced mercantile component; class C, solar central-places – regional administrative centres. With a great deal more archaeological evidence being available, it is evident that the class A sites were numerous in this period, while there were few class B sites. Class C now appears to be a more contentious category.

The most notable addition to the class A sites are the beach sites discovered in the western Baltic and the so-called 'wiclets' in England. The extraordinary number of beach sites identified in Denmark may reflect the fact that these places were used for short periods as the coastline constantly changed (Ulriksen 1994). 'Wiclets', small emporia, are more a matter of supposition; these were places like Sandtun (Kent) (Gardiner et al. 2001), Thetford (Andrews 1995) and Burnham Overy (Norfolk) (cf. Rogerson 2003) – which in many respects grew to be regional markets (or, to use the Continental historical nomenclature, *portus* settlements (for example Verhulst 2002: 91-3)) in the ninth century.

The class B sites such as Dorestad, Hamwic and so on, are familiar as trading places. However, as I have indicated elsewhere (Hodges 2000), large-scale excavations (as opposed to trenching) has revealed the topography of these places. Van Es's decision to strip large tracts of Dorestad to document the centre's topography proved a stimulus to understanding the internal arrangements of places such as Hamwic, Ipswich and Ribe in the same way. These data throw a great deal of light on master-planning and the political economy. The fundamental issue about the foundation of these gateway communities was that they were political entities predominantly intended to serve their regions. As a result, long-distance trade was a limited waterfront activity, of signal symbolic importance for prestige goods exchange, whereas the greater part of the settlement was involved in agrarian and craft production. In other words, the long-standing notion that places like Dorestad and Hamwic, for example, were only ports-of-trade is misplaced; these places were harbingers of regional artisanal production. Morton has illustrated this point satisfactorily at Hamwic (Morton 1992: 55-68); the same has become evident at Ribe, where traded goods are concentrated in a small area by the waterfront (Bencard, Jorgensen and Brinch Madsen 1990). Dorestad, it is now evident, had a large agrarian nucleus (van Es 1990: 154-62).

One issue, however, remains to be examined. The class B emporia were not cities that evolved thanks to some collective memory. These were founded as planned entities in the manner that Augustus and Justinian had founded new towns. The models for these new Dark Age towns did not lie in the immediate past, but presumably upon their founders' perceptions of urbanism as they interpreted it. Interestingly, as in the case of great imperial planned towns, the emporia evolved little over the course of their histories. In other words, the founding notions – enshrined in the topographic arrangements – proved satisfactory until these places were deserted.

The geography of the emporia has changed little over the last twenty years. Major discoveries include the identification of Quentovic near Montreuil-sur-Mer in the Canche valley (Hill et al. 1990), and Rouen (Gauthier 1989). The extent and histories of London, Ipswich and York have become a great deal clearer (Hodges 2000). Perhaps the most outstanding discovery, though, has been the extent and character of Ribe, Denmark's earliest emporium. Thanks to dendrochronological dating, it is clear that the settlement, complete with tenements, was founded in the early eighth century (Bencard, Jorgensen and Brinch Madsen 1990).

Class C sites – solar central-places – were in fact either Carolingian-period monastic centres serving as places to promote the Carolingian renaissance ethos (Hodges 1997a; Devroey 1985; 1993; 2003) or class B settlements which had lost their international status to operate at the centre of regions. These places became important, as I shall indicate below, as the age of the emporia was eclipsed by an intention to develop regional economies.

Little that is new has been added to the history of seafaring in this period over the past twenty years. Strangely, late Roman and Byzantine ship-building, unlike many skills with their roots in Mediterranean society, were not imitated in north-west Europe. Van Es and Verwers have graphically illustrated the restricted cargo capacities of Rhenish shipping in their recent study of Dorestad's imported pottery (van Es and Verwers 1993). The failure of North Sea boat-builders to make deep-draughted vessels in this period (such as the early Byzantine 'Yassi Ada' type that would have carried Anglo-Saxon and Frankish pilgrims to the Holy Land) presumably reflects the limited demand for cargo vessels as well as the emphasis upon transporting limited cargoes of prestige objects as opposed to bulk goods. In other craft production there was far more interchange. For example, the eighth- and ninth-century glassware from Dorestad and Ribe looks similar to the glass production on the Beneventan monastery of San Vincenzo al Volturno (Hodges 1991; see Stevenson 2001). The common link was probably a pool of master glassworkers from either the middle Rhineland or the Veneto. Other crafts, of course, had more regional roots, as the studies of Dorestad's many different objects, ranging from barrels to stone mortars, show (van Es 1990: 163-72). An unknown element in the production of and demand for craft goods is the relationship between the craftsmen who worked in the emporia and those in 'monastic cities' such as St Denis or San Vincenzo al Volturno.

Not surprisingly, 'objects of trade' have been the subject of many studies (Steuer 1987). Not least, the numerous studies of Dorestad's material culture reflect the extensive network of production sites that the emporium drew upon. These studies bear witness to the European nature of trade in this period. Tating ware, for example, the distinctive tin-foil decorated pitchers made in kilns in the Rhineland and north-west France, have been found not only in north-west Europe from Birka to St Denis, but at Borg inside the arctic circle as well (Henderson and Holand 1992: 32; Munch, Johansen and Roesdahl 2003). Evidently made as a prestige good for perhaps liturgical purposes in the Carolingian realm, this distinctive pitcher was favoured for other reasons by merchants in emporia such as Dorestad, Haithabu and Ribe, and imbued with other prestige status – perhaps because of its mercantile and liturgical overtones – by Viking-period merchants in Birka. Clearly, the taste for Tating ware appealed to northern Europe's emerging elites. As a prestige valuable, it may have been made for one purpose in Latin Christendom and interpreted as a vessel of influence by those pagan communities beyond Christendom who associated the pitcher with 'the Other', just as they attached importance to Arabic imports.

Van Es paid special attention to Dorestad's subsistence strategy, noting the importance of the farms which occupied the northern sector of the settlement (van Es 1990: 58). As the emporia served peasant societies, it is hardly surprising that the rural economy was driven by the political systems of which the emporia, after the later seventh century, like the later 'monastic cities', were major manifestations. In other words, the notion that early medieval kingdoms slowly accrued surpluses and on these bases founded urban communities is undoubtedly a fallacy. As a result, it remains important to document the pattern of rural settlement within the environs of the emporia. Dorestad's hinterland is relatively well documented, but still an exception. Only the environs of Ipswich, Ribe and Birka – of the major Dark Age emporia – are well documented. The recent excavations in 1995 of the Whitehouse estate site, 5 kilometres from Anglo-Saxon Ipswich, brought to light an enclosed homestead poor in material culture (Newman 1992). Evidently, furnishing the emporia with resources, as I have indicated with Hamwic, rather like supplying Carolingian-period monastic cities, was a complex arrangement, based upon a spread of far-flung properties (Hodges 1989: 80-92). The key to the prosperity of the emporia was the articulation of these regional systems, as Smith anticipated, and, incidentally, as van Es's colleagues have shown when illustrating the various sources of Dorestad's material culture (van Es 1990).

The emergence of complex regional market-places, taking advantage of estate surpluses, undoubtedly triggered change in the ninth century leading to the demise of the emporia. In *DAE* great emphasis was placed upon Colin Renfrew's concept of the 'multiplier effect' – in essence, a multi-causal, systemic explanation of change. Without doubt, a major factor, however, was the explicit intention of the Carolingians to develop their economies for the purposes of emulating their Roman forebears. Macro-economic factors, of course, played a part, as did growing regional competition between areas such as Aquitaine which were highly monetised (judging from recent evidence: Jeanne-Rose 1996) and those in Italy which were not (Rovelli 2000). There can be little doubt that the emergence of rural market-places in much of the Carolingian heartlands as well as in the wealthier kingdoms of England induced a switch of emphasis from long-distance trade towards investment in regional development. By the 830s this had caused significant economic problems in those regions beyond the immediate rim of the Carolingian realms, notably the western Baltic and central northern Africa, which gave rise to the first sustained raiders from these parts (see now Sénac 2002). Significantly, whatever, the weight of historical emphasis ascribed to the Vikings and Arabs, the introduction of regional markets – a feature of Carolingian legislation following the Council of Frankfurt – took hold, withstanding the political turbulence of the later ninth century. Indeed, the Vikings, when as conquerors and kings rather than raiders they took command of regions, conspicuously adopted the *portus* model, creating solar central-places such as Ipswich, Norwich, Stamford, Lincoln and York. Their leadership led to an infusion of economic activity in previously underdeveloped regions like East Anglia and Northumbria.

The archaeological evidence now invites us to seek the origins of medieval regional markets in the heyday of the Carolingian age. This period marked the beginning of the end of the emporia – places, such as Dorestad and Hamwic, which were in sharp decline long before they were raided by Viking pirates (Hodges and Whitehouse 1983: 164-8; *contra* Hall 2000).

This model places great emphasis upon the relationship between certain individuals in formulating political policies and the collectives that adopted them. The model flies in the face of earlier thinking which placed emphasis upon a less rational, more organic explanation for the evolution of Dark Age economics (see Moreland 2000 for a traditionalist's approach). Explanations of economic evolution which favoured entrepreneurs, population growth, regional surpluses, and the climate as motors of change cannot be ignored. But, the archaeological evidence emphatically urges us to adopt a paradigm which stresses the intervention of master-planners, undoubtedly major kings, in the creation of places such as Dorestad, Hamwic and Ribe. These master-planners were responding to their circumstances in highly creative ways, using their standing as place-makers to strengthen their political standing in the fluid peer-polity arrangements of this age. The written sources shed no light on these great events, yet, thanks to the large-scale archaeological investigations of these places, launched first at Dorestad, we can comprehend the regional strategies almost as if these Dark Age figures were emulating the likes of the Emperors Augustus or Hadrian. To have done this, using Dark Age archaeological evidence, given its often ephemeral and vestigial nature (unlike classical archaeology), is surely one of the great archaeological achievements of the twentieth century. These data, after all, permit us critical insights into the economic roots of a European polity that we continue to share. It is in this context that I should like to pay homage to W.A. van Es's achievement.

6

Charlemagne's elephant

The great rulers of antiquity, like military theorists of more modern times, were very well aware of the dictum in one or another variation that 'war is merely the continuation of policy by other means'. Charlemagne was no exception. His most ambitious diplomatic initiatives were reserved for Harun al Rashid, whose caliphate dominated the erstwhile Persian Empire as well as several provinces of the eastern and western halves of the Roman Empire (Bachrach 1998: 226).

Relations between the Mediterranean and northern Europe in the age of Charlemagne have puzzled archaeologists and historians. At face value the two parts of Europe appear to have been completely separated, despite Charlemagne's famous coronation in Rome in December 800. Furthermore, relations between Latin Christendom, Byzantium and the Abbasid caliphate (based in Baghdad) appear to have been virtually non-existent. Only intrepid pilgrims bridged the ideological divides that separated these three great regions with their different religions in order to visit the Holy Land. What puzzles archaeologists, in particular, is that while the Christian regions of England, France and Germany apparently had little contact with the south and east, archaeological evidence has long revealed that the Viking-age communities of the Baltic Sea enjoyed successful commercial partnerships reaching to Byzantium and the Orient. Moreover, ninth-century Frankish glass and decorated pottery have been found in excavations of Viking-period settlements as far north as the Lofoten Islands (Munch, Johansen and Roesdahl 2003).

Ever since archaeologist Haljmar Stolpe began his excavations in the barrow cemetery surrounding the central Swedish island port at Birka in 1870 (situated in Lake Mälaren), it has been evident that the north-south divide in post-classical Europe was more virtual than real (Ambrosiani and Clarke 1992). Stolpe found numerous ninth-century merchants' graves containing Arab silver dirhems, similar to the thousands found in hoards in western Russia and around the shores of the Baltic. Many of these coins were defaced with Scandinavian runes, as if to destroy their ideological power. Other oriental grave-goods include silks and collapsible balances. Notable discoveries included a finger-ring bearing the legend *Allah* in Arabic from grave 515, and a cylindrical glass vessel of likely Syrian manufacture decorated with bird and plant motifs from grave 542 (Arbman 1937). Similar finds have been found at other trading sites around the Baltic. Hedeby, for example, the Danish-planned emporium situated at the base of Jutland, boasts not only Arabic objects, but also a lead seal dated *c.* 840 belonging to a certain Theodosius, *patrikos*, imperial *protospatharius* and *chartularius* of the public vestiary, chief of the Byzantine emperor's personal security (Piltz 1998).

Did such objects occur in Latin Christendom in the age of Charlemagne? Only a handful of ninth-century Arabic dirhems have been discovered to date, and only one hoard of them buried in the bed of the river Reno near Bologna in Central Italy (McCormick 2001). Silks, Syrian glass and other exotica are similarly scarce. Archaeologists argue whether the dirhems were melted down to make Charlemagne's silver-rich coins, while as yet few places where silk might survive have been excavated. On the other hand, while the written sources rarely describe commerce, special gifts did attract the attention of monkish chroniclers. For example, the Emperor Charlemagne was sent a brass clock by the Abbasid caliph, Harun al-Rashid in Baghdad. According to the Emperor's biographer, it was,

> ... a marvellous mechanical contraption, in which the course of the twelve hours moved according to a water clock, with as many brazen little balls, which fell down on the hour and through their fall made a cymbal ring underneath. On this clock there were also twelve horsemen who at the end of each hour stepped out of twelve windows, closing the previously open windows by their movements (quoted by Duncan 1998: 128-9; also Hill 1996: 232).

For Charlemagne, this extraordinary object must have represented learning and progress, much as a Model T Ford did in an isolated town in the early twentieth century. The clock, however, was modest by comparison with more Harun's fabled present to his Frankish peer.

Befitting Charlemagne's image of himself as a Roman emperor, Harun sent Charlemagne an elephant, called Abu l'-Abbas, which had originally been owned by an Indian raja before Harun's predecessor, Caliph Al-Mahdi, acquired it (see now Dutton 2004: 189). The gift of the elephant did not come out of the blue. The embassy to the Frankish court was led by the governor of Egypt, Ibrahim Ibn al-Aghlab, in response to a mission despatched by Charlemagne to the caliph's court in 797 – the first of three embassies sent to the caliphate (the others set out in 802 and 807 respectively). Ibrahim crossed the Mediterranean and disembarked at Pisa. From there, in part following the old Via Cassia from Rome to Turin, the embassy journeyed over the Alps to Charlemagne's court in the Rhineland. Once in Germany, Charlemagne presumably built a house for Abu l'-Abbas, where the creature lived for the best part of a decade. We know only one further detail of the elephant's colourful life. The Frankish annals record that when King Godfred of the Danes seized traders from a place called *Reric* – possibly old Lübeck – and installed them at a place that the annalist calls *Sliastorp* (probably Hedeby near Schleswig in north Germany), Charlemagne took the elephant with him on his march to quell the trouble. The two great casualties of the campaign were Godfred, who was assassinated during a revolt in the Danish camp, and Abu l'-Abbas. The elephant died at Lippeham on Luneburg heath.

The story of the elephant draws the thinnest of historical threads together, forging connections between the Arabs, Latin Christendom and the Vikings: between Muslims, Christians and Nordic pagans, setting in motion a cycle of entangled relations. But we should be cautious of taking the story at face value. Inevitably Harun's gift begs many questions: what kind of boat was used to carry the beast to Pisa? It could not have been accommodated on any of the known late Roman or high medieval wrecks so far discovered in Mediterranean waters (cf. McCormick 2001: 513). Are we to assume that the deep-draughted cargo vessel could be docked against a quay at Pisa? How did Ibrahim's embassy progress to Germany? Did Charlemagne build elephant houses at his palaces of Ingelheim, Aachen and Nijmegen? How did the elephant, a tangible commodity from another culture, influence his attitudes to that culture and, consequently, to the re-examination of his own ideology? Was it old Roman imperial vanity that persuaded him to take the creature on the Danish campaign?

The clock and the elephant cannot have failed to open Charlemagne's eyes to the expanding horizons of the ninth-century world. Like the Vikings, he must have been aware of the silver-rich mines of the caliphate and perhaps of the harbours in China open to foreigners since 792. Quite clearly, he must have known that the Abbasids were a source of silks and spices. Less conspicuous gifts such as these are regularly noted from the later eighth century onwards by the *Liber Pontificalis* (Book of the Pontiffs) in the possession of Rome's churches (Delogu 2000). Similarly, a rare description of the rich treasury of the Benedictine monastery of Monte Cassino lists silks and exotica (Citarella and Willard 1983). Excavations of Monte Cassino's sister monastery at San Vincenzo al Volturno in Central Italy have produced sherds of an Abbasid polychrome dish, glass-making following the Syrian tradition, and a sword chape made of nephrite jade derived from China (Hodges 1997a). Yet aside from these objects, oriental culture is notably absent.

Why was this? The principal reason is that this was an agrarian society. The engines of production were royal estate centres and monasteries as towns had not survived beyond the seventh century in Latin Christendom. Rome, of course, never truly died as an urban centre. Recent archaeological excavations in the Forum of Nerva show that north European pilgrims and tourists (such as the retired eighth-century West Saxon king Ine and the young Alfred the Great) would have discovered town life squeezed between the constellation of monasteries that occupied the eternal city in post-classical times (Meneghini and Santangeli Valenziani 2001). Yet Rome was not so much a town in the sense that it had been in the age of the Emperor Augustus with streets and public buildings and residences, as a collection of elite centres with thousands of inhabitants that necessitated a bare minimum of production and procurement services. Rome, without doubt, became a town again in the later eighth century when, with Carolingian political support, it entertained a new vigour, situated as it was midway between the centres of occidental power in the Rhineland and east Mediterranean. Many great churches in the city – basilicas such as SS Quattro Coronati and Santa Prassede – remain a testament to this important revival of its post-classical fortunes (Krautheimer 1980).

North of the Alps, town life was revived around 700 in a particular and almost quarantined sense in a few great places occupying the edges of the North Sea littoral: Rouen, Quentovic, Dorestad, Hamwic (Southampton), Lundenwic (London), Ipswich, Eoforwic (York), Medemblik, Hedeby and Ribe (Hodges 1982; 2000). These places went largely unnoticed by contemporary chroniclers, yet possessed the hallmarks of later medieval towns: customs, quays, warehouses, gridded streets regularly maintained, tenements and industrial zones.

These emporia (trade centres) are archaeology's special contribution to Dark Age history. Like modern shopping malls or airports, they were non-places, in the sense that they were overlooked by contemporary historians (cf. Augé 1998). Their rich material culture was first noted in the mid-nineteenth century. Then famished peasants plundered the bonefields of Dorestad (at the mouth of the Rhine), and at the same time Southampton's inquisitive citizens were digging up parts of Hamwic, the eighth- to ninth-century town on the low-lying brickearths in the Itchenside suburb of St Mary's. But only in the last fifty years, following excavation sponsored by the Gestapo at Hedeby on the eve of the Second World War, has the geography of these places become apparent. Hamwic, we now know, was shaped by a rectilinear street grid, not unlike an ancient city, with groups of dwellings clustered in each *insula*. Initially, Hamwic was interpreted as a traders' town, an emporium humming with foreigners. But closer analysis of the rubbish pits shows that it was in fact a centre for regional craft production. Sunk deep into the brickearth, these pits are brimming with refuse as well as rubbish such as animal bones. The first, distinctive English coins known as *sceattas* also occur in striking numbers (Metcalf 2003).

The same features have now been found at the other great centres of this age. Lundenwic, occupying rising ground west of the deserted Roman walled city, was quite as rich in imported and local material culture, as excavations beneath the Royal Opera House and even in the grounds of 10 Downing Street have shown. Ipswich, initially no more than a riverside nucleus, was furnished with a street grid rising well away from the river Gipping. In one sector the distinctive grey burnished pitchers known as Ipswich ware were made in huge quantities. South-east of York's Roman walled city, beside the river Foss, a similar tract of a Northumbrian emporium known as Eoforwic has been excavated. Again it is singularly rich in finds. The pattern is repeated at Quentovic, the great Frankish emporium, now a green-field site near Montreuil-sur-Mer, and Dorestad, where in advance of a housing development in the 1960s, a great swathe of the Rhine-mouth emporium that served the interests of the Carolingian manufactures in the Bonn-Cologne region was excavated. In common with the line of later eighth- to ninth-century craft workshops found in the central Italian Benedictine monastery of San Vincenzo al Volturno, these places were awash with material culture, much of which has been left for archaeologists to study.

What the emporia lacked distinguishes them as centres. The secular and ecclesiastical elite were absent. Traces of timber or stone palaces like those found at Northampton, for example, simply do not exist in these towns. Churches rarely occur. Hamwic boasts possible examples made of slender posts, as does Dorestad. However, minsters built of stone such as Brixworth (Northamptonshire) or small rural basilicas such as Escomb (Co. Durham) are missing. In a sense, the excavated dwellings, known to archaeologists from the holes vacated by their posts or earthfast beams, follow broadly vernacular forms and reveal only limited variation. Paradoxically, of course, the elite were present in spirit. No archaeologist seriously doubts that the emporia were created by powerful leaders to channel the exchange of prestige goods and to control regional production. Outside Hamwic lay the royal palace of Hamtun; Mercian kings maintained estates at Chelsea near Lundenwic; the Bishop of Utrecht held property in Dorestad. Understated though the ambitions of these places were, we should not underestimate the eagerness of kings and clerics to profit from them.

Hamwic covered more than forty hectares; Lundenwic covered perhaps sixty. As many as 5,000 people lived in these places at their zenith, a figure at least fifty times larger than a large village or royal estate. In each the gravelled streets were regularly repaired, just as the plank-made jetties stretching out into the river at Dorestad were lengthened and maintained as the Rhine bed shifted away from the town.

Did such places exist on the north shores of the Mediterranean? Many historians believe that Venice was possibly as ambitious a centre, replacing Marseilles as the conduit leading from the Mediterranean into central Europe (cf. Ammerman 2003; McCormick 2001). Thousands of traders lived on the islands, if we accept the accounts of Frankish chroniclers of Charlemagne's dogged attempts to conquer the archipelago. As yet, too few archaeological excavations have been possible, but glimpses of the ninth-century levels are intriguing. Several historians believe that Comacchio further south, at the mouth of the river Po on the Adriatic, was another emporium (Balzaretti 1996). Recent survey ahead of a prospective excavation would appear to affirm Comacchio as a critical point on the Adriatic, though its exact chronology will prove to be of great interest given that Ravenna's role as a Byzantine capital seems to have been in sharp decline in the later seventh century, judging from current excavations at Classe by Andrea Augenti.

In complete contrast to Rome, the emporia were without history or memory, ritual or monuments. As such these places could not be central to Charlemagne's vision of a renascent Christendom, with its architecture, art and cultural spirit rooted in the glory of ancient Rome. Convinced of the need to extend the market system beyond these monopolistic centres, Charlemagne promulgated laws intended to introduce regional markets. At the same time laws were issued to encourage the use of a common silver currency based on a closely monitored weight. After 793-4 money-brokers, from Naples to Hedeby, minted silver *deniers* to the new euro-standard (Grierson and Blackburn 1986). It would be foolhardy to suggest that all Europe subscribed to the new economic order, any more than it subscribed to Charlemagne's cultural revolution. It did not. Nevertheless, there was an incremental increase in productivity and trade.

Certainly new towns were created in flourishing regions such as Mercia, Wessex, Flanders and central Italy, while extra-mural markets grew up outside the walls of many monasteries. The archaeological remains of these incipient market towns are often fairly vestigial. In Mercian towns like Hereford and Tamworth, at Winchester in Wessex and Norwich in East Anglia, emergent urban nuclei clearly existed, presaging the planned towns of the late ninth or early tenth centuries. The same is true in places like Ghent or Huy, while further south in Italy new towns like Sicopolis, near Capua, and Centocelle near Civitavecchia were laid out rather in the image of the mid-ninth-century Leonine city filling the zone between the Vatican and the river Tiber at Rome (Marazzi 1994). These were secular versions of the *vici*, the extra-mural market settlements described by chroniclers outside the holy precincts of monasteries such as Monte Cassino (Italy) and St Denis (France) and now identified as clusters of timber buildings in the extensive excavations at San Vincenzo al Volturno, little different from a sector of a north European emporium (Lebecq 2000).

Known to King Alfred from his pilgrimage as a youth to Rome, these places must have been in his mind as he instructed the shift around 886 from Lundenwic to Lundenburg, within the old walls of the Roman city. A wall-painting in London's Royal Exchange, painted in 1912, depicts King Alfred on a piebald horse amid the ruins of the Roman city, sagely approving an architect's plans for the new capital. The image may be a little farfetched, but excavations now reveal a block of 30 hectares laid out in a rectilinear grid mirroring, perhaps, the Middle Saxon field system that had existed here, and clearly resembling the earlier town-plan of Lundenwic to the west. Alfred, we may suppose, the quintessential proponent of Charlemagne's ideas on cultural values and government, was locating his premier city in a place that possessed the spirit of antiquity – a place with a memory, as opposed to a non-place (Hodges 2000: 112-15). At the same time the Anglo-Scandinavian rulers of Eoforwic abandoned the Foss-side emporium for the security and traditions embedded within the Roman walled town of York; the same happened at Rouen, where its Frankish rulers undoubtedly made the same connection between safety and memory.

The rise of towns, of course, reflected rural productivity and a burgeoning demand for craft production at all levels of society. Excavations of villages from all parts of Carolingian Europe show a growing emphasis upon improved animal husbandry as well as crop management. Villages such as Kootwyk, occupying marginal ground in the sparse sandy Veluwe region of the Netherlands, were remodelled, in this case as its iron ore extraction activities lent the community a new significance (Heidinga 1987a). Even beyond the bounds of Christendom, the effects of the new order were felt. Recent excavations of the Viking-age village of Vorbasse (Jutland) brought to light traces of a horizontal-wheel water-mill, a technological device which historians once imagined to exist in Denmark only when it was an established Christian nation in the twelfth (Hvass 1986; 1988). The archaeological evidence suggests that Carolingian-period Viking magnates were every bit as aware of the new technologies as their Christian contemporaries who possessed similar water-mills on their estates at, for example, Old Windsor in Wessex and Tamworth in Mercia. In a nutshell, ninth-century Scandinavians, it is now clear, were tied in not only to the trade in prestige goods emanating form the Abbasid caliphate but also to the new technological information emanating from the heart of Latin Christendom. Nothing better illustrates the integration of Europe as Charlemagne, using new architecture, arts and literacy, promoted a new age of cultural politics.

But precisely who provided the bridge between Christendom and the Orient? As we have seen, much of the evidence is uncomfortably slight. Certainly, after *c.* 800 references in the chronicles to pilgrimages to the Holy Land increase as significantly as the references in the *Liber Pontificalis* to gifts of silks to Rome's churches. Is it coincidental that this was the moment that Abbasid silver dirhems first occurred in Swedish towns like Birka, when the clock arrived in Aachen and when the monks in San Vincenzo al Volturno's workshops made lamps using Arabic techniques? Surely not.

Whether Charlemagne and his contemporaries were influenced by the pilgrims who had been to Palestine and had seen the great Abbasid cities of the Levant (where town life persisted uninterrupted in its Arabic reformulation of classical townscapes) is a matter of conjecture (cf. McCormick 2001). Any contemporary mention of such admiration by a Christian chronicler was heresy. Yet, as the archaeology of the eighth and ninth centuries becomes a little more familiar, we must seriously envisage that, just as the Baltic Sea was regularly in contact with the Abbasid caliphate via the long riverine route passing through western Russia to the Black Sea, so the Carolingian, Byzantine and Arabic worlds were far more interconnected that the media of this Dark Age would have its readers believe. Beyond, the Silk Route, taking in great centres like Merv, connected the west with China, and south, new excavations in east Africa have revealed a string of emporia prompted by Abbasid venturers (Horton 1987). Such contact, as the celebrated Belgian historian Henri Pirenne long ago surmised, was the scaffolding on which the Middle Ages were constructed.

San Vincenzo al Volturno and
the Plan of St Gall[1]

The monastery of the blessed martyr Vincenzo which is situated near the source of the river Vulturno and is now celebrated for its great community of monks... (Paul the Deacon, *History of the Lombards*, translated by W.D. Foulke: Book IV, Chapter XL, 283).

The discovery of the ruins of San Vincenzo al Volturno was quite unexpected. The immense body of data associated with these remains brings a new dimension to the archaeology of the Early Middle Ages. In some ways it is as though a new chronicle had been discovered – not in a well-known archive or familiar place, but in a territory which until now had figured modestly in the history of the first millennium AD. The original intention of the project to indicate the size and extent of the monastery and at the same time to examine the archaeology of its villages, has proved difficult to achieve simply because of the magnitude of the archaeological remains. Nevertheless, it is appropriate to recall the aims of the project and to consider what light these discoveries shed on the Plan of St Gall and the concept of a Carolingian monastic design. This question is bound up inherently with the other principal aim of the project: the determination of the extent to which San Vincenzo depended upon its territory in its rise to become one of the great places of Charlemagne's Europe. First, however, it is necessary to examine the chronology of the medieval settlement. The phasing of the sequence of monasteries at San Vincenzo al Volturno constitutes one of the most important discoveries made during the project.

The phasing

The essence of modern archaeology is not what has been termed the 'Pompeii premise' – the prospect of finding a place fossilised from one

[1]This chapter principally describes the 1980-6 excavations at San Vincenzo al Volturno, concentrating upon the northern sector of the monastery as opposed to the area of the ninth-century abbey-church, San Vincenzo Maggiore, and its associated workshops. For a more detailed account of the excavations see Hodges (1993a; 1995b; 1997), Hodges and Mitchell (1996), Mitchell and Hansen (2001), and Bowes, Francis and Hodges (forthcoming). The excavations have continued since the conclusion of the San Vincenzo Project in 1998, though no coherent reports are yet available.

moment in time (Binford 1981) – but the reverse, the opportunity to record how a place has evolved through time. Time-depth, in the form of a stratigraphic sequence spanning a millennium, can be traced on one spot. The archaeological sequence at San Vincenzo embodies not only the form of the settlement, but also information about production, distribution and consumption, and about the ideological attitudes of the people who lived there. Together, this information, normally so elusive for this period, permits some scale to be placed upon the many levels of history embodied in the monastery. At one level it enables us to assess the details of the twelfth-century *Chronicon Vulturnense*, a source compiled long after the principal events described in its pages. At another level the excavated data allow us to evaluate the impact of European influences belonging to mainstream political, economic and cultural history. The phasing, of course, throws light on all aspects of the place: its artistic history, its architectural history, its religious history, its technological history and so on.

Yet we should be clear about the nature of the phasing. None of the medieval phases were dated by coins or radiocarbon dating; medieval coins were intriguingly rare (cf. Rovelli 2000), while funds were insufficient to consider radiocarbon dates. Instead, a relative sequence has been devised, framed largely by the chronology of San Vincenzo as described in the *Chronicon Vulturnense*, and dated more closely by the material culture. The paintings in the Crypt Church, for instance, were considered to be a fixed dating point when the project began, and have remained a benchmark when assessing the chronology of the stratigraphy in the Crypt Church and 'South Church' areas (Hodges 1993a: 31-2). Many of the excavated remains, as it happens, belong to the age of these paintings. Indeed, one is tempted to think of San Vincenzo as a Pompeii of the Carolingian Renaissance – a place trapped, archaeologically speaking, in a moment in time. It is an illusion, of course, because the ninth-century monastery was formed over several generations, during stratigraphic phases 4 and 5. (Given the ambitiousness of the phase 4 building project, it is prudent to recall that some buildings probably took the entire span of a phase to construct. Churches such as Cologne, Reims and Saint Denis, for example, were the work of several generations of masons [Riché 1978: 157-8].) Then, no sooner was the building programme finished than there is evidence that the place was beginning to fall into decline, even before it was sacked by the Arabs in October 881 (Hodges 1997b). Nevertheless, this cataclysmic end, marked by a spread of burning across the site, within which tell-tale Saracenic arrowheads occurred, is reminiscent of the infamous volcanic eruption that overwhelmed Pompeii.

The sequence of settlement areas seems to be as follows (Figs 7.1 and 7.2).

81

Phase 3a

The first monks arrived at San Vincenzo to discover the dilapidated, but far from completely ruined, buildings of the late Roman settlement. This settlement covered an area of about half a hectare, and in all likelihood the fifth-century residential tower (on Terrace 2) made it a prominent landmark at the north end of the Rocchetta plain. Like the better-known tower at Torba, Castelseprio, it was a conspicuous place in which to found a monastic community (Mazza 1978-79; Bertelli 1988a; 1988b). The archaeology of phase 3 at San Vincenzo is difficult to interpret. The late Roman funerary church was rebuilt and appears to have been transformed into the first abbey-church, while the adjacent Crypt Church, to the north, was either used briefly or not at all. The *Chronicon Vulturnense* leads its readers to assume that the abbey-church founded by Paldo, Tato and Taso in 703 was situated in the same place as the large church built by Abbot Joshua in 808, called San Vincenzo Maggiore by the chronicler. In practice, the excavations have indicated the likelihood that San Vincenzo Maggiore occupied a new site (see below). Hence, we have termed the first abbey-church as San Vincenzo Minore, to distinguish it from the later, ninth-century building. San Vincenzo Minore made use of the pre-existing funerary church (Hodges and Mithen 1993). The residential tower on the terrace above almost certainly became the focus of the monastic cemetery, while it must be assumed (at the moment) that late

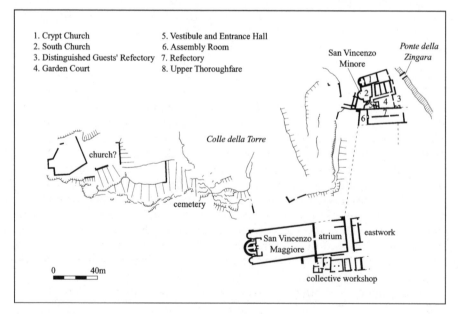

1. Crypt Church
2. South Church
3. Distinguished Guests' Refectory
4. Garden Court
5. Vestibule and Entrance Hall
6. Assembly Room
7. Refectory
8. Upper Thoroughfare

7.1. Plan of San Vincenzo al Volturno: excavations 1980-98.

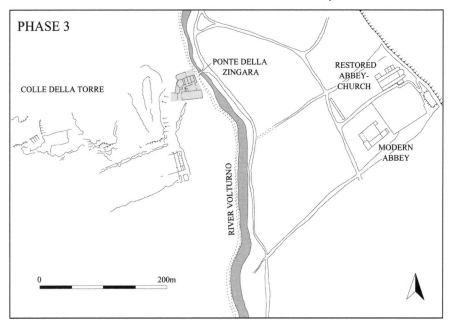

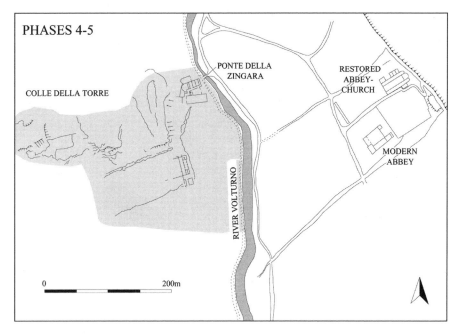

7.2. Settlement plans [1995] for phases 3 to 5 at San Vincenzo.

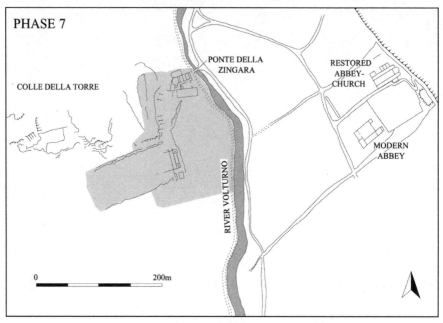

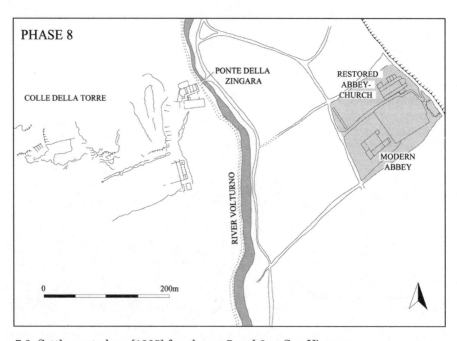

7.3. Settlement plans [1995] for phases 7 and 8 at San Vincenzo.

Roman buildings to the south of the 'South Churches' provided the community with accommodation.

Little else found in the excavations can be assigned to this phase. The material culture of the monastery in the early eighth century was almost certainly impoverished.

Phase 3b

The first major change to the form of the settlement was the demolition of most of the late Roman Crypt Church and the construction of the new Crypt Church. This latter building had a short, poorly built nave, which was bonded onto the late Roman apse. The nave was built upon the remains of an earlier republican structure, and had a façade embellished by the re-use of cornices to support its corners (reminiscent of the use of *spolia* in the façade of the more or less contemporary Spoletan funerary chapel, known as the Tempietto di Clitunno (Emerick 1998)).

The idea of a small chapel flanking the mother church on a parallel axis was not uncommon in this period. Such a feature has been noted at Saint Martin, Angers from the early eighth century and at Saint John at Müstair and at Farfa from the later eighth century (McClendon 1987: 56). A second change of some significance was the creation of a primitive ambulatory for San Vincenzo Minore by constructing a rudimentary wall to close off the south end of the passage which existed between the apse of this church and the rock-face beyond. The effect resembles the primitive later eighth-century church of Santa Maria Annunziata at Prata di Principato Ultra, near Avellino, where an ambulatory lay between the painted apse and the natural rock-face (Belting 1968; Pavan 1990: 291-5). In the case of S. Vincenzo Minore, the construction of this short stretch of wall, comprising rubble and a clayey mortar, resembled the poorly made remains of the nave wall of the Crypt Church. However, this addition cannot be more precisely dated. There had been an ambulatory of sorts between the late Roman 'South Church' and the rock face below Terrace 2 during the fifth century. The presence of the ambulatory perhaps reflects the assimilation of a late Antique scheme by the monks. The ultimate model may have been the ring-crypt built into the apse of Old Saint Peter's in the time of Pope Gregory the Great (590-604), which became the model for many similar crypts, not only in ninth-century Rome, but also in the Frankish kingdoms from the later eighth century onwards (Krautheimer 1980: 86; McClendon 1987: 58). However, the primitive nature of their achievement must be emphasised; no architect as such designed this new construction.

Phase 3c

The first elements of a monastic plan can be attributed to this phase. As Fig. 7.4 shows, it comprises San Vincenzo Minore (the 'South Church'),

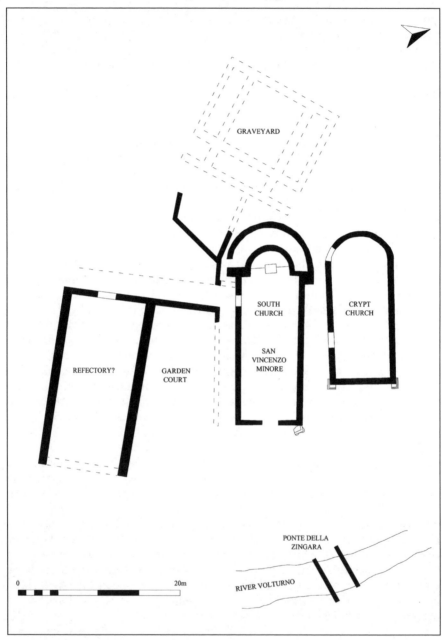

7.4. Plan of San Vincenzo [1995] in phase 3c.

with a church (the Crypt Church) on its north side, a possible passage (the south corridor of the 'South Church', leading from the Ponte della Zingara along the north side of the Garden Court to the ambulatory of San Vincenzo Minore), and a comparable north-south passage leading from the south doorway of San Vincenzo Minore along the west side of the Garden Court to a large rectangular building tentatively identified as a refectory.

San Vincenzo Minore was significantly altered. A finely built new ambulatory replaced the simple symmetry of the new addition to the church, its level coursing and hard lime mortar rendering, distinguished this from the earlier buildings in the monastery. The painted altar found in the apse of this church also probably belonged to this phase.

North of the 'South Church', the (late Roman) apsidal end of the Crypt Church was rebuilt at this time. Its scheme of decoration may date from this period; it was more or less contemporary with the painted apse of the phase 3 'South Church', incorporating bands of blue-grey, dull red, pale orange-red, cream and yellow, with thin white lines along the divides. Traces of figurative painting were also found.

An arrangement of corridors around the pre-existing Garden Court appears to date from this phase. The south corridor beside the 'South Church', defined on its south side in phase 4 by wall 506, probably followed the line of a late Roman enclosure was which had bounded the south side of a cemetery at that time (Hodges and Mithen 1993: 172). This corridor provided a means of access from the Ponte della Zingara to the new ambulatory. The corridor turned south at the western end of the Garden Court. Here, leading through the south doorway of San Vincenzo Minore, the passage, defined on the east (Garden Court) side by wall 468, led to a building sealed beneath the later Refectory. The outline of the earlier building, possibly an earlier refectory, could be made out from the undulations in the tiled floor of the phase 4 Refectory and was confirmed in the re-excavation of the modern pipe-trench that bisected this building. This building was approximately 11.6 metres wide by 21 metres long, sufficiently spacious to accommodate about a hundred monks dining at tables.

Several points can be made about these alterations. First, a new plan was being grafted onto the existing one. Secondly, this plan embodied rather more clearly, and much more competently, the features introduced to San Vincenzo in phase 3b. Thirdly, the new ambulatory was possibly the most proficient construction discovered in the excavations from any phase. The exactitude of the symmetry (despite the fact that the ambulatory was constructed against the rock-face), the level coursing, and above all the distinctive hard mortar rendering stand out in contrast to the rustic efforts of phase 3b. San Vincenzo's masons could not have changed so suddenly; the services of a *sapiens architectus* – an architect-builder – must have been responsible for these works. Lastly, the context for this redevelopment, if the building beneath the phase 4 Refectory was a phase 3c Refectory, must have been the rapidly increasing size of the monastery's community. It is tempting to identify this remodelling as a response to the changing needs of the great community at San Vincenzo which Pope Hadrian and Paul the Deacon described in the late eighth century (*Codex Carolinus: Monumenta Germaniae Historica [MGH], Epistolae Merowingici et Karolini aevi I* (= *MGH Epp. III*.66, 594); *HL*: 283).

Phase 4a

Great changes, far exceeding those envisaged in phase 3c, were made in this period. Unlike the phase 3c programme, when new parts were grafted onto old ones, most of the phase 4 building programme was conceived as a new venture in which the pre-existing structures were modestly accommodated.

The major change was to shift the ritual axis of the monastery from its position beside the Ponte della Zingara (that is within the late Roman settlement) to a new site on the southern edge of the old remains, overlooking the Rocchetta plain (Fig. 7.2). It is proposed that San Vincenzo Maggiore was constructed upon a high, terrace at the base of Colle della Torre, dominating the plain, and visible from the mountain road from Isernia to Sulmona, above and to the north-east of Cerro al Volturno. As a result, the 'South Church' no longer served as the principal church of the monastery; instead, it is proposed, it was radically transformed into a grand guest-hall.

The exact plan of the monastery at this date is very far from known, but its bare outlines can be tentatively pieced together. The new abbey-church (Hodges and Mitchell 1996) was almost certainly the pivot around which the monastery was spread out. Immediately south-east lay collective workshops, where glass and fine metalwork for liturgical and secular use were made (see Chapter 8).

On the north side of the abbey, beside the river, lay the claustrum. The architect was expedient in devising this complex. The phase 3c (?) refectory/range was enlarged into a great thatched barn of a refectory in phase 4. The kitchen and stores must have been situated close by, and it is probable that together they formed an east wing, with convenient access to the river. In this general area, too, it is likely that there was a dormitory for the monks. This might have formed a south wing of a cloister, if the complex took a standard medieval form. While the exact layout of the claustrum remains a matter of speculation, it is clear that unlike the Plan of St Gall (see Fig. 7.5), as well as many later Romanesque monasteries, the claustrum was not situated immediately alongside the new church. Instead, it seems to have been placed at a little distance, much as seems to have been the case, for example, at Saint John, Müstair (Switzerland) (Davis-Weyer 1987). The size of the Refectory may offer a clue on this score. Several hundred monks needed to be accommodated in this complex. Evidently, the architect, while calculating the space necessary for such large buildings, decided to retain a significant part of the old (phase 3) nucleus. Otherwise, it might be deduced, he would have constructed the claustrum in the fields due south of the new abbey-church (where the collective workshops were in fact built). The integration of the new complex with the original monastery is a feature of the phase 4 plan. Two long passages linked the new abbey to the old northern sector. The Lower Thoroughfare, which included the Assembly Room, connected the monks' quarters to the abbey-church. This passage, furthermore, continued through a small covered courtyard (the Vestibule) to the distinguished guests' quarters situated in the old phase 3 nucleus. The Upper Thoroughfare followed virtually the same route, but outside the claustrum and at a higher level (on Terrace 1). This passage almost certainly provided access to buildings on the terrace above, as well as linking the abbey-church (San Vincenzo Maggiore) to the distinguished guests' quarters. A wall at the back of Terrace 2, on which remains of a painted decoration were found, follows the same line as these two passages, emphasising the existence of a coherent plan in the arrangement of the new monastery.

The Assembly Room, at the north end of the Lower Thoroughfare, immediately outside the monks' Refectory, may conceivably have served as a place of meeting. Its principal purpose, however, was as a space where the monks might gather before proceeding to the Refectory. The paintings in this room were certainly outstanding. The line of prophets along the west wall was by artists working in a fashionable Lombard idiom, while the scheme of (painted) marbled panelling around the room, as in other rooms, reveals the aspiration to recreate the elegant grandeur of the Roman past.

The old 'South Church' (San Vincenzo Minore) was entirely rebuilt. It incorporated a chapel at its west end (half the phase 3c church, including the altar). This was separated by a cross-passage(s) from a two-storey hall: on the ground floor there were three rooms while on the first floor there were apartments. The quality of the paintings, as well as the marble *opus sectile* floors associated with these first-floor rooms, indicates that this was a grand building. Like the Assembly Room, the first-floor hall of this building had a scheme of overlapping parti-coloured scales reminiscent of late antique practice, perhaps decorating wall-benches, as well as dados painted in imitation of painted marble panels. There were also traces of fine figurative decoration similar in style to the Prophets in the Assembly Room. One section of the room, however, contained a painted dado in red porphyry and red speckled grey granite, arranged in such a way as to suggest cut marbled panels. This was a decorative scheme of the highest quality. Below the hall, the ground-floor rooms included stabling for horses and simple accommodation. A south corridor, painted with a dado in imitation of panelled *opus sectile* revetment, led visitors from a narthex in front of the Ponte della Zingara to a grand marble staircase (in the Entrance Hall), situated on the south side of the aula. In its new function, therefore, the 'South Church' incorporated grand apartments in its upper storey, a chapel, a small stable and possibly primitive ground-floor accommodation. This range of features points to the building being the Hall for Distinguished Guests (see, however, Fentress 1996). Its model was the duke's palatial complex at Salerno (Peduto 1990: 320-6), or the much-admired palatial complex at Benevento, in the vicinity of Santa Sofia (Peduto 1990: 319). Such building complexes are well-known from Carolingian Europe. For example, the ninth-century reformer, Abbot Haito of Reichenau, informs us that '(the) auditorium of the abbot lies between the claustrum and the gate …, so that he can receive in conference the brethren without inconvenience to the guests, and the guests without inconvenience to the brethren' (cited by Horn and Born 1979: vol. 1, 22).

Next to the Entrance Hall lay the small porticoed Garden Court. The east portico was particularly fine. Here, re-used fluted columns supported the roof, while, in classical Campanian fashion, the arrangement was skilfully evoked in the paintings on the back wall of the portico. Following Roman fashion still further, it is likely that a large second-century marble vase either stood either in the centre of the Garden Court, or between two of the columns around it (Mitchell and Claridge in Mitchell and Hansen 2001: 147-9). To the immediate east of the Garden Court, and entered from the colonnaded east portico, was a long narrow 'building' which contained fine paintings. The scheme of decoration was badly burnt in 881, but traces of Egyptian blue were found, suggesting that this was no ordinary room. The presence of a smashed vessel-glass of fine quality in this room, destroyed in 881, lends weight to the hypothesis that this was the refectory for the distinguished guests, which was entered from the Garden Court.

The Crypt Church was probably not altered at this time. It could only be entered from the south, by a cross-passage, at ground-floor level leading from the Lower Thoroughfare through the 'South Church' complex.

Whether the late Roman residential tower remained in use in this phase is not known, but on Terrace 3 above it is likely that another church stood at the north end of the terrace. The remains of an eleventh-century church identified in Trench R almost certainly were associated with an earlier eighth- or ninth-century church founded on this prominent point on Colle della Torre. Remains of another large building directly overlooked the new abbey-church on the south-facing slope of Colle della Torre. This building seems a likely candidate for the abbot's palace. Further up the hill was situated a large cemetery. Only a small sample of the cemetery was investigated. Nevertheless, it seems probable that at least several hundred people were buried here over a comparatively short period of time. A few were buried in fine tombs, including two rock-cut arcosolia, while others were placed in simpler rock-cut tombs (Hodges 1995a). Further up the hill, occupying the summit of Colle della Torre, was yet another complex of buildings.

It appears that the phase 4 monastery spread well beyond Colle della

Torre. During the ploughing of the fields on the east bank of the river Volturno, traces of a further stretch of buildings came to light. The spread of debris here covers almost a hectare (Bowes, Francis and Hodges forthcoming). It suggests that there was some kind of 'extra-mural' *borgo*, possibly containing the dwellings of craftsmen, traders and lay dependents, like *Eulogimenopolis*, the *borgo* later known as San Germano on the Via Casilina below Monte Cassino (see below, Fig. 7.6) (Leccisotti 1987: 38; Delogu 1992: 307).

During phase 4, San Vincenzo became one of the largest monasteries in Europe. With an estimated population of at least 300 monks in the early to mid-ninth century, judging from the dining space in the Refectory, and, as was normal (Horn and Born 1979: vol. 1, 268), possibly as many lay dependents would have ranked amongst the largest monasteries in Latin Christendom. Contemporary texts offer population numbers of monastic communities of comparable size. Centula boasted 400 monks under Abbot Angilbert, Fontanella (Saint Wandrille) may have briefly had as many as 300 monks, whilst Fulda, with an estimated 270, and St Gall, with about 120, were smaller than San Vincenzo (Horn and Born 1979: vol. 1, 343). In terms of settlement area, the ninth-century monastery at San Vincenzo far exceeded the better-known ones at Farfa (McClendon 1987), Monte Cassino (Pantoni 1973), Müstair (Davis-Weyer 1987: Müstair, it should be noted, had consistently less than fifty monks at its zenith during the ninth century), and Novalesa (Cantino Wataghin 1985; 2000).

Three features of the phase 4 monastery stand out. First, there is its sprawling size; secondly, the fact that virtually every room and passage was painted; and thirdly, the conscious use of classical *spolia* and classical ideas in every part of the complex. The paintings associated with this phase suggest that it dates to either the last years of the eighth or the first years of the ninth century. The *Chronicon* offers a clear context for this colossal enterprise when it describes how Abbot Joshua (792-817) rebuilt the abbey-church in 808 with the assistance of Louis the Pious. As Wickham has shown (1995), Louis the Pious's contribution may be a legend of little substance. Nonetheless, if Joshua extended his building works to include not just the abbey, but the entire monastic plan, there is little doubt that his later reputation as an abbot with royal connections was in certain respects justified. The distinctive, if expedient, construction technique common to all these buildings suggests the work was executed rapidly over a short period. In many cases it became necessary to repair the buildings at a later date. The two thoroughfares and the back wall of Terrace 2 are the best index of the common purpose behind this project. These formed the spine of the new monastery, connecting the new abbey-church to the distinguished guests' sector. Around this spine, we may suspect, the other buildings were constructed. There can be little doubt that a plan of sorts was put into effect, executed under the direction of a *sapiens architectus*, involving the creation of an enormous monastic city similar in concept to the new Italian towns of the age (Marazzi 1994). Much of this work was probably undertaken by the monks and lay people using locally available materials. A good deal of the stone, for example, was probably found on Colle della Torre. But at the same time the scale of the enterprise, the inclusion of distinctive architectural concepts then in fashion, such as the hall for distinguished guests, the extensive use of glass windows, tile pavements and classical *spolia*, as well as the presence of northern Lombardic idiom in much of the decoration, all indicate that this settlement was the product of many connections and influences, masterminded by an abbot as ambitious as any in Europe in this period of intense ecclesiastical development (*contra* Devroey 1993: 239).

Phase 4b

Minor alterations were made to the rooms on the ground floor of the 'South Church'. Note should also be taken of the sub-phases of the workshops in use during this time (see below, Chapter 8).

Phase 5a

The construction of the annular crypt in San Vincenzo Maggiore almost certainly belonged to a major rebuilding of the basilica and its east end. It seems likely that on acquiring the relics of St Vincent, the abbey aggrandised its primary cult centre, constructing an elevated atrium with a raised eastwork reached by stairways in its two flanking towers (Hodges and Mitchell 1996). This colossal new endeavour was the occasion for other re-building elsewhere in the monastery.

It is my contention that the alterations to the Crypt Church occurred as another phase of the major works was undertaken throughout the monastery. The portrait of Abbot Epyphanius in the crypt of the Crypt Church dates the paintings here to his period in office (824-42). The crypt itself, it now seems clear, was made in this period; a good case has been put forward for it being designed as an elaborate funerary chapel of a kind that was in fashion in the Carolingian age. Above it, the sanctuary of the Crypt Church was remodelled as well. In addition, an atrium was now created at its east end and the building might be entered directly from the Ponte della Zingara. A number of fine tombs were inserted into the atrium.

These changes, like those in earlier stages of the monastery's history, accompanied a programme of rebuilding of the 'South Church' guest hall. The alterations necessitated the closure of the north-facing doorways of the 'South Church' undercrofts. These could no longer be used as stables; instead, the building(s) north of the Crypt Church (found in Trench EE) might have provided these facilities. In the west end of the 'South Church', the chapel was filled in, and a high third apse was constructed. The high third apse of the 'South Church' would have necessitated the demolition of part of the late Roman residential tower on Terrace 2 (although it should be noted that the tower may have been demolished before this). The aggrandisement of this building was probably accompanied by the addition of a monumental loggia-like extension to the Entrance Hall (with its arcading reminiscent of the façade of the church of Santa Maria delle Cinque Torri at Monte Cassino [Scaccia Scarafoni 1946]), on the south side of the building, and by the addition of a finely painted bench in the east portico of the Garden Court. In sum, the entire complex appears to have been refurbished, with, in functional terms, the old chapel within the 'South Church' being replaced by the Crypt Church. The alterations to the Entrance Hall may have been the occasion for the construction of a bridging passage, westward from the first floor of this building, over the hitherto open yard in the Vestibule to Terrace 1. This caused the Vestibule below to be covered, at which stage its walls were decorated and a tiled pavement was laid. Here, within a generation or so, a fine tomb was inserted. In time, it may be surmised, the conspicuous break between the monks' quarters and the distinguished guests' sector was made increasingly less apparent. Above the ubiquitous marbled dado in this room were several images of young, gaily painted saints. The artist responsible for these figures was working in the tradition of those who in phase 4 had painted the Prophets in the adjacent Assembly Room, but a generation later. At about the same time, the Refectory was extended eastward with the addition of an annexe.

The monastic community had reached its zenith.

Phase 5b

The patched cracks in the lower walls of the 'South Church', as well as the bowed form of its south wall, could relate to the earthquake of 848 (Guidoboni 1989: 614-15). Generally, however, few other building works and virtually no decoration could be attributed to the central and later decades of the ninth century. The monastery's heyday was plainly over.

Phase 5c

The widespread burning throughout the monastery, in some cases associated with heavy arrowheads, as fired from a composite bow, must have been the result of the Arab sack in October 881. The most dramatic evidence came from the workshops on the edge of the Rocchetta plain. Here the door had been burnt down, probably by fire-arrows, and had crashed inwards onto shelves or cupboards inside the east room (Hodges 1997b). The entire building then ignited. Scrap bronze, similar to that excavated in this building, was found in a pit (D 320) in the Upper Thoroughfare, perhaps hastily concealed, or abandoned, during the attack. Arrowheads were also found in the distinguished guests' Garden

Court. These were probably shot from the Ponte della Zingara, and may have been intended to fire the thatched Refectory. Both refectories burnt to the ground, leaving little but ash. A timber beam, however, crashed into the east portico beside the Garden Court, and remained where it fell for over a hundred years. The fire swept along the south ground-floor corridor of the 'South Church' (the distinguished guests' quarters), and through it, to the edge of the Crypt Church. Parts of the Entrance Hall were badly burnt, while the tiled roof of the Vestibule collapsed. The roof at the north end of the Assembly Room also collapsed, blocking the doorway leading to the Vestibule. Traces of the fire were also found in the building(s) behind the Crypt Church. Without any doubt the sack was devastating

Phase 6a

The vestiges of the monastery occupied in the tenth and early eleventh centuries tell a sorry tale. The Crypt Church possibly fared the best; only its atrium fell into delapidation. The 'South Church' ground-floor rooms may have been used intermittently, but the state of the apartments above is not known. Tombs, however, were cut into the apsidal end. These were probably part of the cemetery focused upon the Entrance Hall. In the Entrance Hall itself tombs were inserted into many of its rooms, and there is a strong impression that it had become a martyrium housing, initially, those who perished in 881. In the 'South Church' corridor, alongside, as well as beside the Upper Thoroughfare and on Terrace 2, there were still more tombs. In addition, a tomb was cut into the north bench of the Refectory immediately beside the Entrance Hall.

The Refectory itself was devastated, but a small room of some makeshift kind was made within the northwest corner of the old building. A rough doorway was chopped through the Refectory wall here, providing access to the Entrance Hall and to the 'South Church'. Further south, we must presume the abbey-church stood in ruins, while the workshops were burnt out. It is tempting to interpret the ruins as an index of San Vincenzo's dismal fate in the tenth century. The community, according to the chronicler, had shrunk to a handful of monks who used some buildings and were unable to repair others. The integrated plan no longer functioned, but the Entrance Hall cemetery may have been intended to inform visitors of the dreadful calamity suffered by the community. Was the Crypt Church the Santa Maria beside the gate, (re)built, as related by the twelfth-century chronicler, by Abbot Rambald soon after the monks returned from exile? Is San Salvatore, the church which was, the chronicler informs us, used while the abbey stood in ruins, to be identified with the building situated on the summit of Colle della Torre? Between these surviving buildings – islands in a sea of ruins – there were doubtless thickets of brambles concealing the devastation of October 881.

Phase 6b

The demolition of the monastery was a systematic affair. All but the apse of the 'South Church' was levelled to below first-floor height. This level then became the height of the demolished Entrance Hall, and filling-in level of the Vestibule, the Assembly Room, the peristyle Garden Court as well as the refectories. The buildings behind the Crypt Church were also pulled down at this time. The tips in some cases were nearly two metres deep and contained a great deal of ninth-century material which presumably had been lying about for 150 years. The Crypt Church, however, survived. New building works were also underway as the demolition progressed. A large mortar-mixer bedded on the initial tips overlying the east portico of the distinguished guests' Garden Court is some indication of this. Elsewhere we have associated this mortar-mixer with Abbot John V's major redevelopment of the monastery in about 1055. It should be noted, though, that the scale of the demolition and the ruthless disposal of ecclesiastical objects provides a modest glimpse of the new energy behind San Vincenzo's eleventh-century revival as a community.

Phase 7

The abbey-church (San Vincenzo Maggiore) was almost certainly rebuilt in the late tenth century by Abbot John IV (cf. Hodges and Mitchell 1996). Later, under Abbot John V, a new claustrum was constructed on its south side. An enclosure wall probably belonging to this period, still surviving to a height of almost a metre, appeared to define the new south side of the Romanesque complex. To the north, however, little of the original ensemble of buildings survived. With the exception of the Crypt Church, which appeared to have remained in use throughout the eleventh century, the other ninth-century buildings in front of the Ponte della Zingara were levelled and were mostly sealed beneath a yard reminiscent of that around the great eleventh-century monastery of Cluny (Conant 1968). The Crypt Church itself was altered at some time in the eleventh century when its sunken atrium was filled in. All that survived of the 'South Church' was an enigmatic gate in front of the Ponte della Zingara, a low wall on top of the old south wall of the hall, and the apse (see Hodges and Mithen 1993: 177-8, 190). This presumably separated the area where the 'South Church' had once stood, and perhaps also the Crypt Church, from the yard immediately to the south. The wall might also have drawn visitors crossing the Ponte della Zingara either towards the apse of the 'South Church' or along the corridor once beneath the 'South Church' to the south doorway of the nave of the Crypt Church. The survival of the 'South Church' apse and the Crypt Church is difficult to explain: perhaps there was a tradition associated with these buildings, relating to the foundation of the monastery, which led to their exemption from the otherwise thorough demolition at this time.

In the yard itself traces of a small brick-built kiln were found, set up against the largely demolished back wall of the Lower Thoroughfare. The kiln was probably used for making pottery, though no wasters were discovered in the excavation. Close by were traces of post-built structures as well as pits. These may have related to short-lived and small-scale industrial activities concentrated in this area.

Phase 8

Late in the eleventh century Abbot Gerard decided to abandon the old settlement and to shift the community to a more readily defendable site on the edge of the Rocchetta plain. Gerard, formerly a monk at Monte Cassino when Desiderius was abbot there, may have been seeking to emulate the achievements of the Cassinese. It is as likely, though, that he was conscious of the vulnerable location of the abbey at a time when the Borrelli family was becoming increasingly powerful in the upper Volturno valley (Wickham 1985a; 1985b).

Parts of the grand Romanesque abbey were excavated by Pantoni when the building was restored in the 1960s (Pantoni 1980), and some evidence of the plan of the monastic ranges survives (see Bowes, Francis and Hodges forthcoming). It was here, during the twelfth century, that the monk John compiled the *Chronicon Vulturnense*, recalling the great history of his forebears at San Vincenzo. As he was writing, the old site was being turned into terraces which were cultivated more or less continuously until 1980.

Discussion

Before considering the implications of the phasing, one point needs to be emphasised. The phasing represents a sequence of archaeological time-slices: these may be equated to historical time in certain instances with some precision; in others only broad indications are possible. For example, the chronology of the ninth-century (phase 4-5) building works at San Vincenzo appears to be fairly exact (cf. Chapter 8, where the workshop chronology is described). However, the sub-divisions of phase 3 are relative to one another and must be treated as time-slices of as yet unknown numbers of years in the eighth century. Likewise the chronology of phases 6 and 7 must be treated as time-slices of which only the limits are exact in historical terms.

The morphology of the monastery: 703 – c. 1100

The overall form as well as the individual components of the monastery altered greatly between the eighth and twelfth centuries (see Figs 7.1 and 7.2). The phase 3 monastery covered about half a hectare in area; the

96

ninth-century monastery covered between five and ten hectares; the size of the phase 6 monastery is impossible to estimate, given the present state of our knowledge; the phase 7 monastery may have covered two or three hectares at most; and the phase 8 monastery covered just over two hectares. These rough estimates are as much as we hoped to achieve at the start of the San Vincenzo project. We need to note that the earliest (phase 3) monastery was essentially a modified Roman villa. In common with many monasteries throughout western Europe at this date, the founders made use of existing classical buildings. In phase 3b, however, there was a conscious attempt to alter the existing 'South Church' and the Crypt Church, perhaps to meet new liturgical needs. However, the first great changes occurred in phase 3c. The new buildings display an architectural capability that was never again equalled at San Vincenzo. The contrast to the phase 3b additions could not be greater. The Refectory, believed to belong to this new complex, was capable of accommodating about a hundred monks at a sitting. Evidently much had changed in the monastery. Not least, to judge from the phase 3b building works, the quality of the construction implies that an architect must have been employed to manage the work. A good parallel for this exists from precisely this time. The Frank, Walcharius, archbishop of Sens and apparently an engineer long in the confidence of both the papal and Frankish courts, was summoned to Rome to act as a consultant to Pope Hadrian on the project to refurbish St Peter's (Krautheimer 1980: 112). In the case of San Vincenzo it is tempting to regard the outcome as an image of the large community to which both Paul the Deacon and Pope Hadrian referred (Del Treppo 1955). Wickham (1995) argues that it was Carolingian patronage granted to Abbot Paul that made this new layout possible. Here in the late 780s and early 790s, just as at the abbey of Farfa (McClendon 1987: 6), we might surmise that the mixed rule in practice at the abbey since its foundation was replaced by the exclusive use of the Rule of St Benedict, a move in keeping with Charlemagne's precepts for monastic reform. However, the phase 3c monastery was a small undertaking by comparison with what happened under Abbot Joshua's direction. San Vincenzo's buildings expanded to cover an area approximately ten times larger than Paul's monastery. Moreover, the community of monks (and probably their lay dependents also) almost certainly tripled or quadrupled in number. Preeminent amongst the new buildings was a grand abbey-church, San Vincenzo Maggiore. Paradoxically, although references were made to classical antiquity in almost every part of the new complex, Abbot Joshua's monastery marks a break with the classical villa form and the beginnings of a medieval layout.

The decoration and material culture of the monastery, however, embody the spirit of the Lombard cultural revival of the mid-eighth century (Belting 1968; Mitchell 1990; 1994; Mitchell and Hansen 2001), although the new Frankish political and cultural presence in northern and central

Italy may be evident in the scale and design of the monastic buildings and in certain aspects of their ornamentation. Classical *spolia* were prominently positioned throughout the monastery. Cartloads of Antique capitals, columns, bases, inscriptions and furniture were incorporated into the phase 4 buildings. The ninth-century paintings, as in other parts of Italy during this period, employed certain ideas and motifs commonly found in antiquity. The decision of the abbot and monks to build ambitiously and to embellish their buildings with rich painted schemes was largely determined by the practice of the Italian Lombard courts in the preceding generations. The Lombard king and his dukes, in an open spirit of mutual rivalry and emulation, had devised traditions of spectacular cultural display in which classical reference and resonance were always present. The Carolingian invaders of Italy were to adopt these strategies and to deploy them widely and effectively in the next century. The *Chronicon* also leads us to suppose that much emphasis was placed upon the traditional importance of the place as *Samnium* (J. Patterson 1985; La Regina 1989). It remains contentious whether this was an invented tradition, in so far as the eighth- to ninth-century community could have known almost nothing of what *Samnium* looked like. Finally, there was a pronounced Beneventan dimension to the monastery's outward appearance. Abbot Joshua must have found a body of skilled (and, in all probability, prized) craftsmen to serve him in this great enterprise. Even though the monks may have assisted in the work, as the chronicler asserts, a glassmaker would have been needed to make the windows and the lamps vital for lighting; tile-makers would have been required to instruct in the production of the thousands of tiles used in the floors and roofs; smiths would have been needed to make the huge number of nails employed in the roofs; and masons would have been needed to mix the mortar and design the buildings. The archaeological evidence confirms Lynn White's contention (1962) that the diffusion of technology in medieval Europe was the achievement of a Carolingian-period monastic movement, such as has been discovered at San Vincenzo.

The phase 5 additions to Joshua's monastery took two forms. First, the guest-house facilities were aggrandised, and secondly, to judge from the changes to the Vestibule, the integration of the monastic plan was improved when the complicated phase 4 steps linking the Upper Thoroughfare to the northern sector were replaced by a first-floor passageway which bridged the Vestibule, arriving at the first floor of the Entrance Hall. The painted decoration in the monastery took a new form in this period too. The northern Lombard idiom apparent in the phase 4 decorations was further assimilated and its implications developed by a second generation of painters (Mitchell 1994).

However, after the fury of changes and building spanning the period *c.* 790-830/40, the momentum slowed. Little evidence exists for mid- to later ninth-century renovations or buildings of any substance. The phase 6 monastery was seemingly a sad, decrepit place, where the levels of artistic and of artisanal practice matched those exhibited in the eighth century. But ninth-century skills were not entirely forgotten and lost. In the eleventh century the monastery was refurbished and then entirely rebuilt entirely on two further occasions. These Romanesque monasteries were more compact, less ambitious versions of the ninth-century model, and rooted in a central Italian tradition almost certainly springing from Monte Cassino (Carbonara 1979).

The arrangement of the settlement also betrays interesting attitudes to space and form through time. The compact eighth-century monastery, with its small abbey-church (the phase 3 'South Church'), was markedly different from the succession of plans which followed it. The phase 3c additions, notably the ambulatory, suggest increased emphasis upon ritual connected with the dead and that sufficient visitors were either anticipated or present to warrant the building of special areas to promote the abbey's relics.

The phase 4 monastery was very different. Apart from the overt scale of the new buildings, the settlement was seemingly separated into zones or modules linked by a network of passages and corridors. A large increase in the population at San Vincenzo inevitably caused it to be divided and probably stratified in some way. Monks and lay people would have occupied different quarters and possibly have taken different routes through the monastery. Similarly, distinguished visitors appear to have been allocated palatial quarters, while ordinary pilgrims were probably accommodated in more modest parts of the monastery (possibly close to the main bridge in front of the abbey-church). The cemeteries of this new monastery reveal the same stratification. Some individuals were buried in front of the Crypt Church (perhaps members of the secular élite); ninth-century funerary inscriptions from the areas around the great elevated atrium of San Vincenzo Maggiore suggest that the monks' cemetery lay close to the abbey-church, as it is shown on the Plan of St Gall (the Reichenau cemetery: Zettler 1988: TA 35); and the secular cemetery may have been the one situated on the hill overlooking the principal church and, significantly, the fields where the monastic dependents had once worked.

The tenth-century monastery provides a marked contrast to its predecessor. Collective burials, individual burials in large and small, undecorated and decorated, tombs seem to illustrate the inchoate ideology of this transitory age. The sequence of eleventh-century monasteries begins to emulate the extensive scale of the ninth-century settlement. There was a new cloister, a refurbished abbey-church, probably new workshops and farms; several churches were furbished by Abbot Ilarius, including one identified in Trench R on Terrace 3; the old cemeteries were still in use; and new quarters were probably built for the abbot and distinguished guests.

The changing attitude to space manifested in the plan of the monastery can be found also in the history of individual buildings.

All the earliest buildings in the monastery (in phase 3a) owed their origins to antecedent late Roman structures. The environment was primitive, with beaten earth floors not unlike a house from the period. Likewise, the clay-based mortar and the rough-hewn rubble walls belong to an age of primitive technology. Clearly, the eighth-century community had little knowledge of construction techniques. By contrast, the buildings of phase 3c and 4 showed considerable competence. The ambulatory and the south wall of the 'South Church', in particular, were skilfully built with hewn and re-used stone (there being no evidence that stone was quarried until phase 7, the mid-eleventh century). Unlike the poor clay-based mortars of phase 3a-b, those used in phases 3c and 4 are lime-based and rather harder.

The form of some phase 4 buildings, such as the hall and the porticoes around the Garden Court, owed a good deal to the construction techniques of classical architecture, but some at least mark the beginnings of a medieval tradition witnessed elsewhere in the principality of Benevento (Belting 1968; Peduto 1990). The Crypt Church was a modest building, quite consistent with eighth- to ninth-century churches found throughout western Europe. The 'South Church' guest hall, by comparison, was a 'triclinium' of a type adopted by the secular and ecclesiastical élites (Polci 2003). Its origins were Roman, but in many respects the particular type was medieval. Such palatial complexes appear to have existed at Benevento and Salerno, as a result of the revival of fortunes in the region under Arichis II (Delogu 1977: 26-32; Peduto 1990: 319-26; Delogu 1992; Mitchell 1994). Certainly, the passages, the Entrance Hall, the refectories and the workshops – some with tiled roofs, some thatched – belong to an incipient medieval architectural tradition. A notable feature of this early medieval building tradition at San Vincenzo was its perilous expediency. Buttresses had to be incorporated into the Refectory, the Entrance Hall and the Assembly Room of the Lower Thoroughfare to reinforce the unstable phase 4a-b walls. The roofs too betray the same expediency. A multitude of long nails discovered in the excavations reveals the surprising inability of local carpenters to make neatly jointed roof timbers. Instead, it appears that the beams, trusses and supports were nailed together. This is a feature which would be most unusual north of the Alps at this date. However, Pierre Toubert, in his monograph on the estates of the abbey of Farfa, commented on the rarity of wooden dwellings mentioned in the early medieval sources (1973: 334ff., 660-3). Likewise David Andrews drew attention to the absence of timber buildings in modern times in Italy, and suggests that stone buildings with tiled roofs may have been preferred since classical times (1982: 2-3). However, numerous excavations in recent times have shown that after *c.* 500 most domestic buildings in Italian towns and villages were constructed on timber (for examples, see Brogiolo 1989, 1992 for Brescia and neighbouring villages, and Ward-Perkins 1981 for Luni). Construction of buildings in timber and

the use of thatch for roofing appear to mark a genuine break with antiquity. Even the small classical farms in the upper Volturno valley had
been roofed with tiles. Either the monastic tile-maker(s) found the task of
covering these many roofs too great, or (more probably) the builders
considered the poorly-built walls too weak to support a tiled roof on so
large a building. Straw and reeds for thatching were readily available on
the Rocchetta plain, and while thatch was perhaps considered a covering
of inferior status it was nevertheless cheap, easily repaired and retained
the heat in the winter. Less rubble and *spolia* were included in the
Romanesque buildings. The use of more ashlar appears to distinguish this
phase.

This archaeological evidence about the sequence of monastic plans,
including the layout and architecture of the settlements and their individual buildings, makes it possible to study afresh the Plan of St Gall, one of
the original aims of the San Vincenzo project. Obviously, the excavations
do not reveal an entire plan with which to make comparisons with the
ninth-century drawing. Nevertheless, we are in a position to test empiri-
cally the theory of a standardised plan spread throughout the Carolingian
territories. San Vincenzo, *contra* the view expressed by Lawrence Nees
(1986: 4), is not peripheral to this problem.

San Vincenzo and the Plan of St Gall (Fig. 7.5)

The Plan of St Gall (Stiftsbibliothek, Ms. 1092) has been analysed and
lavishly published by Walter Horn and Ernest Born (1979). The drawing
is composed of five separate pieces amounting to 0.77 x 1.12 metres in size.
Just on the grounds of its size it is an extraordinary document of its age.
The plan of the monastery was drawn in red ink and had been annotated
by the architect. A dedication discloses, so Horn and Born argue, that it
was made in the scriptorium at Reichenau (now in south Germany),
having been drawn up at the request of Abbot Gozbert who presided over
the nearby monastery of St Gall from 816 to 836. Horn believes the author
was Haito, bishop of Basle (803-23), and simultaneously abbot of
Reichenau. Haito, according to Horn, was a leading participant in the
reform synods held at Aachen in 816 and 817. The synods debated
Benedict of Aniane's proposals for a universal rule (*una consuetudo*) for
the spiritual and temporal conduct of monastic life, to replace the mixed
rule (*regula mixta*) that had prevailed in the preceding period. The outcome of the synods was a compromise between the liberals and ascetic
reformers like Benedict. These views, Horn argues, were embodied in the
Plan of St Gall, which he contends is a paradigmatic blueprint drawn up
by Abbot Haito as a model for future monastic building (Horn and Born
1979: vol. 1, 21-2). Horn argues that it demonstrates the defeat of
Benedict's attempt to recreate the simpler, egalitarian monastery of an
earlier age. Some stratification was retained within the rules of the

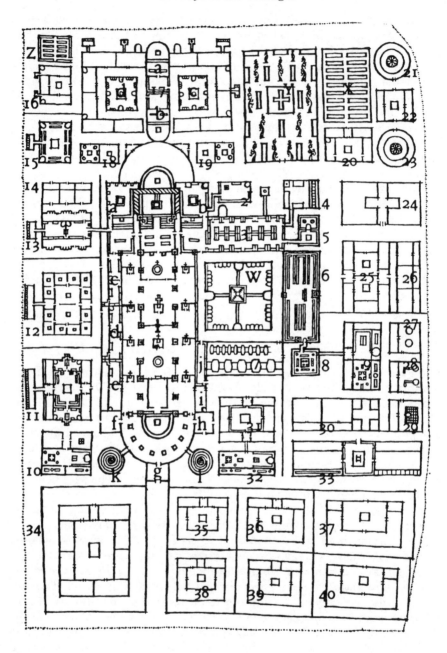

7.5. Schematic drawing of the Plan of St Gall.

monastery, notably permitting the abbot separate facilities (ibid.: vol. 1, 22). Horn asserts that the Plan of St Gall reveals a 'consummate conceptual and technical homogeneity ... a mosaic of perfect order and rationality. This order is tight and consistent. It does not show, at any place, the kind of break or formal incompatibility that one associates with an architectural composition pieced together from heterogeneous parts' (ibid.: vol. 1, 53). This homogeneity, in Horn's view, stems from the blueprint for unity (*forma unitatis*) encompassed by the directives for canons and canonesses framed at the synods of 816 and 817. Yet, as he acknowledges, the unity of empire of which the unity of the church was a precondition had been a prevailing aspect of the Carolingian world since the late eighth century: 'the drive for uniformity was programmatic and universal' (ibid.: vol. 1, 22). Consequently, Horn seeks the union of schematism and reality in the Plan of St Gall not only in Roman military plans, but also in the planning inherent in existing churches such as Cologne cathedral (ibid.: vol. 1, 27-31). Indeed, he concludes that the Plan of St Gall displays 'a *largesse d'esprit* that appears more akin to the educational and administrative policies promoted by Charlemagne and his advisers than to the constrictive atmosphere prevalent in monastic life a the time of Louis the Pious' (ibid.: vol. 1, 27).

Horn's thesis owes much to the tradition of art and architectural history which emerged in the late nineteenth century, and was widely admired in the 1930s. Erwin Panofsky (to whom Horn and Born dedicated their book), in his *Renaissance and Renascences in Western Art* (1960), offers a clear statement of this tradition: 'when Charlemagne set out to reform political and ecclesiastical administration, communications and the calendar, art and literature, and – as a basis for all this – script and language ... his guiding idea was the *renovatio imperii romani*' (Panofsky 1960: 44).

Hardly surprisingly, the publication of Horn and Born's book generated much controversy. The most substantive charges have been made by Paul Meyvaert (1980), Dom Adalbert de Vogüé (1984), Warren Sanderson (1985) and Alfons Zettler (1990), all of whom contend that the dedicatory inscription on the plan, which (as was noted above) Horn and Born took to be axiomatic evidence that the plan is (i) a copy, and (ii) officially prescribed, indicates quite the contrary! The critics, who accept Bernhardt Bischoff's translation of the dedication (1962), believe that the plan concerned a specific building project at St Gall, and thus cannot be interpreted as paradigmatic. The critics appear to have a solid and convincing argument (Jacobsen 1992; Zettler 1988). Jacobsen, in particular, has demonstrated that the plan was not a copy, as Horn and Born suggested (1979: vol. 1, 15-19), but a palimpsest of complex drafting (Jacobsen 1992: 35-106). But does this entirely undermine the central tenet of Horn and Born's study? In some ways it appears to. For example, Lawrence Nees, in a review of the volumes, describes this as a 'severely antiquated' approach which has distorted and produced 'a rather one-sided view of Carolingian art' (1986: 5). Yet he, like all the critics, offers no alternative approach, except to emphasise the importance of understanding the detail of the Plan of St Gall as part of the Carolingian movement. It seems that he (and most of the other reviewers) would prefer to consider the Carolingian renaissance as an assemblage of loosely connected traditions rather than a single, clearly directed movement of the kind proposed by Panofsky. But there are just as many dangers in particularism as in the generalisations that underpin Panofsky's sweeping perspective of the Carolingian age. The Plan of St Gall surely offers us a remarkable model for a ninth-century monastery, even if it is not a blueprint? The pendulum of opinion on this matter has swung between generalisation and particularism, much as it has on many other historical issues during the twentieth century. To a large extent this is a consequence of the restricted nature of the database. Jacobsen, in his recent study of the Plan of St Gall, has been able to examine the church thanks to the countless excavations over the past century, but the other buildings, and thus the plan as such, remain beyond the scope of all but the bold because the archaeological data still do not exist (Jacobsen 1992). The San Vincenzo excavations, however, shed some new light on the issue, not simply because they provide new information on monastic plans, but also because the monastic complex as a whole has been sampled using modern archaeological methods as opposed to being investigated using antiquarian techniques. As a result a number of significant observations can be made about the Plan of St Gall.

Three different plans can be identified at San Vincenzo during the Carolingian age:

1. the phase 3c plan of the 780s/790s (Abbot Paul's plan);
2. the phase 4a plan of the period 792-817 (Abbot Joshua's plan);
3. the phase 5a revisions to the phase 4a plan in the period 824-42 (Abbot Epyphanius's plan).

Abbot Paul's plan

The phase 3c plan, although little of it survived, appears to have had the aim of enhancing the primitive phase 3b monastery. Two features stand out about this phase: first, the high calibre workmanship involved, and, secondly, the imposing ambulatory added to the small eighth-century abbey-church (San Vincenzo Minore). These features point to a programme of works designed to replace the disparate parts of the earlier eighth-century monastery with an integrated plan. In addition, there was an emphasis upon the promotion of San Vincenzo's relics. However, there was no evidence to show that the new plan included the variety of additional settlement units, such as a farm and workshops, which figure in the Plan St Gall. The principal evidence for this is the virtual absence of materials such as glass and tiles in this phase, notably in the phase 3c levels sealed beneath the phase 4 floors in the ground-floor rooms excavated in Trench G, the 'South Church'. Workshops and other facilities may have existed, but these were not situated in those areas in which there have been excavations.

Abbot Joshua's plan

The phase 4a plan was conceived on an urban scale. It included a great many different sectors, in addition to an enhanced emphasis upon the ritual focus of the monastery in the form of San Vincenzo Maggiore. Workshops for glass-working, fine metalwork, iron-working, the carving of bone and horn, carpentry, tile-production, and many other crafts, occupied at least one sector. Other sectors, it might be surmised, included Terrace 3, with a church, in all probability, at the northern end, and the hilltop of Colle della Torre, separated from the main body of the monastery by the cemetery. But was it a planned settlement in the sense that its architecture was working from a blueprint?

Several features suggest that parts of it were planned, in so far as someone designed a new, much larger monastic layout than had existed in the phase 3c monastery. The principal evidence to indicate the presence of an architect working with a blueprint of some kind consists of the two long corridors (the Upper and Lower Thoroughfares), as well as the back wall of Terrace 2, which appear to have been built first, as the axis, linking the old abbey-church to San Vincenzo Maggiore: the rest of Abbot Joshua's monastery was developed around this axis. These corridors simultaneously divided and connected the component parts of the settlement. The means to undertake this work, of course, was a critical factor. The architect must have had available a pool of artisans, who were familiar with mixing lime mortar, with monumental construction techniques, with making tiles for pavements and roofing, with making window panes and glass lamps for lighting, and many other allied crafts. Abbot Joshua's achievement was not a piecemeal enterprise, but the ambitious creation of a settlement which exceeded the ambitions of Christendom's new town-builders (see, for example, Haslam 1987 on ninth-century Mercian towns and Marazzi 1994 on ninth-century new towns in central Italy). Phase 4 was a 'monastic city' in the sense described by McKitterick (1994). Its closest parallel, it may be supposed, was Monte Cassino, where Abbot Gisulf at this time built a new town, called *Eulogimenopolis*, immediately east of Roman *Casinum*, astride the ancient Via Casilina (Fig. 7.6) (Leccisotti 1987: 38). Other parallels are to be found at Fontanella (Saint Wandrille), Saint Riquier, where in 831 2,500 houses were grouped into specialised quarters around the monastery (Riché 1978: 38-9), and Saint Denis (Fig. 7.7), where parts of the *borgo* have recently been excavated (Héron and Meyer 1991; Meyer 1993).

But Abbot Joshua's monastery, while it embodies a unity of purpose and

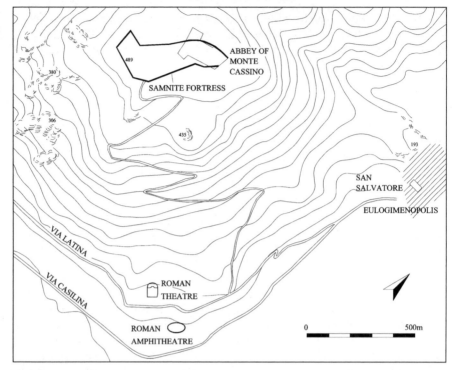

7.6. Map showing the location of the abbey of Monte Cassino and ninth-century *Eulogimenopolis*.

spirit, is not readily comparable to the Plan of St Gall (Fig. 7.5). The modular character of the Plan of St Gall bears witness to a hierarchy within the place, yet, in the absence of passages or corridors, paradoxically it appears that there existed a fluid access between all parts of the settlement. The layout, on the other hand, offers no hint of the history of St Gall – of pre-existing buildings, modified, for example, to the needs of a new liturgy (see, however, Zettler 1990). At San Vincenzo, by contrast, it is important to note that the architect decided to retain the old monastery, albeit in a remodelled form, within the loosely ordered structure of his new plan. Reason and history were grafted together in an intriguing form. Thus the architect resisted the opportunity of creating a new settlement on the Rocchetta plain, as Abbot John V, Desiderius of Monte Cassino's ambitious contemporary, was to do in the mid-eleventh century. The configurations of the landscape, as a result, also prevented the architect from creating an ideal symmetrical scheme. In addition, the bridges, long corridors, yards and gardens, intersections of a sort, served to break up the plan and to accentuate the differences between the sectors.

San Vincenzo in phase 3c had been dominated by its abbey-church, San

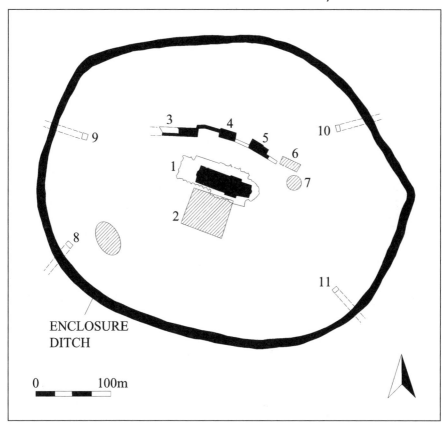

ENCLOSURE
DITCH

0   100m

7.7. The monastic city of Saint Denis *c.* 869: 1. Carolingian abbey; 2. Monastery; 3. Guest house; 4. Church of St Bartholomew; 5. Church of St Peter; 6. Church of St Paul; 7. Church of St John the Baptist; 8. Paris gate; 9. Compoise gate; 10. Bazoin gate; 11. St James gate.

Vincenzo Minore, with its pronounced west end including the enlarged ambulatory. By contrast, the monastery in phase 4 was dominated by two buildings roughly at either end of the settlement: at the south end, the new abbey-church of San Vincenzo Maggiore (measuring 36 *passus* (paces) by 16 *passus* and raised on a platform built to command the southern aspect of the place) (Hodges and Mitchell 1996), and, towards the north end, the 'South Church' (measuring 31 metres long and 14 metres wide), completely remodelled as the abbot's guest-house for distinguished visitors (Hodges and Mithen 1993). Long corridors connected these two nodal points in the monastery, much as we are led to believe that Charlemagne's audience-hall at Aachen was connected by a long passageway to his palace-chapel (Heitz 1980). Essentially, the plan and profile of the place lay emphasis not upon unity, but upon the twin pillars of society, the

107

Church and the secular élite. In short, it is tempting to interpret the phase 4 monastic plan as an expression of the transition from the early Carolingian concept of unity to a monastic zeal where for a while, at least, abbots recognised and sought to influence the aristocracy.

Abbot Epyphanius's plan

The phase 5 revisions to the phase 4a plan almost certainly belonged to the age of Abbot Epyphanius. The essential layout of the monastery was not altered, but significant parts of it were aggrandised. Visitors would have found it to be an even more impressive place. The distinguished guests' complex was enlarged with a new, high west apse. Associated with this was a fine arcosolium tomb in the corridor leading beneath the 'South Church' to the refurbished Crypt Church with its exquisitely made crypt. The emphasis upon refurbishments can also be found in the Vestibule, where the yard separating the claustrum and distinguished guests' sector was roofed and the area was decorated. The Entrance Hall was also decorated, using an imposing pilastered façade with an arcaded loggia in the upper storey. Concomitant alterations were also made to San Vincenzo Maggiore at this time: the apsidal west end with its crypt as well as the great elevated atrium with its raised eastwork facing visitors approaching from the river Volturno was doubtless completed in this period.

Individuals were certainly being given greater emphasis in the refurbishments. There was a new cemetery in the atrium of the Crypt Church. It is argued that the crypt itself was constructed for the child of a donor. However, this point is most explicitly illustrated by the portraits of Abbot Epyphanius himself, two deacons and the occupants of the tomb in the cycle of paintings in the crypt.

Discussion

How are we to interpret this sequence of plans at San Vincenzo in the light of the discussion of the Plan of St Gall? The Plan of St Gall was drawn up in the wake of Charlemagne's death, at a time when the relationship between the nobility and the Church was beginning to come under strain. Whether it was a paradigmatic blueprint or simply a design for a major monastery, as a unique artefact it is of a paramount importance for any interpretation of the Carolingian age. How are we to judge its significance?

The Carolingian empire was the largest political entity in western Europe between the end of the Roman empire and Napoleon's short-lived polity a millennium later. Unlike the Romans and, indeed, Napoleon, Charlemagne had few administrators at his disposal – only learned churchmen like Alcuin and Einhard – and no legions. To unify this polity, as most historians agree, he sought to make use of the Church rather than armies. Christian ideology was explicitly fashioned to bind the disparate regions together by restraining the political aspirations of potentially hostile aristocrats. The Church, in short, provided a constitution for the empire, a *Klosterpolitik*. Monasteries were no longer retreats, but out-ward-looking centres of civilisation promoting the new ethos (see, for example, McKitterick 1994). Senior churchmen were well aware of their growing power in the empire, especially after the loss of Charlemagne's charismatic leadership. As a result, the synods of 816 and 817 were designed not only to build upon the spirit of reform, then already two generations old, but also to develop the role of the Church in the formation of the State.

Central to these meetings was the part played by Benedict of Aniane, sometimes described as Louis the Pious's vice-regent. According to Ardo, Benedict's biographer, it was the reformer's intention to promote 'such a state of unity that it seemed as though they had been instructed by one master and in one place' (Noble 1976: 249). But was this spirit of unity already jeopardised by a generation of discussion, dispute and, above all, the passing of Charlemagne? By c. 820 the stability of the empire rested upon the twin pillars of society, the nobles and the senior churchmen, and the use that they made of an incipient third order, (skilled) workmen (Duby 1980; Le Goff 1980; Andreolli and Montanari 1983: 129-45). Benedict of Aniane's monastic concept had necessarily been superseded by a more pragmatic entity (Heitz 1980; Jacobsen 1992: 321-32). Monasteries modelled upon Aachen, in which long passages played an important axial role, connecting, yet separating, secular and ecclesiastical poles, already existed at Centula (Saint Riquier [Taylor 1975]) and, in all likelihood, at Farfa (McClendon 1987: 64ff.) and Monte Cassino (Pantoni 1973, where he illustrates the sequence of abbey-churches). This was the inevitable consequence of Charlemagne's strategic use of the Church in the later eighth century. He had directly and indirectly invested power in the ecclesiastical élite in order to control the secular aristocracy (Schmid 1972).

Such a policy meant that monasteries needed rooms for public recep-tions and for accommodating guests, to bring spiritual influence to bear on their aristocratic visitors – to involve them in the new Benedictine ideo-logy. The Plan of St Gall – this unique artefact betraying a contemporary perspective of a centre of civilisation – illustrates the comparative impor-tance of visitors. Four separate houses are allocated for the reception of royal visitors, according to Horn: '1, a house for the emperor and his immediate entourage; 2, an ancillary building containing the kitchen, bake and brewing facilities pertaining to this house; 3, a house for visiting servants; and if my interpretation is correct, 4, a house for the emperor's vassals and others of knightly rank travelling in the emperor's train' (Horn and Born 1979: vol. 2, 155). Horn and Born calculated that the total surface area taken up by these houses and their surrounding courts amounted to a little over a fifth of the surface area of the entire monastic complex. Nevertheless, unlike the distinguished guests' complex at San Vincenzo, with its own access over the Ponte della Zingara, and which was then connected by a corridor to the abbey-church, the great abbey-church on the Plan of St Gall dominates the guests' quarters in its shadow. St Gall's guest-houses were evidently lesser buildings. The Plan of St Gall, of course, may reflect the circumstances where the authority of Carolingian government was strong and abbots were not called upon to manipulate local élites (that is in the Rhineland and the transalpine region). On the other hand, beyond the core region of the empire the reverse may have been more likely to have occurred. In the principality of Benevento, for example, which was intermittently (although not after *c.* 790) compelled to pay tribute to the Carolingian empire, it seems likely that the authority and skill of individual churchmen (and their craftsmen) to manipulate the aristocracy would have been an issue of enormous, indeed critical, significance. Accordingly greater importance was attached to the independence and grandiosity of the guests' accommodation.

In sum, San Vincenzo took part in a cultural renaissance, much as St Gall did. In San Vincenzo's case, the need to cultivate the local élite was more necessary than at St Gall, and this purpose is more explicit in the layout of the phase 4 monastery that it is on the St Gall plan. On the other hand it would be misguided to interpret everything from San Vincenzo as explicitly Carolingian in origin when it is clear that the monastery was Beneventan, and conspicuously displays strong cultural affinities with the southern and northern Lombards. On reaching this conclusion, it is appropriate to consider the other aim of the San Vincenzo project, the context of the monastery.

The context of the monastery

Chris Wickham (1995; see also Wickham 1985a; 1985b) has outlined the historical context of San Vincenzo as a great monastic landlord. As he describes it, the monastery's history fit satisfactorily within the broader sweep of Beneventan history (Del Treppo 1968; Peduto 1990). Its eighth-century phases mirror the circumstances of the duchy of Benevento in the age before Arichis II, whereas its great expansion appears to have followed hard upon the changes wrought by him; and the monastery suffered from the political ramifications of the Beneventan civil war, after the second quarter of the ninth century; only late in the tenth century and during the first half of the eleventh century did circumstances revive once more (Wickham 1981: 159). In fact, it seems that the *Chronicon Vulturnense* was the last great achievement of the abbey. Thereafter, the place passed into obscurity. The achievements of San Vincenzo's great builders, abbots Paul, Joshua and Epyphanius, seem all the greater because of the apparent remoteness (in modern terms) of the monastery.

Far from the heartlands of the principality of Benevento, the monastery lies in a mountain valley, almost equidistant from the coastal littorals of the peninsula. Significantly, the settlement is located at the intersection between two climatic zones: that is, the Mediterranean zone and the mountain continental zone. In the continental zone winters are hard and long with a good deal of snow, while summers vary between temperate and humid high temperatures, with many thunderstorms. By contrast, mild wet winters and long hot summers typify Mediterranean climates. Apart from the obvious differences in living conditions, climate has major implications for agrarian regimes. The Mediterranean climate supports polyculture with olives, vines and cereals, but the upper limit of this cultivation is at the 800-metre contour. A continental climate, by contrast, chiefly gives rise to stock-raising and the cultivation of hardy cereals. The nineteenth-century sheep-fair held beside the abbey clearly illustrates this point, for it was the place where shepherds and peasants working two entirely different landscapes met.

It appears that this strategic location was first occupied in later Samnite times when a *vicus* was founded at San Vincenzo. This settlement was located a little over half way between Venafro or Isernia (both situated in classic Mediterranean territory) and Alfedena (located in classic continental upland territory). The half way point, as the crow flies, occurs at about Colli a Volturno. But the half way point on foot, bearing in mind the steep climb from San Vincenzo up the mountainous face of the Mainarde to Alfedena, is roughly on the Rocchetta plain.

However, the potential of such location could only be realised fully once intra- and interterritorial exchange became possible and important, at that point in time when the bulk production and distribution of regionally-specific agrarian goods could be coordinated by society. The archaeology of the upper Volturno valley demonstrates that this momentous change occurred in the last centuries BC. At this time the hilltop settlements were finally abandoned in favour of sites where the agrarian resources could be efficiently exploited. A local family or a provincial government may have established a sanctuary site at San Vincenzo, which, over the course of several generations, became the hub of a small, loosely aggregated, urban settlement. This settlement, while perhaps inheriting some traditions from local hilltop sites, was explicitly situated at the northern end of the Rocchetta plain on poor but readily defensible ground where full advantage might be made of communications up the valley, on the one hand, and, on the other, of the potential of the plain for grazing stock and growing cereals. It remains a matter of speculation whether this was the site of *Samnium* (J. Patterson 1985; La Regina 1989).

The complex history of San Vincenzo's classical antiquity led the form of the settlement to alter from a *vicus* to a villa. Nevertheless, over 600 or 700 years the location advantages of the place must have changed little until classical society and its economy collapsed. The late Roman settlement was the final relic of the integrated economies that connected the

111

mountains and the Mediterranean (Hodges 1993b). Perhaps as much for a tradition spanning many centuries as for its immediate late antique past, after its desertion in the sixth century, it continued to be used intermittently as a burial ground by local peoples who upheld the tradition of burial at this place. But these peoples were few in number; they were occupying hilltop locations, such as the hills around Colli a Volturno and Vacchereccia, for a variety of reason, and their impoverished material culture expresses the drastic downswing in the economy of this region (see Chapter 9). In effect, this inland valley had returned to its prehistoric condition, where the mountain resources might satisfactorily maintain only a small population.

This economic potential may have been recognised, in a sketchy sense at least, by the Beneventan founders, Paldo, Tato and Taso, in the early eighth century, but its full potential was certainly not realised by them. Of course, it is unlikely that the monks chose the site for its economic qualities; instead, they were guided, we may suppose, by such matters as the historic association of the place, close to the source of the river Volturno, which had enjoyed 700 years of virtually uninterrupted settlement, as well as by its position close to the Beneventan frontier.

According to the *Chronicon Volturnense*, the monks were given a largely defunct landscape. The chronicler describes it as a wild, abandoned zone, evoking the image of a pioneering age (Wickham 1985a: 13-23; 1994: 157). (In this instance, Le Goff's analysis of the desert-forest image in texts of this period, wherein later chroniclers attempted falsely to conjure up origins that resembled biblical primitivism, is now all the more interesting as the archaeological evidence for settlement continuity is very limited (Le Goff 1988; Wickham 1994: 157; for a review of the archaeological evidence see Hodges 1990; 1992c).) In one sense, however, the founders of San Vincenzo may have been seeking a mystical isolation that had parallels with the history of the people of Israel (Le Goff 1988). The Duke of Benevento's generosity needs to be measured in these terms. At Benevento, as in many southern Italian towns, it is very likely that the classical community had dwindled to little more than an élite settlement (Peduto 1990: 312-19; *contra* La Rocca Hudson 1986; Brogiolo 1987; 1989). The nearby colony of ancient *Venafrum*, for example, appears to have lost its bishopric by the seventh century, after which only its northwest corner was occupied by the fortified residence of a count (Morra and Valente 1993: 29-30, 89). Nevertheless, some elements of classical life outlasted the regional devolution of the Roman state. Notions of Roman property ownership survived the eclipse of the empire (Wickham 1981: 92-114; 1994: 99-118). Was the duke's largesse towards Paldo, Tato and Taso designed, therefore, not only to secure his vulnerable northern frontier, but also to encourage the development of what was a marginal zone? Were the monks part of a modest plan to revive the integration of mountain and Mediterranean resources within the duchy? If an early medieval fair had been located at San Vincenzo, it would have eluded the archaeological investigations for two reasons. First, it would have been located, in all probability, outside the monastic perimeter, possibly on the Rocchetta plain or on the east side of the river Volturno (cf. Bowes, Francis and Hodges forthcoming). Secondly, bearing in mind that we have failed to pinpoint the locus of the nineteenth-century fair witnessed by the Hon. Keppel Craven (1838: 62-5), identifying the remains of such a temporary (seasonal) activity would prove very difficult.

According to the chronicle, pre-eminent in the minds of San Vincenzo's founders was the development of a religious retreat dedicated to Saint Vincent. Within a century, though, the tiny sanctuary had been developed beyond the imagination of any early eighth-century monk. Similarly, one wonders if the Samnite founders of the sanctuary at San Vincenzo would have recognised the *vicus* at its apogee in the early first century AD, covering as much as ten hectares and including the numerous monumental buildings which grew up around it. One reason may have been San Vincenzo's acquisition of the relics of St Vincent in the early ninth century (Mitchell et al. 1997; Geary 1978: 166-7). A second reason is revealed by a comparison of the patterns of settlements in the region in republican and early medieval times.

The field survey of the upper Volturno valley shows that the republican settlement formed part of an extensive system to which many small farms or cottages belonged. Small farms were dotted at regular intervals around this territory. This is an index of the integrated competitive market system of which each settlement was one part. By contrast, the monastic settlement system before 1000 was altogether different. Very few medieval farms were found in the field survey. Excavations at Vaccherreccia, however, suggest that the farms of the seventh century onwards were small, unprepossessing settlements already situated on hilltops (Hodges et al. 1984). These excavations, as well as those at Colle Castellano (tenth-century *Olivella*) (Bowes, Francis and Hodges forthcoming), show that these farms had an impoverished material culture up until the age of *incastellamento*, at about the turn of the millennium, making them archaeologically difficult to identify (Hodges 1990). In short, the survey as well as the excavations of villages within the two differing ecological and climatic zones constituting the *terra* indicate that San Vincenzo was slow to develop its own domain. Only small churches, possibly *plebes* (Settia 1991: 3-4), such as that excavated at Colle Sant'Angelo (above Colli a Volturno), offer any illustration of San Vincenzo's extraordinary wealth (see Chapter 9). Modest churches such as Colle Sant'Angelo, it appears, rather like the sanctuaries surrounding the great Samnite hilltop settlement of Monte San Paolo, were the monastery's limited investment in diffusing its spirit as a centre of civilisation to the dispersed families in *condumae* in its immediate environs. San Vincenzo evidently looked further afield for its resources.

Wickham (1995) shows that San Vincenzo acquired numerous estates in the heartland of the principality of Benevento, places illustrated by Peduto in his recent appraisal of the duchy (Peduto 1990: 362ff.). The scale of Abbot Joshua's achievement, as Wickham argues, cannot simply be measured in terms of the phase 4 monastery, for in his period as abbot San Vincenzo became one of the great landowners in Italy. Clearly, the monastery managed to influence many of the lower-ranking Beneventan nobility at a time when the old Lombard duchy assumed a new political shape as a coalition of princely households, and as the territory began to sense its precarious position between the two superpowers, the Carolingian and the Byzantine empires (Cilento 1966: 209; Delogu 1977; 1990; Peduto 1990).

The significance of the estates donated to San Vincenzo lies in their location. Almost all were close to the major centres within the principality, on the Mediterranean littoral as opposed to in the mountains. A fortified centre of this kind was investigated at Santa Maria in Civita in the Biferno valley, 30 kilometres from the Adriatic coast, again close to the northern frontier of the principality (Bowes and Hodges 2002).

At Santa Maria all the features (for example, the enclosure wall, a church serving the community, associated cemeteries, a non-nucleated habitation pattern) of a late tenth-century *castello* in the upper Volturno valley were found to exist in the early to mid-ninth century. The settlement was processing and storing cereals in some quantity (Van der Veen 1985), and in receipt of mass-produced pottery as well as some glassware. It exhibits some of the traits of the Carolingian agricultural developments documented on other estates in the early ninth century (Andreolli and Montanari 1983). In this respect it constitutes a part of the scientific and technical development encouraged by the Carolingians, illustrated in many other forms in Abbot Joshua's monastery, but notably absent in rural settlements such as Vacchereccia in the upper Volturno at this time. Put another way, the archaeology of Santa Maria in Civita strongly suggests that the expansion of agricultural production was taking place within parts of the Beneventan heartland, but not within the upper Volturno.

But why did San Vincenzo seek to acquire estates around Benevento, Capua and Salerno, where similar agrarian developments were perhaps under way, when it failed to invest in its own *terra*? In part, of course, land, especially in these areas, was a measure of status and power. Benevento and Salerno had experienced a significant urban revival under Arichis II (Delogu 1977; 1990; 1992; Peduto 1990), not so very dissimilar from the revival of Rome itself (Delogu 1988; Hodges 1993b). Not surprisingly, San Vincenzo's neighbour, Monte Cassino, had built up a similar reputation as a landowner in Benevento (Toubert 1976), and, under Abbot Gisulf (797-817), was able to rebuild the abbey-church on a large scale, as well as found the new town beside the ruins of ancient *Casinum* (Leccisotti 1987;

Pantoni 1973). Neither San Vincenzo nor Monte Cassino could have consumed the produce of their estates, and much of it must have been redistributed to their many dependent houses. Some of it doubtless was also traded to the monasteries' mountain communities in the Abruzzo. However, it is tempting to speculate that some small part of it was traded via middlemen beyond central Italy.

The excavations at San Vincenzo permit us to show how there was a programme embracing not simply the revival of classical imagery, but, more lastingly, the reintroduction to élite centres, at least, of classical technology. Yet to enlarge this picture we need to examine the monastery's farms, probably located on the Rocchetta plain, and more of the extramural settlement situated on the east bank of the river Volturno. Beyond this, the archaeological data remain frustratingly slight. It still remains imperative that we examine the material culture of the peasantry to establish the extent of the reverberations of this programme. Santa Maria in Civita provides a clue, as, in a rather different, ideological measure, does the church at Colle Sant'Angelo, that local communities were being 'cultivated' to support the new spirit. In rural German contexts, for example, Heiko Steuer has illustrated the development of more effective, fixed management of rural resources in this period, associated with the construction of local stone-built churches (Steuer 1989); Theuws has demonstrated the same in the Kempen region of eastern Flanders (Theuws 1991). Even in Anglo-Saxon England there is evidence to show that the adoption of the new estate practices accompanied the ideological reorientation of this age (Hodges 1989: 116-49). At the other end of Europe were abbots like Joshua attempting to introduce similar, more intensive forms of resource control? In so far as this remains a matter of speculation, the San Vincenzo project failed to achieve all its objectives.

In conclusion, the archaeology of San Vincenzo sheds light on the significance of the Plan of St Gall, illuminating both what it is and what it is not. The large-scale investigations at San Vincenzo lend some qualified support to Horn's sweeping contention that: 'Superbly executed, and possibly the most accomplished architectural creation of the age of Charlemagne, the Plan of St Gall owes its existence to a striving for cultural unity that pervaded the whole of Carolingian life: unity embodied in a common language, Latin; a common belief, Christianity; a common legal and spiritual authority vested in the offices of the Emperor and Pope; and unity of monastic custom and observance. It was the search for unity in the conduct of monastic practice – *unitas regulae* – that by inner necessity also required creation of an ideal scheme to standardise and guide monastic architecture for the future' (Horn and Born 1979: vol. 1, 356). Yet, as is now clear from excavations at Reichenau and St Gall, Horn plainly overstated the significance of the ideal scheme to standardise. Nevertheless, the archaeology of San Vincenzo at its apogee splendidly illustrates a striving desire to evoke a spirit of unity and renaissance far from the

115

source of its conception. The paintings, the prolific display of script, the explicitly positioned pieces of classical *spolia*, and the revival of technology, show that San Vincenzo's abbots sought to be part of a programme that drew upon Lombard and even Frankish connections, as well as to exploit fully the renaissance of Beneventan political life that followed the reign of Arichis II. This led to great monastic riches, lifting the monastery out of its natural and social context, and, paradoxically, in this manner contributing to its inevitable demise.

8

The ninth-century collective workshop at
San Vincenzo al Volturno

Shortly after his election to the abbacy of San Vincenzo al Volturno, Joshua, a Frank by origin, launched a plan to transform the hitherto unprepossessing eighth-century Beneventan monastery. Excavations have revealed that the Beneventan founders employed the ruins of a fifth-century estate centre as the foundations for the first monastery established in 703. A late Roman funerary basilica was rebuilt as the abbey church, San Vincenzo Minore. This became the centre of a cluster of monastic buildings occupying no more than a hectare. The unexceptional architecture was matched by the poverty of the monastery's material culture. Yet, it was here that Abbot Ambrosius Autpert composed the biblical commentaries that made his name as a theologian of European repute. In 787, following Charlemagne's passage through Italy, San Vincenzo was granted immunities from taxation as well as other privileges. Almost at once the monastery acquired donations of land, and at this moment, it is believed, the abbey-church was re-modelled with a substantial ambulatory (San Vincenzo phase 3c). Joshua's election in 792 coincided with San Vincenzo's expanding fortunes (Hodges 1997a; for the phasing of San Vincenzo see Hodges 1993a: 31-2).

Joshua's project was immense in design. The new focus of the monastery was to be the abbey church of San Vincenzo Maggiore, situated below the southern flank of Colle della Torre. The site had to be landscaped and terraced. An axial corridor connected the new church to the old one, beside which new cloister buildings were erected. New ranges of buildings were also constructed on the terraces on the slopes of Colle della Torre. A church and associated ranges was even sited on the crown of the hill. New bridges, including one described as being of marble, provided access to the east bank of the river, where over the next half-century, our excavations have shown, a *borgo* established itself.

Spread over as many as ten hectares, Joshua's immense building site was dominated by the erection of one monumental structure – San Vincenzo Maggiore. When the basilica was consecrated in c. 808, it was approximately 63.5 metres long and 28.3 metres wide, its aisled nave supported by 24 marble columns apparently taken as *spolia* from a Roman temple at Capua. Almost as soon as Joshua had died, his successor, Abbot Talaricus (817-23), set about aggrandising the basilica, adding a ring crypt

117

below the west-facing apse and a massive vaulted eastwork and atrium (San Vincenzo phase 5a) (Hodges and Mitchell 1996). With some resemblance to St Peter's at Rome, the abbey-church plainly lent great prestige to San Vincenzo, from which up until the 830s the monastery acquired a rich array of gifted properties (Wickham 1995). This was to change dramatically. Civil war broke out in the Carolingian kingdoms and then in the Kingdom of Benevento in the later 830s and 840s. Matters thereafter worsened: in 848 an earthquake severely damaged much of the monastery, including the great church (San Vincenzo phase 5b). The excavations show that the subsequent repairs to the fabric were expedient; San Vincenzo's fortunes, it appears, were waining. The end came on 10 October 881 when a band of Arabs in collusion with the Bishop of Naples attacked the abbey from the south, and once they had forced an entry, savagely sacked the great renaissance centre (San Vincenzo phase 5c) (Hodges 1997b).

The Arabs forced their entry through a line of buildings on the south side of San Vincenzo Maggiore, comprehensively putting them to the torch. When the monastery was later remodelled in the eleventh century, these remains were levelled and partly protected by a proto-Romanesque new cloister. The archaeological stratigraphy, as a result, was well preserved and rich with the contents of these buildings from that morning in 881. The contents showed beyond doubt that this had been a line of craft workshops and dwellings. Moreover, behind this building were, first, mounds of refuse pertaining to its last occupants, which in turn sealed the construction levels of the church, which themselves sealed well-preserved remains of the first workshops erected hereabouts – temporary workshops utilised by the craftsmen employed in Abbot Joshua's enterprise. The picture of archaeology, architecture, art and history conjured up in these layers sealed by the charcoal spread of 881 is, to say the least, as evocative as it gets in any excavation.

The first workshops: the temporary workshops and first collective workshop

The earliest phase of workshops has been defined as the temporary workshops (Hodges and Mitchell 1996: 51-4; Hodges 1997a: 94-101; 149-50). A sequence of workshops, each replacing the next, making first tiles, then bronze and copper items, then glass, and finally a bell-casting pit, were located at the eastern front of San Vincenzo Maggiore (Fig. 8.1A). These workshops belonged to the period in which the new basilica and, perhaps, the new cloisters were constructed (phase 4a). In addition, south of these – that is, more or less alongside the basilica – lay a line of pisé buildings probably comprising five rooms (two of which were E and F, described below) (Fig. 8.1A). The remains of this palimpsest of workshops in front of the east end of the basilica were levelled to make the platform on which the eastwork, cross-passageway corridor and atrium of San

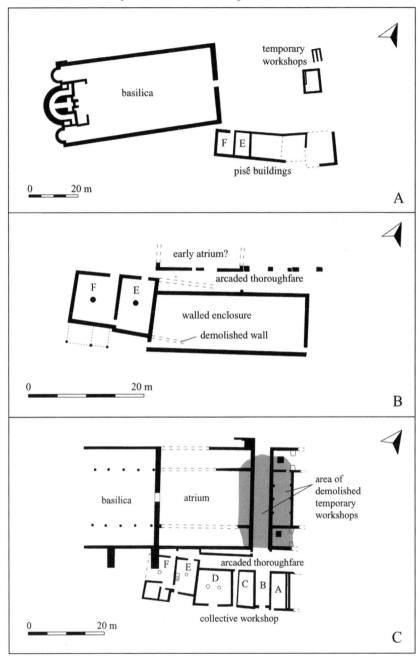

8.1. Schematic plan of the workshops at San Vincenzo al Volturno, *c.* 790-881: (A) the phase 4 temporary workshops; (B) the phase 4b first collective workshops; (C) the phase 5 collective workshop.

119

Vincenzo Maggiore were built, probably between 808 and 823. At the same time, the line of pisé buildings to the south was substantially modified to create a new arrangement comprising rooms E and F and a walled enclosure (Fig. 8.1B). The construction of this complex took place at the same time as the first atrium, or soon after. The new building, which extended for 28 metres from east to west and was 11 metres long, probably represents accommodation of some kind with an attached yard or enclosure. The floor of the yard was roughly paved with cobbles, made of small pieces of limestone and quartz and broken tiles. On the eastern side of the yard, dumps of ash and charcoal, containing large quantities of glass, crucible, semi-precious stones and metal objects covered the cobbles. As this complex was associated with craft activities, we have tentatively described it as the collective workshop, following the terminology used by Horn and Born for the workshop depicted on the ninth-century Plan of St Gall (Horn and Born 1979). The new atrium of San Vincenzo Maggiore and the first collective workshop (rooms E and F, and the enclosure) were separated by a narrow corridor and, to the east, an arcaded thoroughfare, 3.5 metres wide and paved with yellow mortar. Stone-arched doorways at specific locations along the route and the presence of roof tiles, suggest that it was covered.

Shortly after its construction, the enclosure was remodelled when four walls, aligned north-south, were inserted to make from, east to west, rooms A, B, C, and D. Together with the earlier clay-bonded rooms E and F, these new rooms formed the second collective workshop which is the subject of this chapter (Fig. 8.1C).

The second collective workshop

The six small workshops on the south side of the atrium were initially divided into front and back rooms, with narrow doors in the south-facing elevation leading to a rough cobbled yard. The covered thoroughfare still separated the space between the workshop and the atrium of San Vincenzo Maggiore. Little is known from the first phase of this building, dating to between *c.* 820 and the earthquake of 848 (phase 5a). However, after *c.* 848, structural debris was cleared and dumped above the remains of the collapsed roof of the thoroughfare separating it with San Vincenzo Maggiore. The structural alterations associated with this new phase (phase 5b) include the introduction of timber partitions and in some places the laying of fine *cocciopesto* floor surfaces. Changes in access were also made by closing routes that had existed between and through the separate rooms. Emphasis was placed on access to and from the yard to the south. This was accomplished by the introduction of large doorways, wide enough for carts, in the southern walls of the rooms – a change which may have had fatal repercussions in 881 when the Arabs forced their way into the monastery at this point.

8. The ninth-century collective workshop at San Vincenzo al Volturno

Let us now examine each workshop in turn (Fig. 8.1C).

Room A measured 6 by 11 metres and was poorly preserved on its eastern side, surviving to just above floor-level (Fig. 8.2). Initially, two narrow doors may have existed at the southern ends of the east and west walls. The floor was crude, consisting of the quartz and tile cobbled surface that had been laid within the large enclosure. Ash dumps used to level the floor contained a rich assemblage of industrial waste derived from the earlier workshops. Over 1,500 fragments of glass were recovered, including gilded sherds (see Stevenson 2001). Crucible fragments, glass tesserae and beads were also found, together with a silver-plated gem-setting, bronze strips and an iron knife-blade or tool. A layer of clay, which had been heavily trampled above the cobbles and ash deposits, probably represents the occupation and activity within the room during its first phase. From this layer also come two silver deniers of Prince Sico of Benevento (817-32). The coins, probably acquired as a source of silver for silvering metalwork, furnish a date in the 820s or early 830s for the first phase (phase 5a) of activity.

During the second phase, a bench was constructed along the east wall of room A and a layer of yellow mortar was placed over the trampled clay floor. Plaster traces adhering to the side of the bench show that the room was decorated and probably painted. The renovations were completed by the addition of a fine, tiled pavement, evident from surviving fragments and where absent, from distinct impressions visible in the mortar foundation. A second, silty occupation layer which had formed above the remains of the floor, showed that the room had fallen into disrepair by 881. Clues to the function of the room between 848 and 881 are provided by a number of remarkable objects found in two significant deposits. The occupation layer above the tile floor contained a number of bronze objects including a ring, an iron chisel, a small tack, sheet fragments and pieces of beaded wire. The second deposit, a rich, black layer of charcoal and vitrified material, belongs to 881. This contained fragments of bronze sheet, strips, beaded wire and pins; iron rods, hooks and fittings; glass fragments, crucible sherds and glass cabochons. Three special finds are a damaged tray of enamel depicting a long-stemmed flower, a Roman gemstone – a carnelian engraved with a figure making an offering, and an intact small tray of cloisonné enamel (Mitchell 2000; 2001b). Room A, it seems probable, was an enamel workshop in which objects such as reliquaries, book-covers and processional crosses were assembled.

Room B, the narrowest of all the workshops, measured 5 by 11 metres (Fig. 8.3). Initially, the room was open at its north end and narrow doors provided access into adjacent rooms A and C. It was floored with cobbles, many of which were worn smooth. Soon after its construction, a new yellow clay and beaten earth floor was laid over the cobbles in room B and pieces of bone, glass and pottery and several bronze objects including a pin, were

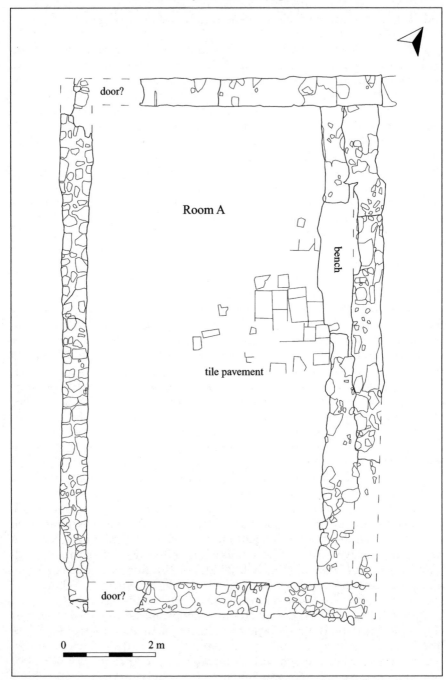

8.2. Plan of room A.

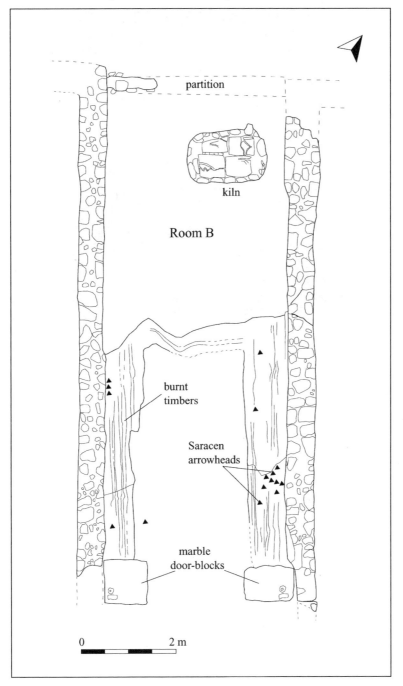

partition

kiln

Room B

burnt
timbers

Saracen
arrowheads

marble
door-blocks

0   2 m

8.3. Plan of room B.

8.4. An ivory monk's head with blue glass eyes
found in deposits behind room B.

found trampled into the surface. Several small clay hearths containing
fragments of glass and crucibles, located close to the side walls of the
workshop, provide clues to its function during this phase (phase 5a).

After 848, the vaulted thoroughfare north of workshop B was used as a
dump for refuse. In places this rose to a metre in height. In excess of 23,000
fragments of animal bone were found, principally the waste from the
working of bone, horn and skin (Clark 1997). There were over 100 pieces
of worked bone, including combs, decorated trial pieces and needles. Ivory
also appears to have been worked: a small latch and the finely carved head
of a monk with blue glass eyes were found (Mitchell 1992) (Fig. 8.4).
Within the workshops, worked bone was only recovered from rooms A and
B, suggesting that these, perhaps, are the most likely locations of the early
bone-workshop. Evidence for bronze-working is provided by the discovery
of a kilogram of crucible. A range of bronze objects, including lumps, strips,
a gilded ring-setting containing a large gemstone and five penannular
brooches, were also found. Finally, 68 lead objects including window
cames, latticework screens and strips were retrieved. The lead appears to
have been specifically made for the production of portable objects decorated with flat glass.

Other finds from the midden included 55 kilograms of potsherds in the
form of jugs, jars and bowls, and iron objects such as nails, rods, tacks,

124

buckles, horseshoes and knives. Other finds include Alpine soapstone sherds, fragments of vessel and *millefiori* glass, glass beads, glass stoppers, spindle-whorls, pestles and whetstones. More than a hundred prehistoric stone tools, including a miniature green schist axe were also present; it seems these served as amulets and alchemy ingredients during craftworking.

After 848, a wide doorway was made at the south end of workshop B. Two re-used Roman marble door-blocks were inserted into the side walls. The opening was almost the width of the room, wide enough for a cart or wagon to enter. The north end was later closed off by a simple timber partition. Inside, the room was plastered and painted. The earlier small hearths were sealed beneath a yellow mortar floor, which was probably paved with tiles similar to the one in room A. Here also, the floor was obviously in a state of disrepair by the time of the Arab attack. The main feature associated with room B was an oval kiln or hearth measuring 1.6 by 0.5 metres. The outer wall of the kiln was constructed of travertine boulders. Four inscribed tiles, with their flanges removed, had been placed within it to create a level working-platform. Along the sides of the room, close to the walls, a number of possible metalworking hearths were located. A line of burnt posts found close by suggest that two, long wooden structures, possibly work benches or shelves stood along the east and west walls.

The finds show that room B was in use in 881. The room was quickly abandoned and subsequently destroyed as a result of a fierce fire. The carbonised remains of the south door were found lying above the mortar floor. Part of a lock mechanism, hinges, bolts, nails and two keys were discovered within the burning. Eighteen arrowheads, some embedded in the charcoal remains of the door, were also found. Within the room, the painted walls and the mortar floors were heavily scorched. The wooden door lintel and the shelves along the walls had been completely destroyed. A deep, black deposit of charcoal and silt, containing the remains of the tile roof, covered the floor. Scattered and broken objects were found within the blackened remains. Once again, these permit us to reconstruct the room's layout and purpose prior to the fire. Many objects lay in the burnt remains of the shelves on which they had been stored. Several red-painted jugs and bowls were shelved on the west side, close to the door. On the shelves opposite was kept a valuable, lathe-turned Alpine soapstone jar, which may have been used as a crucible (Patterson 2001). The jar appears to have been stored with metalwork including an iron spike, a knife, a ring and a rein-shackle (Mitchell 2001c). Pieces of copper sheet and strip were found, together with a hammered bronze rod with a soldered handle. Fragments of glass- and bronze-working crucible, pieces of lead and window glass complete the list of finds stored by the door. In the northern half of the room, the objects were all confined to the eastern shelves, close to the kiln. These included two iron spikes – possibly the two halves of a

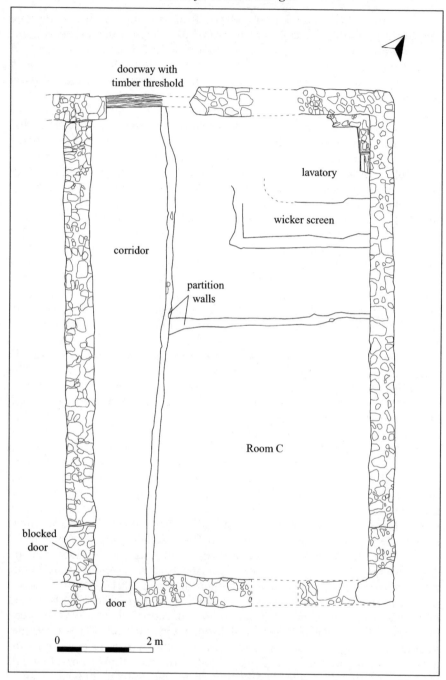

8.5. Plan of room C, the so-called Chamberlain's house.

caliper-type tool, a cut-throat razor, part of a metal sheath, lumps and fragments of bronze and iron, and a little imported pottery. This array of objects as well as the hearths suggests that small-scale metalworking, perhaps for the delicate finishing or repair of objects, took place in the room.

Room C, measuring 7 by 11 metres, was the best preserved (cf. Moreland 1985) (Fig. 8.5). It had two narrow doors in its first phase: one located in the south end of the west wall, giving access to room D; the other in the north-west corner, leading into the thoroughfare. The floor was of cobbles, set in yellow mortar. The first occupation level was an orange clay containing a little glass, crucible, pottery and animal bone. In the south-east corner lay a small, square hearth with a single, heavy tile base, possibly the remains of a chimney (cf. the kiln at Mosaburg, Hungary: Szöke, Wedepohl and Kronz 2004: fig. 2). A small bench-like structure, built of tiles, stood to the east of the hearth, bonded onto the wall. In the north-east corner of the room was a deep pit containing lime and organic material. This was probably a lavatory or waste-pit. Objects recovered from the pit included an almost complete, early ninth-century ceramic jar, and an extremely fine, globular blue glass vessel.

After 848 the workshop was remodelled as a dwelling. Its west door was blocked and replaced by a small doorway inserted into the south wall. Traces of a pathway were discovered in the yard outside leading up to this door. Inside, a wattle and plaster partition wall was constructed within the western side of the room, forming a narrow, raised corridor that allowed direct access between the north and south doors. The remainder of the building was transformed into two rooms. The south room, approximately 5 metres square, had a fine, mortar floor that covered the earlier corner hearth. The walls were plastered and painted along the skirting with a simple design of narrow coloured bands. The north room, which measured 4.5 metres square, was separated by a narrow, timber partition. Its floor was also a mortar surface. The lavatory pit, still apparently in use, appears to have been concealed by a wicker screen and plastered on the tile surround.

Charcoal levels connoting the 881 attack lay across the mortar floors in the corridor and the two rooms. Burnt timbers and tiles mixed within the destruction deposits represent the collapsed roof of the building. All the objects were found in the north room. These included bronze and lead sheeting, lead and iron strips and iron hooks and nails, as well as tools such as awls, chisels, a pair of heavy iron-forging tongs, and a linen-heckle used to prepare wool or flax. The presence of a door-lock mechanism and a key in the north room highlights the importance of this workshop and its contents. From the yard on the south side of this room several moulded terracotta corbels were discovered, suggesting that its outward elevation had been carefully embellished (Fig. 8.6).

Room C comprised what appears to have been a living room at the front

8.6. A terracotta corbel used to embellish the south-facing
elevation of room C.

and a room with a lavatory and a tool store at the rear. Given its situation
in the midst of workshops producing high-quality materials, it is proposed
that it housed either a master-craftsmen or an administrator. The St Gall
plan indicates that the monastery's chamberlain, whose apartment was
located at the centre of the complex, supervised the Great Collective
Workshop (Horn and Born 1979: vol. 1, xxiv, building 25). The lay-out and
decor of room C as well as its contents suggest that its occupant was none
other than the chamberlain of San Vincenzo al Volturno.

Room D was the largest in the complex, measuring 11 square metres
(Figs 8.7; 8.8). Its walls, built of rubble and mortar, butted the clay (pisé)
east wall of room E. Two central posts set on stone post-pads supported its
thatched roof. Three entrances existed in its first phase: two narrow doors
were located in the south ends of the east and west walls, giving access to
room C and round to the southern entrance of room E. A third, wider
doorway was set in the north wall. From this latter door, and from the
adjacent north door of room C, one could pass across the east-west thor-

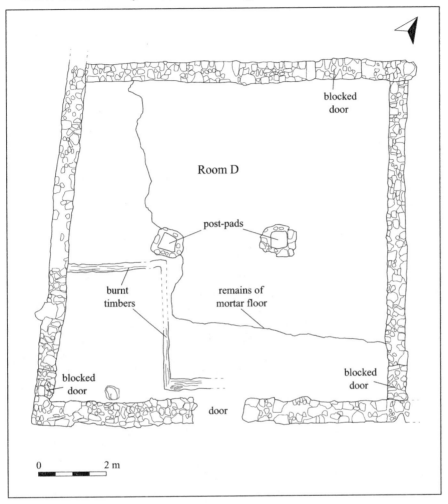

8.7. Plan of room D.

oughfare and through an arched door into the first atrium of San Vincenzo Maggiore. The earliest flooring consisted of makeshift cobbles of small travertine boulders and tile fragments compacted into a yellow clay. The surface survived around the edges of the room and within the three doorways. A range of objects including iron buckles, pottery, bone, painted plaster, glass and crucible were trampled into the cobbled floor.

After 848 room D was radically altered. The first alteration involved a change of access: the three narrow doors were blocked. A new entrance, approximately 0.9 metres wide, was opened in the centre of the south wall. In the central part of the room a surface of crushed travertine and mortar was laid. Although only patches of this surface remained, it was apparent

129

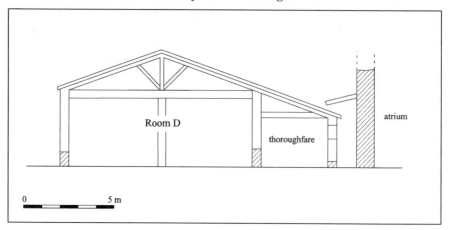

Room D

thoroughfare

atrium

0   5 m

8.8. A hypothetical cross-section (north-south) through room D with the atrium of San Vincenzo Maggiore to the north.

that some kind of division had existed within the floor space. Around the sides of the room was a layer of fine, trampled earth and within it, on the western side of the door, were the remains of timber features. These consisted of the burnt remains of a door lintel, a post and two beams, demarcating the south-west quarter of the room. The timbers appear to represent wooden partitions or some kind of platform structure, burnt *in situ*. Identical structures may have existed in all four corners. On the west side of the room, against the wall was a semi-circular pit, beside which were found the charred remains of a container of grain, possibly a small wooden bucket. The positioning of the timber structures and the mortar floor, combined with the presence of grain and two quernstones which were found outside the door suggest that this was a granary. The interior of the building would have comprised four corner bays, built of timber, in which the grain was stored. Between these, mortared thresh-ing lanes would have formed a cross-shaped floor. A similar building is depicted as the granary on the St Gall Plan (Horn and Born 1979: vol. 1, xxiv, building 24).

In this case, however, D was destroyed before 881. The evidence is unequivocal: the mortar and earth floor was reddened and contained the charred remains of the timber bays and the container of grain. The burnt timbers were covered by a trampled clay surface (the latter was sub-sequently sealed by 881 levels). The fire may have begun accidentally and spread quickly through the roofs of the complex: those of room E, in which the same conflagration is discernible, and F, were also likely to have consisted of thatch or shingle. Whatever the cause of the fire, the trampled clay shows that D was re-used, perhaps as a storeroom or byre up until 881. The clay, which was heavily compacted, contained over 1 kilogram of pottery, including a colander or cheese-strainer, together with fragments

130

of glass, an iron buckle and two small iron clappers from animal bells. Three large wooden posts appear to have been inserted into the walls in order to support the damaged roof, and the front of the building may have been re-roofed with tiles. Its final destruction in 881 was discernible in the form of the collapsed roof and the burnt remains of the door containing round-headed bolts, dome-headed nails and a lock mechanism. A Neolithic stone axe, discovered on the western side of the door, may have been suspended within the roof of the building as a protective amulet or thunderstone (Fig. 9.1).

Room E, together with F, was the oldest building in the complex, having been retained from the complex of workshops and buildings constructed in the 790s (see above) (Figs 8.9; 8.10). It measured 7 by 10 metres. The original walls of the building were randomly built of stone and tile, bonded with clay. The unique alignment on which E and its partner, F were constructed, meant that the two structures encroached westwards towards the south wall of San Vincenzo Maggiore. To the east, they converged oddly with room D. During the first phase of the collective workshop, E was retained in its original form, although the south wall was demolished and re-built a little further south, using stone and mortar. The building retained its two original (phase 4) entrances: the first, located at the east end of the north wall led into the thoroughfare, and the second led from the southern end of the west wall into room F. The charred remains of wooden thresholds were visible in both entrances. The roof of the building was supported by a central post set on a mortar post-pad. The excavations in E are incomplete and consequently, little is known of the building during phase 5a. An early floor made of a layer of brown clay containing mortar and plaster was partially exposed on its east side. Little can be said about the function of the building at this time, except that no evidence of craft activity was found here. Did E provide accommodation or storage for the craftsmen?

After 848, a new door was introduced into the south wall of E. The internal surfaces of the walls were rendered with plaster and slight evidence exists, in the form of clay plinths, for workbenches situated against the east wall. The floor of the building appears to have been refurbished with *cocciopesto* mortar and tiles. At the southern end of the room, the floor led from the new door to a set of well constructed, tile-based, steps. The steps, which measured 0.9 metres high, 2 metres long and 0.9 metres wide, were built against the central part of the west wall of the room, directly opposite the southern entrance. A partition wall probably existed between the door and the steps: a few timber features, yet to be clarified, have been located within the floor. The steps possibly provided access to a loft, perhaps by way of a ladder from the upper platform. The close proximity of the steps to a large tank, situated in the north-west corner of the building, also suggests that the two features are in some way related. The tank, as yet unexcavated, is a rectangular pit

131

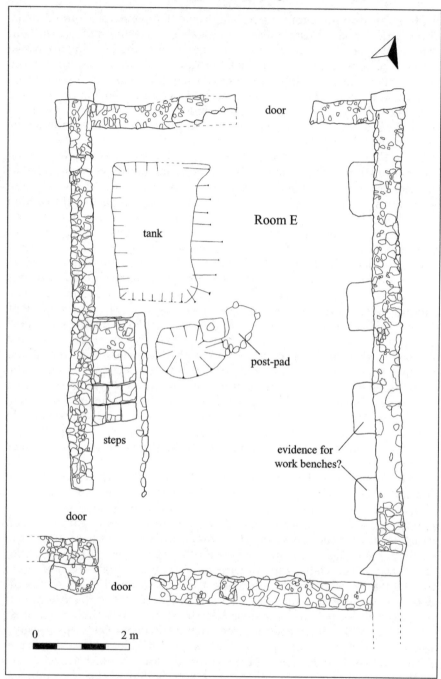

door

Room E

tank

post-pad

steps

evidence for
work benches?

door

door

0   2 m

8.9. Plan of room E.

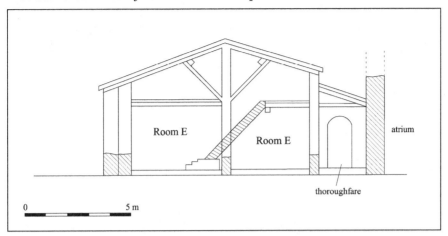

Room E

Room E

atrium

thoroughfare

0   5 m

8.10. A hypothetical cross-section (north-south) through room E with
the atrium of San Vincenzo Maggiore to the north.

measuring 2.5 by 1.6 metres. A large, hollowed block of stone was found close by and together, the two are provisionally interpreted as the tank and counter-weight of an olive press. Alternatively, the tank may represent a grain silage bin, associated with the granary. Before 881 the tank was filled with rubble; this may be associated with aftermath of the fire, observed in D.

Room E appears to have been re-visited after 881: disturbed deposits above the floor probably represent a limited attempt to salvage lost or valuable items. The many objects recovered from the room included a first-century AD Roman coin, fragments of gilded glass and glass vessels, a loom-weight, a bronze ring and molten lead. Many iron objects were also found, including a well-preserved hinge from a large chest with four nails still attached, a slide-key, a drill-bit, a ring, a knife blade, a strap-slide, three large-headed tacks and a bolt. The objects are so wide-ranging, it is difficult to place any secure interpretation on the use of the room, during its final years. Once again, it seems that the poorly maintained building was being used for mixed purposes on the eve of the Arab attack.

Room F is the second building pre-dating the collective workshop (Fig. 8.11). During phase 5a, F retained its original form. It consisted of a single room, measuring 8.5 by 9.5 metres, with clay-bonded walls and a central supporting post mounted on a heavy mortar post pad. It had two, or possibly three doors: the first, leading from the thoroughfare (separating the collective workshop from San Vincenzo Maggiore), was positioned at the northern end of the room and the second allowed access to and from E. A third entrance may have been located in the south-west corner of the building. F appears to have had a timber porch, as wide as the room, which extended 3.5 metres on its south side. Little can be said about its early phase, except that it had a simple, beaten earth floor.

133

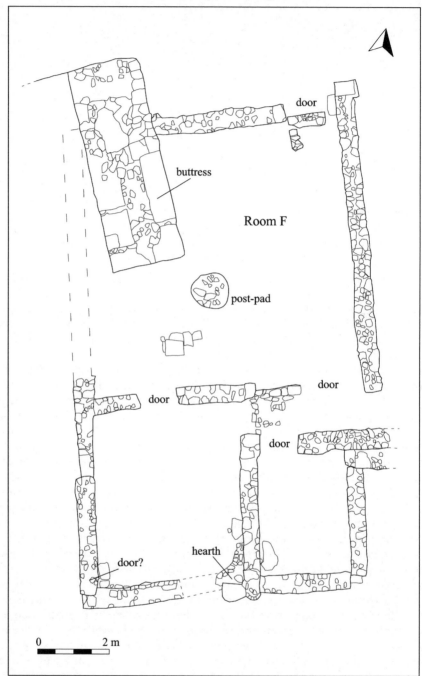

8.11. Plan of room F.

F was significantly altered after AD 848. The south wall of the large room was demolished and rebuilt in stone a little to the north. The timber posts of the porch were left in place and incorporated within a new, stone-built structure making two further rooms. A small east room, measuring 2.5 by 3 metres had a single door in the north wall. A larger west room, measuring 4 by 4.5 metres, had two entrances: one at the north end of the east wall and a second, with a step, at the south end of the west wall. A tile-built hearth or oven was located in the south-east corner. Both new rooms were floored with *cocciopesto*; in the west room this covered the levelled remains of the old south wall. It is not certain whether the large room retained a beaten earth floor: remnants of tiles and *cocciopesto* were located around the doorways. The two south rooms were plastered; traces of painting, vertical red bands framing one corner, survived on the walls of the western one. The main room, now slightly reduced in size, also appears to have been plastered.

Few objects were recovered from the 881 burning layer. The small, south-east room in particular, was devoid of finds. The large north room, which was filled with an ashy destruction deposit, contained only scraps of iron and copper, as well as fragments of pottery, which may have been employed for industrial purposes. The most complete evidence came from the south-west room with the fireplace, where a typical black destruction layer contained an arrowhead. A large iron ring, a quantity of pottery and animal bone and a fragmentary, burnt funerary inscription were also found here. This small number of finds makes it difficult to interpret the function of the building. Nonetheless, the mortar floors, the decorated walls and above all, the fireplace, suggest it served as a dwelling.

The histories of the buildings can be summarised thus:

Phase building history

4a. Temporary workshops. Rubble and mortar constructed glass workshop; pisé buildings (E & F) for accommodation

4b/5a. First collective workshop. Pisé buildings (E and F) with walled enclosure

5a. Second collective workshop. Line of buildings – A to F; A-D constructed of rubble and mortar; E and F in pisé with timber details

5b. Line of buildings – A to F, modified to include two apartments (rooms C and F) and a granary (room D); timber partitions; *cocciopesto* floors

5b1. Line of buildings – A to F; room D destroyed by localised fire; rooms D, E and F used for temporary storage

5c. Line of buildings – A and B in use as metal workshops; C for accommodation; D, E and F used for temporary storage

This detailed description of the line of rooms A to F is intended to illustrate the exceptional character of the archaeological remains. Like the better-known shops found at Sardis, apparently destroyed in a Persian attack dated to AD 613 (Crawford 1990), the 881 sack levels from these buildings at San Vincenzo provide a 'Pompeian premise' snapshot of the buildings and their activities on the eve of the catastrophe (Binford 1981). In addition, the palimpsest of levels dating back to the late eighth century throw light on the building history. The best parallel for a ninth-century building of this type is the so-called collective workshop depicted on the parchment drawing of the Carolingian monastery of St Gall dated to *c.* 820. On the Plan of St Gall, the collective workshop is a roughly square structure, sub-divided into a number of separate but interdependent rooms occupied by diverse craftsmen: shield-makers, sword-grinders, saddlers, shoemakers, curriers, turners, fullers, blacksmiths and goldsmiths (Horn and Born 1979: vol. 2, 189-99). The Plan is a controversial document, but some corroboration for the existence of monastic buildings of this kind comes from the author of the *Chronica monasterii Casinensis*, the late eleventh-century chronicle of San Vincenzo' sister abbey, Monte Cassino. This refers to the workshops that once stood either side of the ninth-century church of San Salvatore, in the *borgo* below the monastery. No workshops of this kind are known from secular contexts; excavations of eighth- and ninth-century north-west European emporia have shown that they were largely composed of clusters (as opposed to a line) of workshops (Hodges 2000: 81-92).

This is not the place to discuss the operations of the collective workshop (see Mitchell 1996; Hodges 1997a). Instead, suffice it to note that on the bases of the industrial waste from the three entirely different complexes, the following can be summarised:

Workshop activities by phase

4a1. Temporary workshops. Tile production with accommodation in rooms E, F and three other rooms

4a2. Temporary workshops. Glass production; E and F etc. in use

4a3. Temporary workshops. Fine metal production; E and F etc. in use

4b/5a. First collective workshop. E and F, and an enclosure; no production debris

5a. Second collective workshop. A (enamels), B (fine metalwork), C (unknown), D (unknown), E and F (accommodation)

5b. Second collective workshop. A (enamels), B (fine metalwork), C (chamberlain's apartment), D (granary), E (olive press?) and F (accommodation)

5b1. Second collective workshop: A (enamels), B (fine metalwork), C (chamberlain's apartment), D (out of use), E and F (accommodation)

The focus of this chapter is the architecture of the complex. Post-built structures, with the exception of the porch added to room F, are largely absent, although most of the buildings had timber features. Post-built construction was very much the vernacular norm at this time in the countryside; indeed, most of the buildings in San Vincenzo's *borgo* were post-built (see Bowes, Francis and Hodges forthcoming). Instead, two types of structures occur here: mortared rubble structures, similar to most of the monastic buildings erected in phases 4 and 5, and simple variations of pisé structures with conspicuous use of rubble in the lower reaches of the walls as well as timber detailing. The promiscuous use of lime mortar in the construction of the phase 4a glass workshop is reminiscent of the lavish lime mortar rendering used in San Vincenzo Minore phase 3c, following the reintroduction of lime mortar to the site in the later eighth century (Hodges and Mithen 1993: 134). After this, lime mortar was used sparingly. Rooms E and F, built in a variant of pisé, merit special attention. Common in classical construction – even in great villas such as Settefinestre – pisé is unknown elsewhere at San Vincenzo (Carandini 1985). Originating in phase 4a, the proposed line of five rooms including E and F, beg many questions. In the wet upland climate of San Vincenzo, pisé was an abnormal construction method which needed to be protected by a good tiled roof. Given the later ninth-century evidence of tile and mortar surfaces in E and F, and the presence of painted plaster in room F, it is tempting to interpret these two and the lost three rooms as accommodation for the craftsmen involved in the construction and furnishing of abbot Joshua's new monastery. Moreover, being a construction form largely alien to the upper Volturno valley, it is no less tempting to interpret these as the work of an architect who, like the craftsmen, was not from the area.

Turning to the details, re-used Roman pieces were used to make the south door of room B from *c.* 848 onwards, just as terracotta modillions – features hitherto associated with church ornamentation – were employed to decorate the south-facing elevation of room C, the chamberlain's room (Mitchell 2001a). *Spolia*, it should be noted, was commonly employed in the main monastic rooms and churches in phase 5a; if anything, the absence of *spolia* in the workshops is noteworthy (Castellani 2000). Modillions, on the other hand, were only found elsewhere at San Vincenzo associated with the Refectory. In his study of the modillions, Mitchell describes them as 'extremely simplified versions of Antique marble acanthus modillions and consoles' (2001a: 117). Ninth-century parallels are known from San Salvatore in Brescia, though the concept is best illustrated by the re-used consoles deployed to decorate the crown of the apse of San Martino ai Monti in Rome. These embellishments may have been made because appropriate *spolia* were not available. This said, although the modillions and painted walls of room C merit our attention, the overall décor of the room was modest by comparison with the grandiosity of the decoration in the first-floor hall of the South Church which accommodated distinguished visitors at San Vincenzo (Hodges and Mithen 1993: 186-9).

Following the earthquake in 848, timber partitions as well as makeshift timber uprights and even a timber threshold (in room F) were ubiquitous throughout the collective workshop. All the signs are that the monastery could no longer maintain its buildings as before, and expedient measures were necessary (cf. the Vestibule connecting the Assembly Room to the Distinguished Guests' Hall [Hodges 1993a; 1995a]). In this complex, this involved the use of timber elements following vernacular norms (cf. the Refectory).

The floors are no less interesting. Ninth-century San Vincenzo boasted a range of flooring including marble, *opus sectile*, terracotta tiled floors, *cocciopesto*, simple mortar surfaces, cobbles and earthen surfaces. The south room of A, the enameller's shop, had a tiled floor. Traces of tiling were also found in rooms B, E and F. Like the well-used corridors and rooms of San Vincenzo, these were perhaps places that, because they were visited by San Vincenzo's patrons, were afforded good flooring. Equally the *cocciopesto* flooring in room C, the chamberlain's apartment, suggests that this was regarded as an index of stature – an index that in the case of rooms E and F suggests that the craftsmen, important individuals in the rhythm of the monastery's life, were accommodated here. Elsewhere, cobbling or earthen floors, as in the undercrofts of the distinguished guests' quarters (in the South Church) were perfectly normal (Hodges and Mitchell 1993: 185).

The furnishing of the rooms was evidently varied. Traces of possible chimneys were found in rooms C and F. Chimneys are unknown at this time, and further research is necessary as the norm were hearths located like braziers away from the wall (see Valenti 1996: fig. 67 for an example at Poggibonsi; also Brogiolo and Gelichi 1997: figs 27 and 35 for examples found at Piadena and Ferrara). The possible chimney in the north-west angle of the glass workshop may have been a prototype for the features found in rooms C and F. The possible latrine in room C, like the one found in the Distinguished Guests' Refectory, was simply constructed with tile, rubble and mortar, yet is an index of the private status of this building (Riddler 1993).

Rooms A, B and C were probably single storied with low-pitched roofs. Room D had a higher pitched roof of thatch supported by uprights set on post-pads – a common feature in modern Molisano vernacular architecture (Marino, Guerrizio and Libernucci 2001). Room E almost certainly had a first floor loft platform (Fig. 8.10). The roofs are no less interesting. Rooms A, B and C were tiled; D was certainly thatched while E and F were possibly roofed with either thatch or shingle. Tile production appears to have been revived in Italy during the later eighth century, as the élite began to build in stone once more with the reintroduction of lime mortar (Gelichi and Novara 2000 on tile production; Gutscher 1980 on mortar mixers). Thatching was undoubtedly the vernacular norm. Indeed, the monks' refectory was thatched, even though it was paved with tiles.

Clearly, tiling most of the collective workshop, just as the principal monastic buildings were tiled, signalled its particular significance. Equally, thatching room D denoted that it had another purpose as a granary at least for part of its life.

Room C, the accommodation for a prominent member of the monastery, merits comparison with known élite dwellings of the age. It was clearly an apartment as opposed to the stone-built, porticoed hall house with an associated storage building found in the Forum of Nerva in Rome (Meneghini and Santangeli Valenziani 2001). The latter bears closer resemblance to the Distinguished Guests' Hall. Nor does it resemble the ninth-century Poggibonsi longhouse, with curved sides, measuring 17 by 8 metres (Francovich and Valenti 1996; Valenti 2004). This, though, had two rooms, and associated with it was a post-built granary. Like the dwelling in the Forum of Nerva, the longhouse had a simple timber porch resembling the south porch of room F. A closer parallel for room C is perhaps the Ferrara town-house, which like rooms C, E and F consisted of spaces subdivided by timber partition walls (Gadd and Ward-Perkins 1991). The association with the granary is particularly noteworthy as it is not at all unique. The ninth-century grain silos associated with the main dwelling at Santa Maria in Civita (Molise) illustrate a simple variant of this arrangement (Bowes and Hodges 2002). A closer parallel is the longhouse and granary at Poggibonsi (Tuscany), and the ninth-century granary found in the seigneurial nucleus at Montarrenti (Tuscany) (Cantini 2003). In each case the granary has been interpreted as evidence of a *curtis* settlement, a proto-feudal manor, receiving grain from its dependent estates (cf. Francovich and Hodges 2003: 76-105). A closer parallel is the tufa-built south-east complex in the ninth-century papal farm at Santa Cornelia (Latium). The three rooms there had had mortar floors, and a Roman threshold lay at the entry to room 2. Christie in his report on the excavations ventures as follows: 'Though the evidence is scanty, one can tentatively hypothesise that this zone formed the administrative centre of the *domusculta,* and that areas for workshops, storage and for accommodation of the estate workers lay close by' (Christie and Daniels 1991: 185). Is the short-lived granary at San Vincenzo, room D, evidence of a semi-independent artisanal community, governed by an official from room C, in possession of their own corn store – a kind of proto-manor within the later ninth-century monastic precinct (see Chapter 9)?

The debris associated with the collective workshop shows that its occupants were making prestige goods that rarely are found in archaeological excavations, but are listed in the inventories of church and monastic treasuries. The artisans who constructed the temporary workshops were probably not Beneventans, but skilled craftsmen attracted to San Vincenzo by its growing international standing. The later collective workshop may have housed those who chose to remain at San Vincenzo, producing enamels, ivories, fine metalwork and glassware that, given as gifts, attracted substantive donations by return. After the earthquake of 848, notwithstanding the high quality enamel and metalworking in rooms A and B, production clearly declined, and the creation here of what amounted to a manorial complex tellingly reveals the changing conditions of the age. The further deterioration of the complex by 881 baldly illustrates the decline of San Vincenzo as a successful player in a regional and inter-regional economy.

Beyond feudalism: monasteries and their management in the eighth and ninth centuries

Would the concern for the management of monastic property become more than an unholy enterprise engaged in by cowled entrepreneurs seeking to ward off worldly corporate raiders while simultaneously enriching themselves if that concern were approached in terms of achieving monastic identity and of anchoring the monastic community permanently in the material world? (Sullivan 1998: 287).

Reduced to a simple formula, the rise of feudalism in Italy, following in the footsteps of the classic French historical texts on the subject, embraces a sequence of stages which leave an imprint of some form in the archaeological record. These are: first, the 'signoria domestica' (essentially, in anthropological terms, a domestic mode of production); second, signoria fondiaria – a system involving those who owe limited obligations to the lord, but the lord does not possess complete hegemony over his community (Carocci 1998: 260); third, the signoria territoriale, where the lord has full jurisdictional power over the community in a classic feudal form. As Luigi Provero puts it, 'the centrality of the land in the socio-political dynamic is a common fact of all societies of the old regime, founded on an economy strongly agrarian in structure' (Provero 1998: 214). This, as it happens, is the context for the transformation of early medieval villages, by stages, into first the curtis, then the castello. Monasteries, by virtue of being major landlords, were necessarily affected by this transformation, as historians of the Carolingian and post-Carolingian ages have long since recognised. Monasteries and villages, in other words, go hand in hand in the history of feudal Europe, as Bloch, Ganshof and Duby, for example, have long since shown (Bloch 1964; Ganshof 1964; Duby 1974; see also Brown 1974 and now Toubert 2004). However, the precise nature of this evolving relationship, not surprisingly, is the subject of much discussion. This discussion has steadily developed in recent times thanks to the excavations of villages where the peasantry, those denied history, can be measured against those, from monasteries who actually wrote and controlled the written record of the age. Not surprisingly, a debate exists between those who believe that the archaeological evidence provides texts of a kind that, in their own way, illuminate the written sources, and reveal that the historical distinction separating the transformation of rural society in late antiquity and the age of *incastellamento* in the later tenth century is no longer tenable (Francovich and Hodges 2003; Valenti 2004).

Put boldly, the primacy of the written sources for this critical period can be contested. No one now doubts that when we find a textual mention, for example, of a *curtis* it equates to a complicated territorial form. We cannot, however, refer the toponym that localised it to a specific settlement or to a site. In the same way, when we come across documentary references to *mansi, sortes* and *case massaricie* (farmhouses) we cannot be certain that they are isolated settlements, because it could be that other proprietors owned houses and land in the same place without there being some form of surviving written record. In reality, often the only way of identifying a place beyond the hypotheses about the names is that of demonstrating by means of painstaking linkage that various mentions of farmhouses refer to one and the same place. Rarely, however, do the written sources from the period before AD 1000 permit us such linkages. Indeed, the sources are invariably too scarce for the construction of a stable glossary of the use of the terms such as *locus, casale* and *vicus* (Ginatempo and Giorgi 2000: 174). In short, the documentation is at best sporadic, and principally offers only qualitative clues. This is why we need measured archaeological data. For the archaeologist no such problems exist as long as stratigraphically dated buildings can be measured and comparisons can be made. Indeed, the material evidence provides quantified data about economic and some-times even social conditions. A monastery, for example, can be measured in terms of its cult centre – its basilica – and its associated rooms and offices providing services. A village, by contrast, is a group of small dwellings, aggregated within a defined space, which with time often comprises further institutional components such as structures indicating the presence of a local power (a tower, a castle or even a large granary) in the settlement as well as the church. It is this definition, rather than the imprecise interpretation of the written sources, which enables us to create models of settlement evolution. Quite clearly, archaeological models can be elaborated as a second step by cross-examining the evidence from the written sources. The early medieval scribe was almost certainly not interested in the problems we are debating here. His focus, understandably, was upon micro-historical matters, above all, legal relationships. By contrast, our focus on the transformation of the Roman landscape necessarily demands a different order of information and a different perspective of the past.

Truth be told, the examination of the post-Roman, pre-feudal country-side has been restricted by the nature of the undiagnostic archaeological evidence. Readily dated archaeological deposits in Italy were rare before 1980 and essentially non-existent before the landmark excavations of the papal *domusculta* at Santa Cornelia, Lazio (Christie and Daniels 1991). Only monastic sites, where epigraphic and art historical evidence occur, have readily provided the fixed chronological (historical) points for launch-

ing investigations of the making of the pre-feudal and early feudal countryside. Foremost of these places in Italy, with ample amounts of
measurable data, is San Vincenzo al Volturno in Molise where issues
about management may be justifiably posed (Hodges 1993a; 1995a;
1997a). In this chapter I wish to examine three issues:

1. the changing form of the ninth-century monastery at San Vincenzo al
   Volturno as a pre-feudal estate centre;
2. the impact of Carolingian-led management changes on the *mentalità* of
   its primary workforce, its artisans of prestige goods, engaged in the
   making of feudal relations;
3. the nature of the monastery's settlements and their limited capacity for
   production.

The pre-feudal farm in the workshops at San Vincenzo al Volturno

The Benedictine monastery of San Vincenzo was founded in 703 beside the
river Volturno in north-west Molise (Hodges 1997a) within the ruins of a
late Roman estate centre. Excavations suggest that the estate centre was
largely or entirely deserted when the founding fathers of the monastery
arrived. The twelfth-century *Chronicon Vulturnense* describes its foundation as though it were in a primeval forest (Le Goff 1988), even though the
place was infused with a long history of Samnite, Roman republican and
imperial occupation and, in Marc Augé's sense, memory (1998). The new
monastery, consistent with the period, was a small nucleus covering less
than a hectare in area with minimal material culture.

Eighty years later great changes occurred at San Vincenzo as in similar
monasteries elsewhere in Italy as the impact of Charlemagne's influence
in the peninsula was felt (see Chapter 7). Granted immunities and privileges by Charlemagne in 787, with resources garnered from its many new
estates scattered across southern Italy, a series of building campaigns led
to a monastic city being constructed on the west bank around and on
the slopes of Colle della Torre. The new monastery was essentially
planned around an axial corridor – a sacred routeway connecting the
old abbey-church, San Vincenzo Minore, to a new one, San Vincenzo
Maggiore, consecrated in 808. As far as can be judged, the new plan was
conceived as a number of modules, ranging from the monastic claustrum on the river side, to collective workshops beyond (south of) the
new abbey-church, and an enclosed church crowning the hilltop. The
settlement extended in modular blocks up the low hill, where half way
up, overlooking the basilica of San Vincenzo Maggiore, was a lay cemetery comprising clusters – presumably family clusters – of inhumations
(Coutts 1995; Higgins 2001).

Around this time, a new settlement for the servile dependants of the monastery (this has been tentatively designated the *borgo*) was created on the east side of the river Volturno, reoccupying the low-lying fields once the site of the pre-Roman and Roman *vicus*. Here, separated from the monastic precinct, excavations in 1995-97 brought to light traces of two areas of dense structures. One area, closer to the river Volturno, contained evidence of post-built and pisé buildings concerned with industrial activity including glass-working and pottery production (Gilkes and Moran 2001; Bowes, Francis and Hodges forthcoming); the second area, set back from the river, comprised a large nucleus of post-built structures covering as much as two hectares (i.e. the area of the recently excavated Tuscan hilltop village of Poggibonsi) (cf. Valenti 2004). These post-built structures produced few finds so it is tempting to interpret them as either dwellings for the monastic servants or storage buildings.

It is perhaps tempting to interpret the ninth-century monastery as an urban phenomenon, taking many of its ideas from contemporary urban circumstances. This might be misleading. The architect's intention may have been to create a city dedicated to God, but the component parts were drawn as much from the countryside as from the incipient towns of the age. To begin with the ritual elements of the monastery followed the Carolingian norms of the age. The architecture of the craft workshops appears to be rural in origin. Similarly, the *borgo*, with its mixture of pisé and post-built structures, comprised a variety of rural building types known both in antiquity and in other Italian rural sites, dating from the early Middle Ages (see Chapter 8).

Particular attention should be paid to the collective workshop immediately south of the basilica and entrance atrium of San Vincenzo Maggiore. The origins of this particular module lay in a series of buildings serving the architects and craftsmen involved in the new abbey-church dating from c. 790-808. These temporary buildings were then remodelled as a linear workshop not unlike those found in late antique towns. These were dedicated to making enamels, glassware, fine metalwork, bonework and ivories – prestige goods that were probably used in transactions with urban and rural patrons in the embryonic principality of Benevento (cf. Mitchell 1996).

The two most interesting rooms as far as the management of San Vincenzo's estate were rooms C and D. Room C, the accommodation for a prominent member of the monastery, merits comparison with the small number of known elite dwellings of the age. Room C measured 6 by 10 metres; it had two narrow doors in its first phase, probably dating to the period 820-848. The floor was of cobbles, set in yellow mortar. In the south-east corner lay a small, square hearth with a single, heavy tile base, possibly the remains of a chimney. A small bench-like structure, built of tiles, stood to the east of the hearth, bonded onto the wall. In the north-east corner of the room was a deep pit containing lime and organic material. This was probably a lavatory or waste-pit.

9. Beyond feudalism

After San Vincenzo al Volturno had suffered the devastating earthquake of 848, the workshop was remodelled as a dwelling. Several moulded terracotta corbels were discovered from the yard on the south side of this room, suggesting that its outward elevation had been carefully embellished. Inside, a wattle and plaster partition wall was constructed on the western side of the room, forming a narrow, raised corridor that allowed direct access between the north and south doors. The remainder of the building was transformed into two rooms. The south room, approximately 5 square metres, had a fine, mortar floor that covered the earlier cobbles and corner hearth. The walls were plastered and painted along the skirting with a simple design of narrow coloured bands. The north room, which measured 4.5 square metres, was separated by a narrow, timber partition. Its floor was also a mortar surface. The lavatory pit, still apparently in use, appears to have been concealed by a wicker screen and plastered on the tile surround.

After 848 Room C was clearly an apartment of some importance. In form, of course, it was architecturally quite different from the better-known elite residences of the age, such as the Distinguished Guests' Hall at the north end of San Vincenzo (Hodges and Mithen 1993; cf. Fentress 1996; Polci 2003). This building with its grand first floor and stores below resembles the first-floor stone-built, porticoed hall house with an associated storage building found in the Forum of Nerva (Meneghini and Santangeli Valenziani 2001) and, in some general respects, the ninth-century Poggibonsi (Tuscany) longhouse, with curved sides, measuring 17 by 8 metres (Valenti 1996; 2004). Workshop room C, though, had two rooms, and associated with it, as we shall see, was a post-built granary, Room D. A closer parallel for Room C is perhaps the Ferrara town-house, which like rooms C, E and F consisted of spaces subdivided by timber partition walls (Gadd and Ward-Perkins 1991). The association with the adjacent Room D (lying immediately to the west), interpreted as a granary, is particularly noteworthy as it is not at all unique. Room D was the largest in the workshop complex, measuring 10 square metres. Its walls were built of rubble and mortar. Two central posts set on stone post-pads supported its thatched roof. Three entrances existed in its first phase dating to *c.* 820-848. The earliest flooring consisted of makeshift cobbles compacted into yellow clay. After 848, Room D was also radically altered. The first alteration involved a change of access, whereby the three narrow doors were blocked. A trampled earth floor was laid around the sides of the room and within it, on the western side of the door, the remains of timber features were found. These consisted of a burnt door lintel, a post and two beams, demarcating the south-west quarter of the room. The timbers appear to represent wooden partitions or some kind of platform or box structure, burnt *in situ.* Identical structures may have existed in all four corners of the room. On its west side, against the wall lay a semi-circular pit, beside which were found the charred remains of a container of grain.

145

Of course, the interpretation of this building as a granary will remain a matter of interpretation. It is presently based upon the positioning of the timber structures and the mortar floor, combined with the presence of grain and two quernstones that were found outside the door. Our interpretation, taking account of the granary depicted on the early ninth-century schematic plan of the monastery at St Gall (Switzerland), suggests that the interior comprised four corner bays, built of timber, in which the grain was stored. Between these, mortared threshing lanes would have formed a cross-shaped floor (Horn and Born 1979: vol. 1, xxiv, building 24).

The identification of Room D as a granary begs comparisons with other known examples from this period. Close to San Vincenzo al Volturno, ninth-century grain silos were associated with the main dwelling at Santa Maria in Civita (Molise), described in some detail below, illustrating a simple variant of this arrangement (Bowes and Hodges 2002). A closer parallel is the longhouse and granary at Poggibonsi (Tuscany), and the ninth-century granary found in the seigneurial nucleus on the hilltop at Montarrenti (Tuscany) (Valenti 1996; 2004); Cantini 2003). In each case the granary has been interpreted as important evidence of a seigneurial presence and, therefore, a defining factor in interpreting each of these places as a *curtis* settlement, a proto-feudal manor, receiving grain from its dependent estates (Van der Veen 1985). Perhaps the closest parallel for the example at San Vincenzo, however, is the tufa-built, south-east complex in the ninth-century papal farm at Santa Cornelia (Latium). The three inter-connected rooms found in the excavations possessed mortar floors; and, reminiscent of San Vincenzo's Room C, a re-used Roman threshold lay at the entry to room 2. Christie in his report on the excavations ventures as follows: 'Though the evidence is scanty, one can tentatively hypothesise that this zone formed the administrative centre of the *domusculta,* and that areas for workshops, storage and for accommodation of the estate workers lay close by' (Christie and Daniels 1991: 185).

Any interpretation of the changing form of these rooms in the collective workshop at San Vincenzo during the ninth century is always going to be controversial. Was the level of craft production declining, necessitating the introduction of a closely controlled granary? Or was grain now more important to the monastery than the prestige goods that had been produced here in a previous generation? At present any interpretation is certain to be speculative. Nonetheless, the short-lived granary at San Vincenzo, Room D, appears to be evidence of the existence of a semi-independent artisanal community, governed by an official from Room C, in possession of their own corn store – a kind of proto-manor within the later ninth-century monastic precinct, literally alongside the basilica of San Vincenzo Maggiore.

The comparison between the rich archaeology of the monastery, particularly the workshops, and the settlements in the region could not be greater. The 1980-81 survey of rural settlement in the upper Volturno valley showed a sharp decline in settlement after the third century, with few nucleated centres such as San Vincenzo being sustained until the later fifth or sixth centuries. After this, it seems highly probable that the much reduced communities moved to occupy selected hilltops. One possible site, occupied at this time is Vacchereccia, 4 kilometres south of San Vincenzo. Village formation in the *terra* of San Vincenzo, however, may have been significantly delayed by the creation of the nucleated village forming part of the large ninth-century *borgo* at the monastery itself. In some respects the *vicus* of pre-Roman and Roman times had been re-established, albeit in a new guise. Not until the monastery was experiencing a recession in its fortunes in the mid-ninth century on the occasion of the civil wars with the Kingdom of Benevento, as well as within the Carolingian empire is there any evidence of investment in the small, rural communities of the upper Volturno valley (Wickham 1995). First, churches were constructed at several key points in the valley in the 830s, one of which, at Colle Sant'Angelo on an exposed hilltop high above the later village of Colli a Volturno, was excavated as part of the San Vincenzo Project. The small chapel at Colle Sant'Angelo was grandly furnished with paintings and window glass. Nevertheless, it was short-lived; by the tenth century it appears to have been demolished, in all probability its building materials being transported to the new *castello* situated at Colli a Volturno, founded in 972 (Bowes, Francis and Hodges forthcoming). From this time, too, dates the small tower residence of Colle Castellano, described below.

In sum, San Vincenzo became a massive manorial nucleus in the early ninth century articulated around a new abbey-church, San Vincenzo Maggiore. Part of this nucleus was an associated *borgo* including craft-workshops and probable dwellings of a lay workforce, such as is described at St Denis in Paris and, closer to San Vincenzo, the suburb of Eulogimenopolis at Monte Cassino – an extramural settlement located far below the Benedictine monastery (cf. Lebecq 2000). The new settlement must have had a huge impact upon the rural communities of the upper Volturno valley. Classic village life was probably delayed, as peasants sought opportunities in the monastery's *borgo*. Only with the mid-ninth-century recession brought about by political squabbling did significant investment occur in rural society in the upper Volturno valley. This was the occasion for the monastery to create its own grain storage in the workshop area under the vigilant eye of an administrator, symbolically distinguishing these resources from any barns and granaries situated in the *borgo*. Small wonder, then, given this apparent separation of resource management, that when the monastery was attacked in 881, the servants disloyally sided with the Saracen marauders (Hodges 1997b).

The subsequent history of San Vincenzo is inextricably entangled with the next steps in the process of village development. First, in the second half of the tenth century, it appears that the monastery invested in developing its properties in the upper Volturno – charters contained within the twelfth-century *Chronicon Vulturnense* register, a classic example of *incastellamento* (Wickham 1985a) . Second, drawing upon its new resources, during the first half of the eleventh century, a nucleated Romanesque monastery was created within the ruins of the ninth-century monastic settlement. Third, late in the eleventh century, dissatisfied with this nucleus, the monks constructed a new community (the so-called New Abbey [Hodges 1997a]) within a ditched and fortified enclosure on the east side of the river Volturno (much of it overlying the remains of the ninth-century *borgo*), demolishing the old site to provide materials for the new buildings. To the new site were taken the remains of Abbot Joshua, architect of the ninth-century monastic city and a central figure in the *Chronicon Vulturnense* written in these new Romanesque surroundings in the twelfth century (Delogu 1996). As Walter Pohl has put it, the 'capital of memory was still at the core of the community as it struggled to keep its inner unity and privileges in troubled times' (Pohl 2001: 373).

Managing production in the monastery

The transformation of the monastery was contingent upon the capacity of its successive ninth-century abbots to promote San Vincenzo as a major centre and manage not only its new community effectively but also its new properties. Clearly, the personalities and connections of Abbots Joshua (792-817), Talaricus (817-23) and Epyphanius (824-42), in particular, should not be underestimated in any assessment of the monastery's ascendant standing in Italy and, indeed, Latin Christendom. Making an urban community where there had been a settlement of village size beforehand was extraordinarily ambitious. Possession of the relics of St Vincent obviously assisted its rise as a centre (Mitchell et al. 1997). No less significant was the monastery's ability to find craftsmen who not only constructed the grandiose new buildings to a master architect's design, but also sustained its regional authority with its network of donors through the production of gifts such as reliquaries and other prestige objects. These moveable objects were fundamental to the management of the monastery's growing number of dispersed estates throughout southern Italy (cf. Reuter 2000: 23 on Carolingian 'positional' goods). Given as gifts to local lords, reinforcing growing social differences at a local, estate level in this proto-feudal age, the monastery in return received benefactions in the form of land (cf. Silber 1995). The prestige goods, in short, were significant instruments in San Vincenzo's accumulation of landed wealth and its ascendancy to a feudal power. As Anthony Cutler has recently written, 'Like goods in trade, gifts functioned as incentives to further consumption and thereby provoked production. They served a variety of ends – social, political, and ideological – and were therefore means to the attainment of objectives rather than objectives in themselves. Moreover, to meet these ends ... [the monks] like merchants made rational calculations, including

148

the selection of recipients, the value of the gifts sent, some anticipation as to the benefits that would accrue from their behaviour and even the decision to move things in and out of commerce' (Cutler 2001).

As we have seen above, excavations have discovered the remains of the temporary workshops used by the craftsmen when the basilica of San Vincenzo Maggiore was being constructed, and then a line of permanent workshops which, after the Plan of St Gall, we have described as the collective workshop. The evidence from these workshops as well as their refuse shows that the craftsmen were producing prestige goods: enamels, glassware, ivories, bonework and elaborate metalwork. These objects involved the craftsmen in complex cycles of production, as the later twelfth-century German scientist Theophilus describes, as well as consumption. Such objects do not occur commonly in either urban or rural excavated sites of this period; quite the contrary. These are items of the kind described in the Treasury of Monte Cassino infamously robbed in 842 (Citarella and Willard 1983).

Fascinating though this gift exchange cycle was, and critical though it may have been to the pre-feudal managerial strategy of San Vincenzo, it is not the most illuminating discovery from the workshops. Because, besides the artefacts and waste from craft manufacture, the excavations brought to light two prehistoric stone axes and a large assemblage of lithics, mostly Palaeolithic tools made from flint quarried on the nearby hill of Monte Santa Croce (Fig. 9.1) (Francis 1994 on the flint sources; Mitchell 2003: 1116-23 for another interpretation).

The prehistoric flint tools are particularly interesting in that they divide quite evenly between the temporary workshops and the collective workshop deposits. Of 63 flints found in the workshops, 28 were contained within the former and 23 were recovered from the latter levels. Many of the tools were contained within structural features, such as kiln linings, floor surfaces and mortar mixers. The remaining 12 flints were not phased. Perhaps the most notable discoveries were two stone axes found within ninth-century deposits: first, a miniature greenschist axe of late Neolithic date, probably derived from the Alpine region or southern Italy (Dr J.E. Dixon [University of Edinburgh], personal communication), was found in the mid-ninth-century refuse tips behind the workshops. Second, a large igneous axe of early Bronze Age date was discovered in the later ninth-century burnt roof levels of the granary (Room D, described above). The provenance and distribution of the workshop tools contrasts greatly with that of 16 flints recovered from the liturgical area of the monastery, which were purely residual and found exclusively within late garden soils and twelfth-century demolition deposits (cf. Francis 2001). In summary, the prehistoric flint tools and stone axes found in the workshops show clearly that the ancient implements were recognised and collected by the Benedictine craftsmen.

Now, it is tempting to give these tools a functional interpretation.

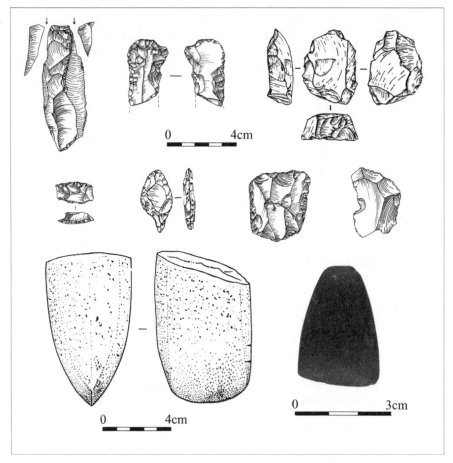

0   4cm

0   4cm

0   3cm

9.1. Two stone axes and a selection of lithics from the excavations of
the collective workshop at San Vincenzo al Volturno.

Perhaps the flints were used in some form of craft production? For example, in his manual on metal and ceramic production, the twelfth-century
scientist Eraclius describes the use of powdered flint for polishing cut
stones, and of burnt thunderbolts mixed with powdered glass for glazing
vases (Le Begue 1967).

   The problem here is that none of the flints or axes found in the workshop
excavations show signs of secondary wear or use. Instead, it seems more
likely that these tools were recognised at the time as special implements
and were deliberately placed in parts of the workshops as apotropaic
instruments. A number of medieval sources attest to the magical and
apotropaic properties of prehistoric tools (e.g. Riddle 1977). Commonly
these are described as thunderstones or *ceraunia*: amulets used to protect
houses and farms against the worst effects of the weather (Jensen 2000).

The weather, after all, was the greatest menace faced by the craftsmen and peasantry alike as they were compelled to increase production to service the new monastic community. Parallels are also known. A large prehistoric jadeite axe was found within the roof levels of a twelfth-century Cistercian monastery in Bonn, Germany. Numerous prehistoric axes were recovered from the remains of eleventh-century houses in the village of Lund, Sweden (Carelli 1997), while a stone axe, now in the Metropolitan Museum, New York, purchased in Istanbul, bears an incised crucifixion and on the other side, the prophet Elijah and the fiery chariot in which his successor Elisha, saw him off to heaven (thanks to Dr Helen Evans of the Metropolitan Museum for providing information on this axe).

How are we to interpret these extraordinary objects? If we accept the interpretation of these objects as magical as opposed to having a utilitarian function, some further insight is shed upon the changing conditions inside the monastery. The basilica and claustrum, like all the main service rooms of San Vincenzo, were decorated with images designed to promote the new renascent spiritual order, as John Mitchell has shown (1997; cf. 2003). It was a spiritual order that depended, to some considerable extent, upon the productive capacity of the workshops to attract reciprocal donations from the monastery's lands. In the workshops, it seems highly likely, artisans from far-flung regions and their assistants drawn from the local communities came face to face with huge new tensions. On the one hand the monastery was now staffed with an army of young men, drawn from all over Italy. This newly created urban environment must have been ruled with firmness to avoid problems. On the other hand it is likely that the craftsmen had to subscribe to an equally artificial life-style, separated from families and confronting the strong ideological authority of the monastery. It is not difficult to imagine the tensions. Nor, we might add, the tensions in the rural communities around San Vincenzo, as the monastery pressed to increase agricultural production in order to feed a population that grew from perhaps 50 to 500 monks in the early ninth century. Fear of the new ideological regime, like fear of the potential affects of bad storms, might help to explain the presence of the prehistoric amulets, especially the stone axe that once hung in the monastery's own granary beside the abbey-church itself. The new spiritual order was reinforced by recourse to age-old beliefs.

Managing the estate

Chris Wickham has described the ample collection of charters in the *Chronicon Vulturnense* that record the boundaries of properties made over to San Vincenzo but are uninformative about the quality or quantity of resources available from these lands (1985a). Against the silence of the sources, Mario del Treppo argued that the lands comprised *curtis* settlements dedicated to providing the monastery with raw materials – raw materials, we might surmise of the kind used in the workshop described above (Del Treppo 1955). Our excavations during the 1980s provide some measure of the underdevelopment of the countryside in the later eighth and ninth centuries, and the staggering expansion of agrarian production in the tenth century.

The hilltop village of Vacchereccia excavated in 1982 produced negligible evidence of production. Although 4 kilometres from San Vincenzo, its modest archaeology is striking in comparison to the post-built structures in the *borgo* of San Vincenzo or indeed the collective workshop (Hodges et al. 1984). Excavations at the southern end of the *terra* of San Vincenzo revealed a settlement at Colle Castellano that had limited productive capacity. Here, on a low hill located in the southern, fertile zone of the *terra*, excavations revealed the presence of a small stone-built tower close to the summit of the hill associated with later ninth- or early tenth-century ceramics (pottery dated by association with the levels found at San Vincenzo belonging to the Arab sack of 10 October 881). The tower measured approximately 5 by 5 metres. In other words, its floor area was similar to the apartment of the administrator in the collective workshop, but appreciably smaller than certain of the workshops themselves. The excavations were too limited to determine whether post-built timber structures were associated with the tower. The stone tower, however, was obliterated when a stone enclosure wall was constructed around the hilltop, almost certainly in the period after 945 when the hill, known as *Olivella*, was designated as a *castellum* (Bowes, Francis and Hodges forthcoming). Neither of these settlements compares in terms of productive capacity with the agrarian unit in the workshop complex, or for that matter with the evidence of *curtis* settlements such as Montarrenti, Poggibonsi and Scarlino (Francovich and Hodges 2003).

However, a possible *curtis* settlement of this kind was excavated at D85 (Santa Maria in Civita), in the Biferno valley 30 kilometres from the Adriatic sea. Santa Maria in Civita, when it was first identified in 1978, was interpreted as a classic ninth-century hilltop village in which timber and simple stone dwellings were found built up against an enclosure wall (Hodges, Barker and Wade 1980). A subsequent re-evaluation showed that the site comprises two residential enclosures, with an associated church situated on the highest point on the hill (Fig. 9.2) (Bowes and Hodges 2002). Traces of a modest tower, not unlike the one at Colle Castellano, now appear to exist in the eastern of the two residential enclosures, where excavations in 1978 brought to light grain storage pits. Detailed analysis of the grain and its weeds showed that it was the product of processing that had taken place elsewhere. These excavations also brought to light a modestly affluent material culture that included glass vessels. Note should also be taken of the presence of bricks and tiles which were very probably made here for specific building projects. Viewed through the prism of the Tuscan sites mentioned above, Santa Maria in Civita was

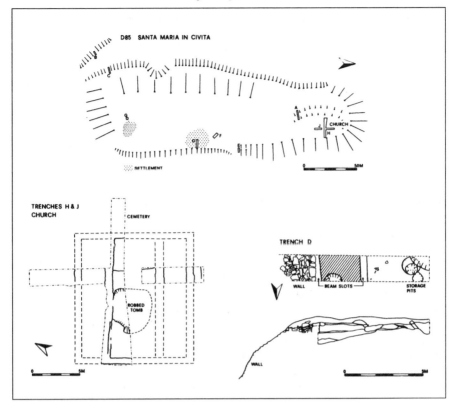

9.2. Schematic plan of Santa Maria in Civita, Molise.

certainly not a hilltop village. Instead, it appears to have been a ninth-century Beneventan élite settlement comprising a household unit (the eastern enclosure) concentrated around a modest tower, an ancillary unit (the western enclosure) and its own church. Santa Maria in Civita was not a *castrum* in the sense of defending a bridge-head (of the type known from the sixth century during the Gothic war [cf. Brown 1978]) – because its tower overlooked its southern side, in fact its grazing area, rather than the nearby Ponte San Antuono leading across the river Biferno – nor was it in form a classical farm. This said, on the evidence of its material, botanical and faunal evidence, it appears to have been the centre of an estate associated with either farms or villages in the vicinity. One further point needs to be made to put this site in context. Thanks to the distinctive ceramics found in the excavations of Santa Maria in Civita, we may be confident that the later Roman farms found in the Biferno valley survey in this area did not continue until the ninth century. No dispersed sites with ninth-century potsherds were found in the survey; evidently, dispersed lowland occupation ceased by the seventh century at the latest (Hodges and Wickham 1995).

153

These small but significant excavations provide us with a few clues about San Vincenzo's management of its agrarian, and indeed, its critical access to human resources. First, the settlements identified so far in the *terra* could not have supported the new monastic city with agrarian produce. Farms of the size of Vacchereccia and Colle Castellano, however much they expanded production, were not arranged on the scale of the *borgo* of San Vincenzo or, indeed, either Santa Maria in Civita or the Tuscan villages like Montarrenti, Poggibonsi or Scarlino. So, either the monastery drew its resources from all over southern Italy, or alternatively its farmers in the *borgo* were intensively cultivating the Rocchetta Plain on which the monastery was located, as well as the valley and hills immediately around the monastery. In short, the creation of a dispersed settlement of new nucleated centres – the classic medieval settlement pattern – was only slowly taking shape in this region before the mid-ninth century. Elsewhere on the coastal plains of peninsular Italy, however, the pattern may have been established before, as the discovery of Santa Maria in Civita shows.

This brings us to an interesting further aspect of the monastery. How did the abbots of San Vincenzo al Volturno obtain the workforce for the *borgo* and workshops after the monastic city had taken shape? Plainly the monks assisted in the construction of the great basilica of San Vincenzo Maggiore itself, as its dedication inscription indicates (Hodges and Mitchell 1996). But it is highly unlikely that the new ideological fervour of the monastery permitted the monks to farm and supply the centre with all its needs – quite the contrary. The five hundred monks probably required as many as 500 staff to support them. Certainly, the monastery housed a large number of servants, as the *Chronicon Vulturnense* describes in its colourful passage recording the savage Saracen attack of 881 when the servants joined forces with the attackers.

The origins of this workforce, no less than the origin of the monks themselves, is intriguing. Certainly, many of the new servants were probably associated in one way or another with the numerous donations of land to San Vincenzo between *c.* 790 and the apparent foundation of San Vincenzo Maggiore in 808. After this, in the period 807-836, San Vincenzo received seven donations of *curtes* or *terrae*, each comprising between three and five families (*condumae*) of *servi*, leading Mario del Treppo to conclude, perhaps erroneously, that the labour force of the early medieval monastery was made up of slaves (Del Treppo 1955). Given the conditions in San Vincenzo itself, this now seems unlikely. A more probable explanation is that the craftsmen were free tenants or theoretically servile *condumae* from the monastery's newly acquired lands. These households may have been offered leases of lands in and near the *borgo* or, perhaps, in the vicinity of the monastery, in return for exercising their knowledge and skills to the monks' advantage. In fact, a *conduma* is known to have occupied lands at Casa Lorenzo, a terraced settlement on the Rocchetta

154

Plain, less than 2 kilometres from San Vincenzo (Hodges 1997a: 184; Bowes, Francis and Hodges forthcoming).

In any event, both the archaeological and documentary records make clear that the building of San Vincenzo Maggiore brought the monastic community into close contact with lay artisans, free or theoretically free persons of low status who were foreigners in the context of the monastery's inner *terra*. From the perspective of the craftsmen, the encounter followed long journeys from places that looked like Santa Maria in Civita or even Poggibonsi dispersed around southern Italy, from Capua or the hills around Salerno, from Canosa di Puglia, Lucera or Siponto, or, further south, from Oria or Otranto. The impact of these newcomers upon the upper Volturno valley and the demands their presence made upon effective management in the monastery should not be understated. Nor indeed, bearing in mind the axes and flints, should the tensions created by the making of this new community.

Conclusions

Archaeology is beginning to throw light on the pre-feudal circumstances of rural Italy. The excavations at San Vincenzo al Volturno illustrate the potential of the material record for further refining an understanding of this transition period.

First, the excavations show the changing economic stages at the monastery as this monopolistic urban centre of the ninth century first flourished before the 840s, then was re-shaped *c*. 848-881, and then again, as a small centre, when it provided the administrative resources for the dispersed feudal villages of the upper Volturno valley created after *c*. 940.

Secondly, the excavations also throw light on the nature of management in this pre- or proto-feudal complex. The manufacture of prestige goods for a gift-giving cycle was highly important to the monastery's economic strategy. However, in contrast to the richly decorated ornamentation of the buildings associated with the new renascent ritual, the workshops were vernacular structures with the single exception of the administrator's suite of rooms. Moreover, the evidence of amulets of a prehistoric nature, probably for apotropaic purposes, illustrates not only the ever-present sensitivity to weather and its effect upon their lands, but also an enduring subscription to pagan forces.

Thirdly, the management of the surrounding landscape evolved slowly. San Vincenzo, like other monasteries in central Italy, was clearly aware of the new forms of rural production centres exhibited at such places as Santa Maria in Civita, but preferred to invest in these forms at the monastery as opposed to its surrounding region. Centralised control was of paramount importance. This managerial philosophy was radically re-evaluated after the sack of the monastery in 881, after which a controlled delegation of management to local communities was skilfully instituted.

In short, between the eighth and ninth centuries the Italian countryside was affected by processes of re-aggregation of the population and the redefinition of the settlement network. The relations between the system of churches and monasteries on the one hand, and the world of hilltop villages on the other, may be perceived in dialectical terms. In the former, there prevailed an ancient model: around the religious centre arose a small scattered settlement destined to grow; in the latter, social relations within the village communities were redefined involving a definitive break with the past. For some centuries these two models confronted each other, but the fact that as early as the tenth century many large monasteries were already starting to decline, and churches were brought within the newly created castles (*castelli*), and not vice versa, indicates how profitable the investment by landed lords in hilltop sites had been. It is tempting to conclude that the monastic city with its *borgo*, like the papal *domuscultae*, were aberrant settlement forms of a proto-feudal age, when the élite, conscious of the classical past, were striving to make a new imprint upon their landscapes.

The debate reviewed in this chapter pitches archaeologists against historians at one level, but at another attempts to move on from such binary opposites as continuity/discontinuity, dispersed/nucleated, and villa/village to re-examine the more complex picture which is now available to us. Further, the model advanced here seeks to assert that archaeology has helped us to rewrite a chapter of the history of rural society for peninsular Italy. In so doing, it sheds light, of course, upon the nature of the written sources and, incidentally, especially in the case of such a famous term as feudalism, its interpretation over the past millennium.

10

Goodbye to the Vikings?

... given the scarce indications from the sources ..., an enquiry into possible sub-periods is nevertheless a step towards a more nuanced approach of the period as a whole (Verhulst 2002: 133).

Medieval history has turned a corner with the new millennium. Almost unnoticed, a new paradigm is being shaped. Ninth-century Europe is being re-calibrated by decades thanks not only to many new excavations but also to the wealth of numismatic evidence being found by tens of thousands of energetic metal-detectorists. The first results cast great doubt upon the role of the Vikings as *deus ex machina* forces in the course of the century. Their role as a catalytic force in terminating an age of peaceful trade between the North Sea kingdoms is open to question as is their part, after a supposed generation of turmoil and cataclysmic disruption, in the making of the Middle Ages and, in particular, in the industrial revolution that characterised the late ninth and tenth centuries. Indeed, the thrust of the new evidence tends in part to confirm that the Vikings only became raiders and invaders when the Carolingian political economy collapsed during the civil wars between the grandsons of Charlemagne.

The traditional history, now the stuff of countless coffee-table books and serious mid-evening television series, goes as follows. The Vikings were bold Baltic Sea merchant venturers who roamed from Russia to north-west Norway plying their trade. However, some dissidents voraciously eyed other sources of income in the form of vulnerable monasteries. Lindisfarne, seat of great Northumbrian learning, was the first major target of these evil marauders in 790. The timeline, so familiar from the books and archaeological sites, runs as straight as a die through coastal attacks in the early ninth century, and on to sacks such as Hamwic, Anglo-Saxon Southampton, in 842 and Dorestad, the emporium at the mouth of the Rhine, in 834. Following the hit-and-run raids come the invasions of Scotland, England and Normandy. The Great (Danish) Army of 865, rather like the panzers of 1940, overwhelmed Mercia, East Anglia and was only halted in Wessex in 878 following a series of Dunkirk-like catastrophes. The Churchillian figure of the age, King Alfred, conceded half of England (which, incidentally, was not his to concede) on condition that the Danish king, Guthrum, was baptised a Christian. From this moment Alfred re-structured his kingdom, founding London in 886 (which had hitherto belonged to the kingdom of Mercia), and initiating a 1944-like re-conquest of the lost kingdoms of England. Alfred's descendents finished the task by 954, ridding England of its Nordic invaders. Meanwhile, York, or Jorvik as it had become under the Danes, like Lincoln, Stamford and other emergent markets in the Danish half of ninth-century England, were suddenly prospering under new west Baltic management (Hall 1984). As the Jorvik Centre in York proudly illustrates to 750,000 or more tourists a year, it was a moment of North Sea brotherhood – an image that has readily engaged European Union support. The Viking monsters had become good citizens, eagerly creating civilised medieval wealth-generating shops within metalled gridded streets.

From time to time historians have pondered how far this picture of the Vikings is pure propaganda issued by the West Saxon court and monastic chroniclers eager to explain how god could have wantonly damned their institutions (cf. Smyth 1998). Cautiously historians have chosen to believe that they have not been hoodwinked. Yet when faced with the first results of the archaeological evidence in the 1980s and 1990s, historians sat on the fence. Towns and trade (including coin circulation), notwithstanding, their significance then as now, to the political economy, were consigned to subsidiary roles in defining the age.

Closer study of the historical and archaeological evidence (especially the coin hoards) reveals a striking binary pattern. The earliest Viking-period towns, such as Haithabu near Schleswig in north Germany, and Birka on an island in Lake Mälaren, central Sweden, appear to have been flourishing in the first thirty to forty years of the ninth century. Then they seem to have declined. Meanwhile, the evidence for Viking raids appears to complement this picture: the number of documented raids increases steadily after *c.* 840, something that is confirmed by the large quantities of Anglo-Saxon and Frankish silver coins in Scandinavian hoards from precisely this period. Trade, it seems, was superseded by raid (Randsborg 1983) (Fig. 10.1).

Coincidentally, the first results of large excavations at the Frankish emporium of Dorestad at the confluence of the Rhine and Lek near Utrecht (van Es 1990) and Hamwic, Anglo-Saxon Southampton (Morton 1992), were demonstrating that these exceptional, monopolistic market-places were actually declining fast when the Vikings first raided them in 834 and 842 respectively (*pace* Hall 2000). Dendrochronological evidence from Dorestad indicates intense investment in building riverside quays up until the 820s with a vibrant mint until the 830s, after which the place sharply declines (cf. Coupland 2002). From about 841 for a period the town was actually in Viking hands. At Hamwic, decline appears to have occurred even earlier, although archaeologists and historians have tried to eke out a miscellany of information to illustrate continuity throughout the ninth century. Not to be outdone, with the discovery of Lundenwic in the late 1980s, centred not in the city (the site of Roman and post-886 London), but in the heart of the West End (notably, under the Royal Opera House in

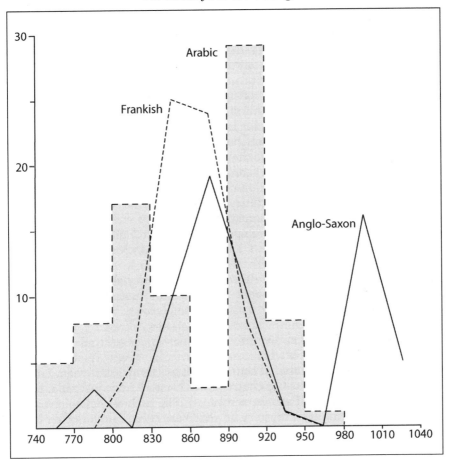

10.1. Graph showing the pattern of Viking-period raids (Anglo-Saxon; Frankish) and trade (Arabic) in terms of coin hoards by date in the Baltic Sea region.

Covent Garden), the same picture has emerged (Hodges 2000: 112-15). The great *municipium*, described by Bede during the eighth century, was clearly in recession by the middle decades of the ninth century. Put baldly, at least a generation separates the abandonment of Lundenwic and the creation of Lundenburg by King Alfred in 886. At York the same picture has been discovered: the Anglian emporium of Eoforwic, located well away from the ruinous Roman colony at the confluence of the rivers Ouse and Foss, was well into recession long before the Great Army passed through the region (see, though, Hall 2000 for an elegant review of the 1970-2000 paradigm). Reassuringly, spectrographic analyses of Anglo-Saxon silver coins in circulation indicate tin-based substitutes were replacing silver as the English courts faced up to depleted treasuries by the mid-ninth century (Metcalf and Northover 1989). Worse still, Northumbrian coins of

159

the central decades of this period – the so-called stycas – contained pitiful measures of silver in their otherwise copper-rich contents (Hodges 1989: 162). How, we should be asking, did the Danish kings of Jorvik suddenly find the silver to replace the devalued Northumbrian currency with a silver-rich coinage meeting international standards? Where, given the disruption in the generations of urban craftsmen and traders, did the architects, merchants and manufacturers come from to people Alfred's new towns as well as those under Danish hegemony?

A significant new dimension has now come to light, nuancing this binary picture. Encouraged by the UK's new portable antiquities act of 1997, metal-detectorists have been sharing their results with numismatists (see www.finds.org). Coincidentally, the numismatist Simon Coupland has challenged the status quo regarding the coin histories of the great Carolingian emporia – Dorestad and Quentovic (Coupland 2002).

Thousands of Anglo-Saxon coins have come to light from fields and deserted sites in southern and eastern England. Some sites, such as Bawsey and Burnham in north Norfolk, Barham in south Suffolk and Royston on the Cambridgeshire-Hertfordshire border, are extraordinarily rich in coins as well as decorated Middle Saxon metalwork (Blackburn 2003; Newman 2003; Rogerson 2003). These places have been christened 'productive sites' in a new collection of essays edited by Pestell and Ulmschneider (2003). The available evidence suggests that these were second-tier markets flush with coins and prestige goods, related in some form to the great international centres such as Hamwic, Ipswich, London and York. Similar second-tier centres have come to light in Frisia, North Germany, Denmark and southern Sweden. The archaeological character of these places remains a mystery as yet. Were these fairs or other forms of periodic markets, or were these places seasonal centres of regional activity? Whatever the case, the Belgian historian Adriaan Verhulst speculates that these are the forebears of the late Carolingian regional markets in the Low Countries and in Charles the Bald's kingdom of Neustria (2002: 134). In England these may be the harbingers of the burhs, the fortified towns which formed the fabric of King Alfred's renewal of his kingdom once he had defeated the Danes. Closer analyses of the coinage from this period, however, suggest to the veteran numismatist, Michael Metcalf, a picture of intense minting and exchanging of coins (Metcalf 1999). Metcalf goes further. He deduces from the overall pattern of single coin-finds, a distribution thinning out towards the west and north-west. More precisely, he writes, 'we may construe it in terms of a greater monetisation of the economy in the east. Set against the political frontiers of the time, this means that there was a contrast between Kent and East Anglia on the one hand, and Mercia on the other, Mercia being significantly less monetised – with whatever social and political consequences that may have had' (1999: 180). The mints at Canterbury, London and Rochester, accounting for 62% of the coins in circulation, appear to have been involved in long-distance trade; their coins are spread throughout southern and eastern England. Coins minted in East Anglia and Mercia are found in the Thames basin and Midlands only. Metcalf attributes the influence of Canterbury, London and Rochester to the enduring cross-Channel exchange of bullion, accounting for the eagerness of successive West Saxon kings from the 830s onwards to have control of Canterbury and London.

Michael Metcalf's booming mid-century economy would have seemed fanciful, given the timeline of Viking raids and invasions, were it not for the incontrovertible evidence of the coins themselves. Now, with Coupland's radical study (2002) of the coin history of Quentovic, the 50-hectare emporium in the Pas de Calais, much is becoming clearer.

The emporium of Quentovic has been identified close to the inland town of Montreuil sur Mer (Hill et al. 1990). Some historians have speculated that it was initially operated by Anglo-Saxon settlers to this region. From the late sixth century onwards it was certainly the principal port for English pilgrims bound for Rome and the Holy Land. Coupland shows, however, that its coins reveal a history that is not parallel to Dorestad, the other great Frankish emporium where massive excavations have played a significant part in shaping our understanding of the centre. Quentovic, it seems, was not booming in the age of Charlemagne. Indeed, the emporium as a mint was insignificant until the mid-ninth century when, as Dorestad was slipping from sight, it suddenly took off, becoming a major place in the last decades of the ninth century. Perhaps it is no coincidence that a recent archaeological survey of the silver mines of Melle in Aquitaine confirms the coin evidence that they were thriving in this age (Téreygeol and Dubois 2003). Coupland, like Verhulst, ascribes much to the political and economic judgement of Charles the Bald, in contrast to his less effective cousins in control of the Rhineland and Italy.

Given these circumstances, it is hardly surprising that the first silver coins minted by Jorvik's new Danish masters in the 890s were for some time believed to be issues from the Quentovic mint (cf. Coupland 2002: 219). Frankish moneyers clearly formed part of the new town government also producing in time imitative West Saxon pennies. Plainly the Danes were looking to emulate successful models for their new investment. Further south, it is hardly surprising too that it is the mints of Canterbury, Rochester and London which were thriving in the 850s and 860s. These were on the road linking London to the coast and a day's boat-ride to the one great centre which had outlived the Carolingian civil war. In short, Coupand demonstrates, while the North Sea commerce was in crisis, trade across the English Channel was not only surviving but intermittently bouyant. In Kent the evidence for this in the form of trading towns has yet to be found, though second tier beaching sites like Fordwich, Sandtun (the site of a recent excavation (Gardiner et al. 2001)) and Sandwich were clearly benefiting. Nonetheless, the spectre of an active

Quentovic engaged with a booming regional economy in south-east England plainly explains why re-founding London, once (after 878) it was under West Saxon as opposed to Mercian control, was such a significant step for King Alfred. This was the key to an export drive that brought in silver and other precious materials – the economic means to drive forward an ambitious political platform for the unification of England under the West Saxons.

What does this mean for the Vikings? First, the timeline needs to be refined in keeping with the histories of not only the North Sea courts but also the political economies of the era. It is hard not to imagine that the Vikings, well aware of the advantages of Frankish life, were seeking to carve out opportunities for themselves not only in hitherto successful ports such as Dorestad but also in failing parts of Latin Christendom, such as Normandy and Northumbria were in the later ninth century (see Bill 2003: fig. 2 on the ninth-century diversification of Baltic sea ship types including cargo vessels). Such opportunism is characteristic of the later Vikings who colonised Iceland and Greenland and joined the Byzantine army as mercenaries. Secondly, it is high time to use modern methods of analysis to examine the thrust of medieval history. The political economies of the age were important factors in shaping the currents of history just as they are today. Contemporary chroniclers were providing their audiences with a skilful propaganda which can only be measured by the material culture. These measures show beyond doubt that the Vikings were not the cause of change in this era but stakeholders in a complex realignment of Latin Christendom in the aftermath of the zenith of the Carolingian empire. We should say goodbye to the Vikings as we have known them, and with the advantage of rich archaeological evidence from Scandinavia to hand, welcome them into the bosom of a new, inclusive history of Europe that melds together written sources with the fruits of digs and days spent metal-detecting ploughed fields.

11

Society, power and the first English Industrial Revolution[1]

Just over a thousand years ago, in 990, Archbishop Sigeric made the journey from Canterbury to Rome to receive his pallium. An account survives of part of this journey; it is a tourist's guide to the great churches of Rome.[2] But the account tells us nothing of the journey to Rome, and only a little about his return trip. Many historians might interpret this as a whim – perhaps only Rome merited a memoir. As an archaeologist, however, I am tempted by another thought: for Sigeric, much of the journey must have astonished him. Not because of the wonders of the Continent, but on the contrary because unexpectedly Anglo-Saxon England must have seemed a developed land. Perhaps this is farfetched, but, as I hope to show, we are only beginning to appreciate the extent of change in England in the *secolo di ferro*. Indeed, I would go so far as to propose that the critical events of English history occurred not in the age of Adam Smith, but during the first English Industrial Revolution of which we know precious little from the written sources, but are now becoming well-informed thanks to the work of a generation of British archaeologists (Hodges 1989). It is my intention to consider the significance of this revolution in three parts: first, its genesis; second, the revolution itself; and third, its implications for society and power in Late Saxon England.

I

Writing of the circumstances familiar to tenth-century Anglo-Saxons such as Sigeric, Patrick Wormald commented: 'England, like all European nations, was founded in a "Dark Age"; we shall never quite understand how. The main objection to belief in the inevitability of English unification is that it is all to easy. It is virtually incredible that what did not happen until long afterwards in countries that were initially subjected to a single political authority should have happened automatically in a country that

---

[1]This chapter is essentially an unaltered version of the paper I read on 19 April 1990 at Spoleto. I am indebted to Professor G. Arnaldi for the invitation to take part in the 'Settimana'. I should also like to acknowledge my debt to Richard Gem, Philip Grierson, Michael Hendy, Michael Lapidge , John Mitchell, the late Timothy Reuter and, in particular, Chris Wickham for discussing aspects of the paper with me during the congress.

[2]I am grateful to Dr David Hill for drawing my attention to the account of Archbishop Sigeric's journey. The text is published in Stubbs 1874; see also Magoun 1940: 268-77.

was not' (Wormald 1983: 128). The Anglo-Saxon achievement, as I have called it (Hodges 1989), was not the result of some inevitable progression. If any single explanation is to be found for the unexpected success of the Anglo-Saxons, it might be in the potentially conflicting desire for a European context, on the one hand, and peer-competition between the patchwork of insular territories on the other.

The first illustration of this mediation between Europe and the complex insular configurations occurred even before the Roman administration left Britain in the early fifth century. Only the brief and eccentric prosperity of some southern British villa estates in the early fourth century punctuates the inexorable path towards dereliction which had begun a hundred years before. The collapse of the state before the final Roman withdrawal is now well attested by numerous excavations. The breakdown of the Roman state was bound to play a significant part in the evolution of the post-Roman peoples. First and foremost, the island was not an obvious destination for Germanic migrants, whose fundamental concern was to improve their circumstances in the wake of the severe economic recession of the third and fourth centuries (Millet 1990; Randsborg 1991). In a nutshell, fifth-century Britain hardly stands comparison with the world of villas and towns to be found in most other provinces of the western empire. Exactly how many migrants journeyed to Britain and why they came, looks likely to remain an intriguing mystery. The archaeology, like the texts, offers us limited assistance in interpreting these epic events (Hills 2003). Suffice it to say that most scholars now favour a small-scale migration, led by pioneers hired by the warring factions of sub-Roman Britain.

A crucial factor in analysing the unification of late Saxon England was the geo-politics of the fifth century. Nearly thirty tribes are described in the seventh-century Tribal Hidage; many more are likely to have existed in the wake of the Roman withdrawal. The archaeology reveals that the economic conditions of this patchwork of communities were extremely simple. The impact of exogenous groups of this fragmented political economy is a matter of speculation. But this was a world far removed from the late antique provincial governments, towns and villa-estates of Gaul or Italy. Fresh light appears in these aboriginal British conditions towards the end of the fifth century. Indeed, it is tempting to ascribe the beginnings of Anglo-Saxon England to this moment. It was at this time, so Ian Wood believes (Wood 1983; 1993), that a Kentish king was drawn into a Frankish political and economic hegemony. Certainly, a new, highly distinctive material culture was adopted in Britain, belonging essentially to the incipient North Sea interaction zone. At approximately the same time a markedly continental funerary rite was introduced to Kent; thereafter, the rite was diffused to many of the patchwork of territories in Britain. As has been pointed out in other cultural contexts, with the intervention of alien traders and connections rivalries were created between the many peer groups; as the rivalries intensified, so identities would have been accentuated (cf. Renfrew 1986). In the sixth century, therefore, a ranked hierarchy of graves occurs in cemeteries though no such ranking apparently existed within settlements or within the settlement system as a whole.

Kingship and lordship as social categories existed before the arrival of the missions. Their exact form may have owed a good deal to the evolution of tribal structures as trading partnerships were made with neighbouring tribes and Merovingians. The Church, as it was to do in Scandinavia later in the millennium (Hodges 1989: 44-53) and in New Guinea in this century (Gregory 1982), provided a conceptual apparatus by which tribal leaders might mobilise labour for public works and military duties. Hence, small pre-Christian communities like Cowdery's Down (Millett with James 1983) and Yeavering (Hope-Taylor 1977) were made into palaces in this period. But the impact of the missions extended far beyond underpinning the concept of kingship. Among the package of ideas introduced by the Church was not only construction in stone using lime-mortar, the making of glass and so forth, but also the notion of time itself (Harrison 1976; Hodges 1989: 43-4), writing (Hodges 1989: 43ff.) and, we may suspect, the 'invention' of languages. These were implements for the storage of concepts and as such objects of distinction. Language – Anglo-Saxon and Latin – was a powerful tool as communications between the patchwork territories were undoubtedly increased by the Church. Change, however, was not limited to one section of society. Here the spade reveals a vital clue about the genesis of the English. The introduction of ecclesiastical settlements – monasteries – of palaces, and of small royal trading-places (Hodges 1982: 50ff.) coincides not only with the final phase of the old funerary rite when some grave-plots were fenced, but also with the construction of fences around farms for the first time in over two hundred years. Land and property were now resources calculated by most levels of Anglo-Saxon society. This may explain the so-called Middle Saxon shuffle – the desertion of many sub-Roman villages in favour of new locations – and the adoption of place-names (Hodges 1989: 65ff.; Hamerow 1991).

Undoubtedly, the Church took advantage of the competition between the numerous Anglo-Saxon tribes to accumulate tracts of land during this period. Yet, in contrast to the metropolitan roots of the Frankish or Lombard bishoprics, as several historians have noted, the Anglo-Saxon Church was compelled to evolve within 'the interstices of local aristocratic lordship' (Nelson 1986: 66) in a landscape containing no towns whatsoever, only their overgrown ruins (described by an Anglo-Saxon poet as 'the work of giants') in such places as Canterbury, London and York. This restricted authority may explain why kings treated churchmen no differently from other powerful laymen.

It is against this background that the pre-conditions for take-off for the first English Industrial Revolution can be pinpointed quite precisely. In the last quarter of the seventh century the North Sea interaction zone

entered a new phase. The exchange of prestige goods between Austrasians, Neustrians, Frisians, Danes and certain Anglo-Saxon tribes was
significantly transformed by the introduction of an incipient trade in bulk
commodities, generated by the marketing of surplus products from the
new management of landed resources. The most significant manifestation
of this new era in European history are the emporia – large, new urban
communities – at which production and marketing were administered.
The size and significance of these centres has been established by archaeologists over the past fifty years (Hodges 2000). The principal places were
Dorestad (van Es and Verwers 1980), Quentovic (Hill et al. 1990), Ribe,
close to modern Esbjerg (Frandsen and Jensen 1987: 164-73) and, in
Wessex, Hamwic. Later in the eighth century, new emporia were to be
founded. Some, like Medemblik (Besteman 1990), were small; others like
Eoforwic (York) (Hall 1988) and London (Lundenwic) (Vince 1990: 13-26)
were much larger. But, in any survey of the genesis of the Anglo-Saxon
society, Hamwic has pride of place.

Hamwic, Saxon Southampton, was built about 680 (Morton 1992). The
concept reveals a far-reaching level of political and economic originality.
The town covered about 45 hectares and had a grid of metalled streets set
within a boundary ditch. Inside the street-grid were buildings sufficient to
accommodate a population of more than four thousand people. Significantly, Hamwic lacks tenemental divisions. Moreover, it is clear that a
variety of industrial crafts were practised in each property.

One must imagine constructing a 45-hectare settlement when the
largest extant place in Wessex probably covered no more than 1-5 hectares. It seems highly likely that the architect behind this great enterprise
was the King, Ine of Wessex. If this is so, we might deduce that Ine was
the first Anglo-Saxon king to use royal power to create a public work that
involved drawing upon mobilised labour from the entire territory (Hodges
1989: 80-92). In his mind, we might speculate, he had some image of a
classical city. The construction was only one issue. Administering this new
level of economic activity necessitated the introduction of new ethics into
this society. It involved feeding and supplying a new force in society. And,
equally, it involved controlling the redistribution of wealth from Hamwic
back to the West Saxon community at large. In short, it was a step towards
creating an integrated economy, involving exchange between town and
country. Ine, it must be surmised, was successful in finding support from
the West Saxon lords in the development of a project which maximised
their own hitherto under-developed economic efforts. This partnership set
in motion the pre-conditions for an economic take-off, establishing a
community of artisans in a single place, practising inter-dependent methods of craftsmanship.

Ine's achievement may owe much to West Saxon tribal circumstances,
as well as to the boom in inter-territorial trade in the late seventh and
early eighth centuries (Hodges 1989: 90). It is clear from a combination of

other evidence, however, that not until the mid- to later eighth century, did kingdoms like Mercia, East Anglia and Northumbria fully embrace the socio-economic advances introduced by Ine (Hodges 1989: 92-104). But on the eve of the Carolingian Renaissance similar great emporia existed at London, Ipswich and York.

In a general sense Wilhelm Levison was right when he claimed that English emigrants to the Carolingian kingdoms enabled the Anglo-Saxon to flow into 'the greater river that is usually called the Carolingian renaissance' (Levison 1946: 151). The Carolingian Renaissance, especially as it affects England, is a very contentious subject (Hodges 1989: 116ff.). Yet, just as archaeology begins to reveal the significance of the Renaissance on the Continent, so it sheds light on its reception in England. I am not qualified to argue its importance in terms of law or literature (see McKitterick 1983: 77ff.), but the renaissance in architecture, the fine arts, and material culture went in hand with a scientific revolution, fostered by a revival of interest in the technical manuals of antiquity (McKitterick 1983: 152). The scientific revolution, in particular, played a significant part in Carolingian economic development.

In England recent archaeological discoveries have brought to light several examples of adoption of Carolingian science. For example, lime-mortar was now used for buildings, new methods of metal-production were introduced, as were new means of firing pottery (Hodges 1989: 120ff.). More significantly, it seems that new methods of storage on farms, and managing livestock were favoured in this period (Hodges 1989: 137-8). The success of the Carolingian Renaissance in England, as on the Continent, may be measured in terms of the survival of these concepts and technologies following the political and economic turbulence of the 830s and after. Nevertheless, the civil war in the empire, like the apparent sharp decline in North Sea commerce, did not leave England unaffected (cf. Metcalf and Northover 1989; see Chapter 10). East Anglia, Northumbria and, in all probability, Mercia experienced an economic recession in common with the Danes (Hodges 1989: 148-9). In Wessex, it seems that Hamwic fell into decay, ultimately to be superseded by a network of incipient markets, whose initial shape and size is virtually invisible to the archaeologist, but whose significance ensured a platform upon which King Alfred could build. Now I have reached the Industrial Revolution itself.

II

There are many different interpretations of what a revolution is. In this Anglo-Saxon context I have in mind Fernand Braudel's definition of events in later eighteenth-century England: 'Etymologically speaking, a revolution is the movement made by a rotating wheel or a revolving planet: a rapid movement once it begins it is sure to stop rather quickly. Yet the Industrial Revolution is a perfect example of a slow movement that was barely noticeable at the beginning. Adam Smith lived in the midst of the first portents of this revolution, yet did not realise it' (Braudel 1977: 105). Adam Smith, of course, did appreciate the growing complexity of the English economy, and his studies prepare the historian for its transformation.

No such chronicler prepares one for the quantum leap in England's economic affairs in the late ninth century. Following the division of England in 878 between King Alfred and Guthrum, the Danish leader, after the Battle of Edington, Anglo-Saxon England swiftly began to assume a new identity. Within a decade a hierarchy of new, planned towns, which also served a dual purpose as refuges, had taken shape in Wessex. Devising a modern military basis to safeguard the king went hand-in-hand with the creation of a market system that led to a economic and social revolution. Alfred's biographer Asser muses fleetingly upon the achievement: 'And what of the cities and towns to be rebuilt and of others to be constructed where previously there were none?' It was a task which surely involved mobilising the entire kingdom. Of these towns, London and Winchester were the largest and most important (Hodges 2000: 112-18). The great difference between Alfred's initiative and that of his distant forebear, Ine, two centuries before, is that Hamwic was a single, monopolistic centre serving a territory, whereas London and Winchester were regional central-places connected to a middle tier of markets as well as of periodic markets, serving all parts of the kingdom. The hierarchy took shape within fifty years, by which time a class of artisans making a wide range of commodities served virtually every part of Wessex. The artisan was now a feature of West Saxon society.

But the revolution was not confined to Wessex. In marked contrast to circumstances in Denmark, the Danish conquerors of eastern England developed a ranked network of towns which was as impressive, if not more so, than the markets of Wessex. Excavations in Ipswich, Norwich and York, for example, reveal that this programme of town-planning was introduced to the Danelaw as early as 880s. Here, the will to contrive was even more marked. Whereas Alfred was drawing upon a rich bullion base (Maddicott 1989), as well as a highly centralised government system with roots extending back over two centuries, the Danish conquerors inherited kingdoms that had poor treasuries, and an impoverished material culture. I shall return later in this chapter to examine the nature of bullion in late ninth-century England. However, at this point, suffice it to point out that in the Danelaw, as Veronica Smart has shown (Smart 1985; 1986), Frankish and West Saxon moneyers were deployed to produce a coinage to articulate the new markets. Likewise, in a contrast to the West Saxon potters operating in Alfred's kingdom, Continental potters were drafted in to set up industries throughout the Danelaw. In short, Alfred's achievement in transforming his inheritance in the wake of the treaty with Guthrum, was matched if not exceeded by the Danes. This significant

168

point may help to explain the speed with which England became not only unified, but also the astonishing transformation of the economy and with it, necessarily, English society. For Alfred, Edward and Athelstan, the Danelaw represented an alarmingly successful competitor. Once the Danes were vanquished and England was unified, the house of Wessex ensured that this success was carefully constrained.

Michael Metcalf has described these changes in England's economic and political circumstances during the tenth century as 'a dramatic metamorphosis' (Metcalf 1986). Like other historians he attributes the basis of this revolution to a revival in international trade (Maddicott 1989: 16). I am not convinced by this thesis. Alfred, Guthrum and their successors throughout the tenth century undeniably had intermittently strong connections outside England. The West Saxon royal household, in particular, married into the great houses of France, Flanders and Germany during the *secolo di ferro*. Nevertheless, the weight of archaeological evidence points to an essentially insular economy throughout the tenth century. Not until the second quarter of the eleventh century (Sawyer 1986; Hodges 1988b; Vince 1990: 106ff.), did England, like most of her neighbours, become threaded together in an incipient world system of the kind sketched by Braudel and his disciple, Immanuel Wallerstein (Braudel 1977; 1984; Wallerstein 1974). The key to the dramatic metamorphosis in the tenth century is not, in certain respects, unlike the circumstances in the later eighteenth century. England's agrarian revolution, as Adam Smith pointed out (Wrigley 1985), was fundamental to the evolution of an urban-based capitalism. The countryside of tenth-century Englad bears witness to great changes, revealing a conceptual understanding of the importance of articulating town and country connections. The concept, as Randsborg has shown, emerged briefly in late antiquity in the western empire, before it was extinguished in the Dark Ages (Randsborg 1991: 82ff.). It is a matter of speculation whether this might have been at the heart of Charlemagne's many economic adventures. However, the concept depended upon reforming the structure of the countryside. Tenth-century England witnessed such changes: a climate optimum – shorter, milder winters and longer, warmer summers – facilitated the colonisation the land hitherto regarded as marginal. Drainage of the Cambridgeshire fens had begun before the end of the millennium (Hall 1984). The uplands of Dartmoor and the Pennines were being settled, as were the woodlands of Warwickshire (Fleming and Ralph 1982; Hooke 1985). The settlement structure was also changing in character.

Whereas archaeology affirms the long and stable character of villages in Wessex, the opposite was the case in Danelaw. In Northamptonshire, for example, Glenn Foard has shown an extensive process of settlement nucleation which appears to date from the late ninth or early tenth century (Foard 1985). This settlement shuffle has also been discovered in

Lincolnshire, Norfolk, Suffolk and parts of Yorkshire (Hodges 1989: 166ff.). This may help to explain the incidence of large numbers of Anglo-Scandinavian place-names – names which were introduced as new villages were created, and as David Roffe has shown in the case of Lincolnshire, as new taxation arrangements were introduced (Roffe 1981: 27-36). But the form of England's villages also altered. Beresford's excavation of the manor at Goltho in Lincolnshire vividly chronicles how a hall of ninth-century date was made into a fortified manor with associated buildings for storage in the early tenth century (Beresford 1987; Hodges 1988c: 169-72). At Raunds in Northamptonshire a similar sequence has been identified. Few archaeologists now doubt that the fortified manor – the prototype of the castle – belongs to the Anglo-Scandinavian age. It seems likely to be a close imitation of the fortified castles of late ninth- and early tenth-century date discovered in the Rhine delta by Anthony Heidinga (Heidinga 1987a: 203ff.; 1987b). In short, it may be another illustration of a Frankish concept adopted by the Danes. But do castles of this date occur in Wessex? So far they would appear to be introduced in the later tenth century at earliest (Hodges 1989: 168-70).

The introduction of the fortified manor in pre-Conquest England was accompanied by another new feature of the English landscape, the parish church. Richard Morris, using a capitalist analogy, has described the construction of churches by lay lords in tenth-century English villages as the 'big bang'. Morris calculates that some 4,000 stone churches were built between the mid-tenth and mid-eleventh century (Morris 1985: 49; 1989: 165-7 and fig. 37; Gem 1988: 21ff.). These circumstances, Morris argues, nurtured a class of skilled technicians and laid the foundations for the medieval quarry-industry. Moreover, as numerous excavations show, the simple, early churches were quickly in the pre-Conquest era to accommodate a swelling rural population. The 'big bang' has passed almost unnoticed before now, over-shadowed by rich histories of the great bishops and their abbeys in later tenth-century England. I shall return to consider these two rather separate forces below.

I have surveyed the revolution rather swiftly. Before considering some aspects of power and society in my conclusion, it is perhaps appropriate at this point to substantiate why these changes in late ninth-century England were remarkable in western Europe. Would Sigeric really have been surprised by England's advanced state? Of course his generation was well-informed about the early Capetian and Ottonian worlds through marriage alliances between the West Saxon and the Continental kings. There is equally no doubt that the Anglo-Saxon Church was much impressed by what it knew of the renascent monastic culture at Cluny and Gorze. But, were the monasteries of France or Italy any more impressive that those in England? Of course, in common with many early modern travellers, I suspect the Anglo-Saxon archbishop was surprised by what an Anglo-Saxon poet appropriately described as the 'work of giants' – the ruins of the Roman age. But the archaeology suggests that town-life in France, northern and central Italy, though no longer dormant after several centuries, was yet to develop an industrial infrastructure comparable with that found in England. Only in the Rhineland, it seems, was there a parallel development matching the Anglo-Saxon circumstances. Of course, as in England, new villages were being built with churches and manors, along the entire length of his pilgrimage. *Incastellamento* in Italy, in fact, was very much a feature of the age in which Sigeric was travelling (Hodges 1990: 17ff.). In sum, while the Anglo-Saxon achievement was exceptional, given the peculiar history of post-Roman Britain, Sigeric (like many tenth-century travellers) must have been surprised that 'the work of giants' had not given rise to conditions which were altogether more advanced in industrial terms.

The seeming inevitability of English unification puzzled Patrick Wormald, as it has other historians (see above) (Wormald 1983; 1994; Stafford 1989; Loyn 1984). I would explain it in terms of two factors: first, late Roman culture barely took hold in Britain; with the extinction of the Roman state, what remained was a Romano-Celtic patchwork of political units. Second, this, then, was effectively *terra nuova* when the Church 'returned' to domesticate the savage mind, thereby becoming part of a triangular relationship with the kings, and their people, which intermittently was put under great stress as a result of exogenous circumstances, when the insular culture came under the sway of Continental forces. Let me illustrate this sweeping generalisation by examining each element in it.

The transformation of fifth-century Britain by free German peasants is in all probability mythistory, as William NcNeill would put it (McNeill 1986). Indeed, Patrick Sims-Williams and others have also cautioned us against over emphasising the Anglo-Saxon migrations (Sims-Williams 1983a; 1983b). In fact, the archaeology of the migrations belongs to two or three generations *after* the alleged event, while the language (Anglo-Saxon) belongs to the eighth and ninth centuries (Wormald 1994). To understand the rhythms of this formative age we must focus upon the fact that in Roman and sub-Roman Britain the Church failed to secure a foothold in the towns, and much more significantly, given the desultory history of Roman towns in the western empire after *c.* 500, the Church failed to establish itself in the countryside as it was to do in Gaul and Italy (Hodges 1989: 190; Randsborg 1991). As a result the small British population was composed essentially of a social unit forged in sub-Roman Britain, which in large measure owed its genesis to Iron Age stock, and to the great demographic expansion of the second century.

However, the Church, when it returned, was not at liberty to impose itself on British society, as perhaps it hoped and as it did in the Merovingian world. Already the numerous sub-Roman tribes had established connections within the North Sea system, which around 600 began to increase in scale and significance. Within the emergent ranking of early

Anglo-Saxon society, the Church represented a potential ally. For this reason it flourished *c*. 600-620, while the North Sea interaction zone flourished and there was perhaps some inflation in the circulation of prestige goods (Hodges 1989: 53); but between *c*. 620 and 670, just as the England's overseas connections languished, so did the pattern of church-building. After 670, however, with the beginnings of commodity circulation initiated in the new emporia such as Hamwic and Dorestad, the Church finally established itself in the interstices of the Anglo-Saxon kingdoms. As Nicholas Brooks has tellingly described, the Anglo-Saxon Church attempted to emulate the Frankish model in the late eighth and ninth centuries, in a bid to become a twin force in England. But it largely failed. Indeed, as Brooks also reveals, by the late 860s Alfred was described as an enemy of the Church (Brooks 1984: 150). In fact, as Janet Nelson points out, the pious scholar-king, beloved by the Victorians, 'could adapt policy to fortune; he was in Macchiavelli's sense a virtuous prince' (Nelson 1986: 68). If Robin Fleming is to be believed, Alfred and his successors manipulated the Church as far as possible as buffer territories between Wessex and newly-conquered lands of the Danelaw (Fleming 1985: 247ff.). Its revival coincided with the apogee of West Saxon royal power in the later tenth century. However, by this time the existence of thousands of parish churches symbolised the Christian authority of lords over their land.

The critical moment in Anglo-Saxon history lay in the later ninth century when Alfred was able to implement his ideas because his authority was not vested in the Church, but in the nobles and people whom he successfully led against the Vikings. Alfred, if his biographer is to be believed, may have been a reluctant king, but he preserved not only the traditional values of West Saxon kingship (Keynes and Lapidge 1983: 18ff.), but also consciously examined the philosophy and practice of government. In a recent essay, Martin Carver takes exception to this emphasis upon royal progress in the making of the English. Instead he searches for a crucial role in the part played by lordship in the formation of the seventh-century Christian communities (Carver 1989). As he acknowledges, his perspective is rooted in East Anglia. Carver's point has much to commend it. From the mid-sixth century it is evident that the tribes of England were becoming increasingly stratified, and with the advent of the Church, this was given a conceptual framework as well as a landed one. To use an anthropological term, levelling mechanisms were deployed to prevent the complete investment of power and authority in one person (Hodges 1982: 185ff.). This is why I have stressed the significance of the great emporium of Hamwic; it was a public work which reveals the power and authority of an individual who had overcome the tribal levelling mechanisms, and found some viable means of managing his resources in conjunction with his lords. King Ine was the spiritual father of King Alfred, at least as far as his laws are concerned, while Charlemagne was perhaps Alfred's role model! Ine, however, as I have pointed out elsewhere, was undoubtedly the role model for kings in other territories in England where tribal levelling mechanisms, to the advantage of secular lords, were more embedded. Not until the later eighth century had the kings of East Anglia, Mercia and Northumbria hesitatingly advanced to emulate Ine's achievement (Hodges 1989: 193-4). Hence, there arose at Canterbury in 838 the need for an association, a *cnicht*'s guild, to safeguard the rights of a powerful, yet constrained stratum of the English elite.

But how was Alfred able to take Ine's achievement one step further, laying the foundations for a medieval society of the kind, I would propose, that Charlemagne also had in mind? J.R. Maddicott has explained the unexpected scale of Alfred's initiative in terms of his access to bullion (Maddicott 1989: 4ff.). Maddicott, using the words of Bishop Wulfsige, claims that Alfred was 'the greatest treasure-giver of all kings' (Maddicott 1989: 5). After the treaty with Guthrum, following the battle of Edington, Alfred allegedly dispersed a fortune, while at the same time reforming the coinage, upgrading its silver content (Maddicott 1989: 14-15). Maddicott explains this wealth as the 'spoils of victory' a prize taken from the Danes in 878. It is an attractive hypothesis because it offers a simple source for the huge volume of later ninth- and tenth-century English coinage, which, as I have pointed out already, does not appear to have come via trade with the Continent. The only problem is this: while Alfred was pushing ahead with his revolution, so too were the kings of the Danelaw. Moreover, whereas silver bullion was obviously restricted in Wessex from *c.* 850, compelling the West Saxons regularly to call in their coinage (Pagan 1986: 57ff.; Metcalf and Northover 1989), it was virtually extinct in Northumbria where in the generation before the Danish conquest only a copper coinage was in circulation. Where did the Danes get their bullion? Are we to split the difference, imagining that the Danes had such a huge treasury in 878 that they might afford to provide bullion sufficient to launch town-building in Wessex and the Danelaw? Frankly, this seems fanciful and we must look at the question from a different angle.

In King Alfred's commentary accompanying his translation of Boethius' *Consolations of Philosophy* is a section of supreme historical importance. Let me quote Dorothy Whitelock's translation:

> You know that no man can reveal any talent or rule and steer any dominion without tools and material. That without which one cannot carry on that craft is the material of every craft. This, then is a king's material and his tools for ruling with, that he have his land fully manned. He must have men who pray, and soldiers and workmen. So, you know that without these tools no king can reveal his skill. Also, this is his material, which he must have for those tools – sustenance for those three orders; and their sustenance consist in land to live on, and gifts, and weapons, and food, and ale, and clothes and whatever else those three orders require. And without these

173

things he cannot hold those tools, nor without those tools do any of the things that he is charged to do. For that reason I desired material to rule domination with, that my powers and domination would not be forgotten and concealed (Whitelock 1979: 919).

Alfred, according to Asser, his biographer, was fascinated by his craftsmen: 'giving instruction to all his goldsmiths and craftsmen' (Keynes and Lapidge 1983: 91). As Le Goff illustrates, the West Saxon King is giving expression to a Carolingian concept in which the management of labour is recognised as an important variable in the evolution of the political system (Le Goff 1980: 99ff.). Le Goff, of course, shows that Carolingian labour was immobilised by a network of obligations ranging over the whole sphere of the sacred and profane. Indeed, he seems just a little perplexed that the English were in the forefront of a revolution which only evolved a little later in the Continental realms. The critical point seems to be this: Alfred, judging from his writings, comprehended that his revolution necessitated additional units of labour. The equation, as the Russian economist A.V. Chayanov pointed out, demands that any sense of drudgery is sufficiently rewarded (Durrenberger 1984: 9-10; Hodges 1988a: 12ff.). Let us not be under any illusion, not only did Alfred appreciate this, but so did his Danish peers. The three orders, so to speak, *oratores*, *bellatores* and *laboratores*, were fundamental to the evolution of the unified tenth-century nation-state. But how was this possible?

First, we must go back to the early seventh century. Then, the concept of property rights, it seems, was not only appropriated by the Church, kings and lords, but, to judge from the fencing of house plots in the villages, and the settlement shuffle, by the peasantry as well. A critical symbiotic relationship existed between those who made history and those who, until the advent of modern archaeological methods, lay beyond the vigilant eye of the historian. This then helps to explain my second point concerning the material culture of the peasantry. The archaeology of peasant dwellings between the seventh and ninth centuries is extraordinarily impoverished in Italy and in most parts of the Carolingian realms with the exception of the Rhine-Seine zone. Suffice it to note that the opposite is true in England. The monasteries and farms of Middle Saxon England are notable for their 'knick-knacks', as Patrick Wormald noted (Wormald 1983; Hodges 1989: 108). Let us not talk, though, in terms of potsherds and bones, significant though those are; we must focus upon bullion. Eighth-century silver sceattas are prolifically distributed around the Seine-Rhine region, just as they are within all the Anglo-Saxon kingdoms except Wessex, where sceattas occur in large numbers in Hamwic, but infrequently elsewhere (Grierson and Blackburn 1986: 164-89; Blackburn 2003; Metcalf 2003). Thereafter, before the monetary economy of the tenth century took off, silver coins were seldom lost. But a telling if slight vision of the wealth of Anglo-Saxon England is not Alfred's largesse (*contra*

Maddicott), which is incalculable, but the extraordinary incidence of simple, beautifully made, pure silver strap-ends that occur in every ninth-century context, irrespective of function, as well as in the Viking hoards. As Sir David Wilson pointed out, these Trewhiddle-style objects are ubiquitous (Wilson and Blunt 1961: 120ff.). These are works of art by comparison with the bronze alloy and expedient silver-inlaid versions which occur in the Carolingian realms (Fraenkel-Schoorl 1978). It is my contention that King Alfred and his Danish peers were all aware that wealth of Wessex – indeed of England – lay not only in the treasuries of its monasteries, or lay courts, but in the houses of the English peasantry, accumulated over generations.

The West Saxon royal treasury was sufficient to buffer the kingdom during the recession of the middle years of the ninth century (Metcalf and Northover 1989). But to control this embedded wealth necessitated a revolution that, thanks to Ine's achievement, was not alien to the English. In other words, apart from making taxation more efficient, England's later ninth- and tenth-century kings, by investing in new towns, industry and rural development, liberated a wealth compiled over generations. This was made possible because the West Saxon and Anglo-Scandinavian kings offered attractive incentives in the form of land, gifts, weapons, food, ale, clothes and, as Alfred tellingly admitted, 'whatever else those three orders require' (Whitelock 1979: 919).

A century afterwards, in 990, Archbishop Sigeric might have had time on his pilgrimage to Rome to reflect on these circumstances in his homeland. Perhaps he made the most of his journey and simply eschewed such analysis. On returning, though, he was squarely faced with the consequence of the Anglo-Saxon achievement. Following the battle of Maldon, he was elected to negotiate with the second wave of Danes, attracted, as Peter Sawyer has shown, by the prosperity of England (1965). But, while the author of the poem about the battle of Maldon laments the passing of the old order, and, we may suspect, Sigeric seated at the negotiating table reflected upon the serenity of his recent trip, I feel bound to conclude as an archaeologist, in common with a growing number of historians, that the old order, much evolved, outlived the Danes and Normans and with time laid the foundations of the revolution that Adam Smith witnessed.

12

Conclusions: Pirenne after McCormick

A scholarly Rip Van Winkle who went to sleep over his late Roman or early medieval dissertation twenty years ago would scarcely recognise the age which recent research has unveiled. New methods and tools have sprung up and invite new questions. Together, the new insights and new tools open large vistas to the historian. The time is ripe for trying new approaches to old problems, including this one (McCormick 2001: 3).

Michael McCormick's new book, an encyclopaedic study that effectively pays homage to the perspicacity of Henri Pirenne, essentially invites archaeologists to re-read the history of early medieval Europe and to develop new research strategies. As we have seen in this book, the archaeological data now exist to make such a re-reading possible. The recently published excavations at Borg in the Lofoten Islands, for example, sustain the point that a history based upon over-simplified early modern tenets such as the decline and fall of the Roman empire, the Migrations and the world of Vikings is now over. The rhythms of transformation between later Roman Europe and the ninth-century construction of the post-Carolingian states were complex. They owed much, as McCormick has now shown, to building a network of connections that significantly reached out to the caliphate in Baghdad and, intermittently, to Cordoba, North Africa and even further. This transformation infused the construction of post-Roman Europe with a stability that, in simple terms, meant it never experienced the quixotic pattern of rise and fall that typified later European prehistory and the Roman age. In the age of Charlemagne, we might conclude, a European history starting in the Neolithic took a new and (in modern terminology) sustainable direction.

More specifically, Henri Pirenne concluded colourfully in 1937 that without Mohammed there would have been no Charlemagne. Michael McCormick, making use of new archaeological evidence from all over Europe and a systemic analysis of travellers' accounts, shows that 'the rise – and economic consolidation – of Islam changed the nature of an emerging European economy' (2001: 798). He adds: 'perhaps Pirenne was right' (2001: 798). He concludes that 'communications between the Frankish empire and the eastern Mediterranean world surged in the final decades of the eighth and the first decades of the ninth century ... never again in the history of Europe did they come close to the low levels that prevailed before 750' (2001: 442). He demonstrates that between 753/76 and 800/25 western travellers aiming at points beyond Constantinople abandoned ancient Byzantine routes and began to travel east through the Islamic world. The wealth of Islamic contacts and, indeed, the presence of Islamic coins in Italy and elsewhere in Carolingian Europe is powerfully demonstrated. He graphically illustrates the percentage of Arab coins in Sardinia, the Viking territories, the Adriatic region, the Iberian peninsula and the Rhône valley (McCormick 2001: chart 12.1). The twin-peaks show a decline from a peak in c. 700-724 in the second quarter of the eighth century, then a sharp rise to c. 800, then a fall to c. 850-874. This was an inter-connected world that for the most part lay beyond the gaze of the contemporary sources and, understandably, therefore has been a point of stubborn resistance by modern historians. So, Borg in the Lofoten Islands (Munch, Johanssen and Roesdahl 2003) belongs to later Merovingian and Carolingian Europe, flourishing on the periphery as the centre in the Rhineland reached far to develop its control in places as distant as Miranduolo (Valenti 2004) and San Vincenzo al Volturno in Italy, and tentatively sought to obtain prestige resources by way of inter-connected routes stemming from the Baltic as well as from the head of the Adriatic at Venice. Borg is a metaphor of a Viking age which was, in reality, part of an evolving new Europe.

A more telling metaphor is the watermill at the major village of Vorbasse in Denmark (Hvass 1986; 1988). Marc Bloch, in a celebrated essay, conjectured that watermills were key criteria for the feudal age; that is, instruments of lordly control over production and distribution. Such instruments, he deduced, were only adopted in twelfth-century post-Viking Denmark once it had been harnessed to the Christian European community (Bloch 1935; cf. Toubert 2004: 70). With the discovery of a Viking-age watermill, the excavations at Vorbasse consign this interpretation to historiography. We must say goodbye to the Vikings we have known. Instead, like the Croats or the Komani in the Adriatic regions, these were chiefdoms (Thurston 2001) – building upon generations of stability and development as, for example, the successive village-settlements at Vorbasse show – to participate in not only the exchange of goods but also an exchange of ideas and information.

But how should archaeologists now respond to McCormick's new paradigm? Here are observations on five themes where the archaeological sources merit a fresh re-reading.

Chronology

We now have at our disposal an absolute chronology for the end of the Roman empire and the beginnings of early Middle Ages to set beside the contemporary texts. This new chronology, in outline at least, is compelling.

Henri Pirenne may have 'forgotten' the sixth century, but he recognised the axiomatic importance of the rise of Islam in the seventh century and the Carolingian Renaissance in the making of the Middle Ages. The chronology of this period has been revolutionised by the close dating of ceramics on archaeological sites. In this respect, no book has made a greater contribution to classical archaeology in the last century than John Hayes's *Late Roman Pottery* (1972) which provided the framework for dating African Red Slip tablewares. With this framework, numerous scholars have now dated the transport amphorae of the later Roman world. Finally, with these instruments it has been possible to date many of the local kitchen wares which fifty years ago were normally tossed away by excavators of classical sites. With these data the sixth century (virtually ignored by Henri Pirenne) emerges as an age of change (Morrisson and Sodini 2002). In Italy and the central Mediterranean, with exceptions such as Florence and Marseilles, the collapse of the Roman way of life became unstoppable. Towns began to assume a rural character; the last villas were abandoned and new villages were founded beyond the control of the aristocracy. Trade and distribution systems declined, serving an increasingly marginal sector of society. Further east and in North Africa the collapse was delayed to the earlier seventh century. By the end of this century, though, the Mediterranean world had been utterly transformed with its great capitals such as Constantinople and Rome being reduced to administrative centres connected to a few under-resourced coastal regions. Paradoxically, it now seems, only the Islamic communities of the Near East and possibly in parts of North Africa sustained the bare fabric of Roman socio-economic systems.

McCormick has gauged this transformation accurately, making good use of modern archaeology. He has also gauged how the North Sea, driven by stability within the Frankish kingdoms, was re-invented as a cultural and economic interaction zone exactly at this time. Beginning in the later sixth century, a shared commonality of culture begins to exist, embracing northern France as far west as Normandy, the Low Countries, western Jutland and much of south-eastern England (Näsman 1998). This was the basis of the substantive economic transformation of the 670s, when a silver currency was adopted in place of the high value Merovingian gold issues. Just as significantly, this is when places like Dorestad and Hamwic were created as planned towns. Dendrochronological dating has provided almost absolute dating for this immensely important moment in European history. Ribe in western Denmark, for example, is accurately dated to the first decade of the eighth century. Here, as in the Mediterranean, chronology is no longer an enigma. On the contrary the boom of the early eighth century was followed by a well-dated recession of some kind. Then came the axiomatic moment of modern Europe. All the archaeological evidence now reinforces the impact of Charlemagne, especially after his monetary reforms of 793-4. The next thirty years mark a boom in investment in towns, palaces, monasteries, churches, the countryside, production and, of course, the arts.

12. Conclusions: Pirenne after McCormick

McCormick's book simply and skilfully embroiders Pirenne's thesis using archaeological and newly analysed historical and numismatic data. This was a platform that transformed not just the centre of Europe but also many of its peripheries. Just as Charlemagne owed much to Mohammed, to paraphrase Pirenne, so the Viking tribes owed everything to Charlemagne. This is not a novel conclusion. Holger Arbman appreciated this when, as he worked on the archaeology of the middle Swedish emporium of Birka, he published *Schweden und das karolingische Reich* (1937). But this time boom did not lead to recession. The significance of the early ninth century, as Pirenne signalled, was that it provided a platform for sustainability for the societies not only of Latin Christendom and the Baltic Sea world. The result is clear. We can effectively say goodbye to the Vikings as we have known them. These peoples were Europeans who like their later descendants, the Normans, appreciated how to adapt contemporary developments to their advantage. The vehement and discordant response of the monastic authors of this age who suffered from Viking enterprise, essentially to be eclipsed as power-brokers, should not distract us from recognising the material achievements of this period. Medieval Europe grew stronger in the ninth century, realising the aims and objectives of the Carolingian Renaissance in all its diverse forms.

So what new directions should archaeologists be taking to improve this chronology? First and foremost, more regional chronologies are needed, connecting coins and ceramics (2004). The fruits of the metal detectorists in England show clearly that the chronology of the mid to later ninth century is more complex than many historians had hitherto imagined. Mark Blackburn and Michael Metcalf's models, based on finds of single coins mostly found by detectorists (Blackburn 2003; Metcalf 1999; 2003), serve as a benchmark for similar research on the chronologies of other regions in the seventh and eighth centuries. Parallel to these there exists a need to refine regional ceramic chronologies, as the University of Siena has done recently for Tuscany, illuminating rural development processes in other regions (cf. Valenti 2004). The chronologies of Lombardy in early Carolingian times or Apulia under the Byzantines need to be refined to measure alongside the contemporary understanding of, say, Rome in this period based upon the results of excavations in the Crypta Balbi. Regional chronologies are equally needed to help us understand Catalonia and Provence, to measure the conditions around the peripheries of the Frankish drive to invest alongside the Rhineland and Low Countries. In short, a patchwork of data presently exists. So far it illuminates how more complex the regional circumstances of Latin Christendom were even if, as now appears, there were shared models for development.

Demography

Archaeologists and historians are now more or less agreed about one puzzling fact: the population of the later Roman world collapsed. The question now is the scale of the collapse because this will help us to explain why it occurred.

Plainly, the density of settlements of the earlier Roman period simply does not exist after the later fifth and sixth centuries. Historians may quibble about the nature of the evidence, but after thirty years of extensive and intensive field surveys, the evidence is compelling. Southern Tuscany is a good example. Here surveys have in fact covered approximately 1,929 square metres, equal to 8.6% of the region, and they have revealed 2,521 first- to fourth-century settlement structures, and 201 sixth- to seventh-century structures. As Riccardo Francovich has commented, one major conclusion is apparent (forthcoming). A severe population crisis emerges between the period of greatest population during the first to third centuries and the seventh century, the evidence for settlement structures decreasing by a power of twelve. If we project this data onto the whole region we can estimate dramatic changes in land use. From an average of one site per 1.27 square kilometres in the first and third centuries, the density drops to one site per 4 square kilometres in the fourth to sixth centuries, and to one site per 10 square kilometres in the sixth and seventh centuries. Was this due to plague, changing dietary circumstances, shifting reproduction strategies or a combination of all of these?

The evidence for plague has yet to be convincingly identified, and in any case the population was declining long before the first so-called Black Death of Emperor Justinian's period. Then again, the archaeology of the fourteenth-century Black Death in Europe is astonishingly slight. As for changing diet, it is evident that the decline of commerce restricted the transport of foodstuffs while the rise in pig-rearing in late antiquity has long attracted attention as though it was a forebear of fast-food living. As for shifting reproduction strategies to explain this demographic catastrophe, as Jack Goody once hinted in a study of the place of the Church in later Roman and medieval society, it is an untested hypothesis that merits consideration (Goody 1983). At the Adriatic port of Butrint, though, a new study of a sample population of the town as its economic fortunes ebbed away in the later sixth century shows how they were markedly susceptible to disease (Hodges, Bowden and Lako 2004). Of course, the Butrint study needs to be one of many. Indeed, just as field surveys have pointed to the extraordinary biological transformation of later Roman Europe, now there is urgent need for a comparable number of palaeopathological studies.

12. Conclusions: Pirenne after McCormick

Production and gift-giving

The archaeology of rural western Europe in the early Middle Ages provides a contrasting picture with late antiquity. Now we are beginning to measure the nature of production and, with caution (cf. Moreland 2000), comprehend the entangled issue of gift-giving as a fundamental mechanism in the making of the Middle Ages (cf. Cutler 2001; Reuter 2000). But many more examples of production sites are needed.

Excavations of villages in France, Germany and the Low Countries show settlements comprising large dwellings by Roman or later medieval standards. These tend to occupy large fenced yards at points in under-populated landscapes where, for the most part, it was possible to take advantage of mixed farming resources. The limited evidence suggests agricultural regimes with surpluses. It appears that the Church took some time to recognise the apparent wealth of the countryside, and did not discover the means to impose itself upon local communities until the zenith of the Carolingian era and even later in Anglo-Saxon England and Italy (cf. Hodges 1989: 194; Francovich and Hodges 2003). The example of San Vincenzo al Volturno, illustrated in several chapters in this book, sustains this conclusion. Moreover, these excavations reinforce Georges Duby's view (1974; cf. Boucheron 2003: 249) that with Carolingian patronage a highly rational investment strategy of rural development was instigated by previously inactive monasteries. The key to this strategy was the promotion of the monastery by enhancing its cult standing, and then, generating and, critically, sustaining a network of donors. Timothy Reuter, taking Duby's point a step further, pinpoints a shift in the Carolingian period with the invention of what he terms 'positional' goods. In his opinion, these were investments representing status and power as opposed to utilitarian objects. Gift-giving, he argues, was not simply about displays of largesse but also served to stress socially what one retained and did not give (2000: 23-4).

The gifts in San Vincenzo's case consisted of estates given to the monastery by Lombard aristocrats, mostly in the Principality of Benevento, a territory which paid intermittent allegiance to the Carolingians (Wickham 1995; cf. Toubert 2004: 45). A critical component in the gift-giving cycle was the role of the collective workshop where 'positional' goods were produced. These were prestige goods such as enamels and glassware – invariably liturgical in character – made for donors, who in return had already given tracts of land that produced labour and agrarian surpluses. This entangled exchange system rested upon establishing San Vincenzo's cult status as much as obtaining appropriate craftsmen for the monastery. This rare and remarkable example highlights an important lacuna in the archaeological record: we know too little about the early medieval aristocracy and its way of life. Of course, there are manor-houses such as Barbing-Kreuzhof in south Germany, as well as a growing

181

knowledge of early medieval aristocratic houses in the Forum of Nerva in Rome (Francovich and Hodges 2003: 102-3). Yet their way of life remains largely unknown. Their significant relation with monasteries in terms of generating rural production is the subject of an important paper by Ilana F. Silber who contends that

> The notion of 'keeping-while-giving' brings into relief the framing of such processes in certain perceptions of time, endowing 'wealth' with unique meaning by raising it above the ordinary flux of things, 'outside the present'. In both respects indeed, donations to monasteries may be understood, with due modifications, as a form of 'keeping-while-giving': contributing to the ongoing, and ever-tentative, constitution of solidarity and authentication of differences between monks and laymen, while endowing monastic wealth with unique meaning by securing it in monasteries, at least ideally, for eternity. The crucial difference, however, is that 'keeping-while-giving' in this specific and highly elaborate variant, may also be shown to have the capacity to acquire a collective, even public significance expanding beyond the individual and particularistic interests activating and activated by the gift circuit (1995: 228-9).

Put another way, in the light of the collective workshop excavated at San Vincenzo, Silber's model commends us to consider how the enamels, regalia, glassware and other prestige goods produced in the monastery were used in aristocratic manors. The social implications of the gift-relationship at a local level are well-documented from later tenth- to twelfth-century monastic circumstances. Does the San Vincenzo collective workshop mark the first experiments with this strategy, as the Church and aristocracy vied to situate itself in an underdeveloped countryside?

'A world apart'

It is instructive to look at those regions which fall outside the remit of McCormick's re-working of Pirenne's thesis. It is a theme which, however awkward in the face of regional histories, needs to be faced.

The archaeology of western Britain and Ireland provides an interesting counterpoint. This Atlantic region, actively connected since the Neolithic (cf. Cunliffe 2001), is notable for the poverty of its contact with Carolingian Europe. We need only compare the Lofoten Island settlement of Borg with, say, Dunadd, the early Dalriadic capital in south-west Scotland, scene of Leslie Alcock's incisive if small-scale 1980s research excavations, to adduce the apparent material poverty of the Atlantic communities (Campbell and Lane 2003). McCormick might remind us of the Scottish and Irish monks who along with the Northumbrians followed the pilgrimage routes to Rome. Yet the impact of these great experiences is barely discernible in the archaeological record. Of course, the illuminated manuscripts and ecclesiastical arts bear witness to southern European influences (as the authors of the Dunadd excavation report argue), but the secular society was rooted firmly in the pre-Roman Iron Age. The only obvious extra-regional influence belongs to the end of the Roman Mediterranean, taking the form of the small numbers of sixth- to seventh-century D and E tablewares normally attributed to (later Roman) connections with western France. Quite why these unimpressive pots took the fancy of the western British communities is hard to determine. The pots in question are neither distinguished as minor artistic pieces (such as, for example, the later Roman African Redslipware dishes) nor, it seems, containers of prized commodities like oil or wine (although dyer's madder (*Rubia tinctorum*) was identified in one vessel found at Dunadd). Nevertheless, several generations after the end in *c*. 550 of the long-distance traders who brought (African Redslip) A-ware tablewares and B-ware amphorae to the Atlantic seaboard communities, a strangely similar trading episode appears to have joined sub-Roman Aquitaine with these communities. What is crystal clear is that, unlike the parallel routes traversing the later sixth- and seventh-century Merovingian North Sea, this Atlantic seaboard route never prospered. At its zenith the contact represented by the E-ware sherds amounts to less than 200 vessels, concentrated at monopolistic élite centres such as Dunadd. Moreover, by the later eighth and ninth centuries when Carolingian-period Aquitaine was affluent with silver from the mines at Melle (Téreygeol and Dubois 2003), there is no evidence of continued contact with Dunadd when, thanks to Alcock's excellent excavations, we now know the royal centre was at its apogee in terms of its architecture. So, unlike the North Sea zone (reaching well beyond the emporium at Kaupang in southern Norway up to the Lofoten Islands) which prospered in episodic phases throughout the eighth and ninth centuries, the Atlantic seaboard – and Scotland in particular – remained outside the rim of pan-European economic expansion described, for example, by McCormick. Here was, as McCormick admits (2001: 539), 'clearly now a world apart'.

Another region that was a world apart yet beyond the imagination of Latin Christendom in post-Roman times was Umayadd Spain. The sheer urban dimensions and wealth of Cordoba with (slight later) palaces like Elvira Medina bear witness to a culture that owed its energy to the same Islamic forces of production and distribution that underpinned Abbasid enterprise in the Euphrates and Tigris valleys (Ewert 2002). The great palace mosque at Cordoba, like the great mosque of the Aghlabids in Kairouan (Tunisia), ranks alongside the sprawling earlier ninth-century Abbasid palaces of Samarra as opposed to any of the imitative architecture of Charlemagne's empire, including his palatine chapel at Aachen. Similarly the palatial economies of the Cordoban caliphate bear comparison with the investment in contemporary farming in Mesopotamia, as opposed to the limited proto-feudal efforts of the Franks even in the colonisation of uplands beyond the Rhine (Nitz 1988). Finally, to take one illustration of

183

the gap in technical know-how: the use of polychrome glazed dishes in Cordoba, made to Persian standards, pre-dated by centuries their production in any part of Latin Christendom. The solitary comparison was the thick green glazed Forum Ware of ninth-century Italy, an unimaginative imitation of a Roman type. No wonder, then, that the Carolingians vacillated between seeking a foothold in the Iberian peninsula and making pacts with Cordoba (cf. Sénac 2002). This was a world of staggering conspicuous consumption, dwarfing anything invented in the monastic or royal minds of Carolingian Europe. However, it was connected directly or indirectly through North Africa to the great reservoirs of wealth being tapped around the Indian Ocean and beyond. For the most part, as Phillipe Sénac (2002) has shown, intercourse with Latin Christendom was rigorously restricted to the acquisition of relics and in episodic deflationary moments to a piracy that menaced southern France, Corsica, Sardinia and the western Italian coast.

Byzantium

Archaeologists and historians of Byzantium are now agreed on the dramatic discontinuity that distinguishes the later seventh, eighth and ninth centuries from what went before. Yet, again, the real scale of Byzantine society lacks measurement between the early seventh and later tenth centuries. Archaeological evidence would permit the empire to be comprehended alongside the rise of Carolingian Europe and the towering ambitions of the Caliphate.

Towns, the key points of early Byzantium, simply disappeared altogether or, as in the case of Constantinople, were hugely reduced centres of population. It is amazing to visit Monemvasia in the southern Peloponnese and imagine that the citizens of this place, allied with the much-reduced army from Athens, Nauplia and the Cycladic Islands in 727 set out to besiege Constantinople (Klaus and Steinmüller 2001: 11). The military expedition was a failure but the ambition that these tiny communities might gang up on the centre of the empire shows how topsy-turvy the world had become. Describing these places, John Haldon (1999: 15-16) writes:

> I would suggest that what we are confronted with here are small but distinct communities whose inhabitants regarded themselves (in one sense, that of domicile, quite legitimately) as 'citizens' of the city within whose walls their settlement was located; that the *kastron,* which retained the name of the ancient *polis,* provided a refuge in case of attack (although in many such cases it may not necessarily have been permanently occupied, still less permanently garrisoned); and that therefore many of the *poleis* of the seventh to ninth centuries survived as such because their inhabitants, living effectively in distinct villages within the area delineated by the walls, saw themselves as belonging to the *polis* itself, rather than to a village.

12. Conclusions: Pirenne after McCormick

The issue, therefore, is not necessarily whether places like Middle Byzantine Butrint, presently in southern Albania, were occupied, but rather what form did the occupation take? What role did the town play within its local region, bearing in mind that during some periods it may have played no role at all? Did this change after the seventh century? Are we looking at thriving urban centres which were hollow parodies of the classical town, housing little but ecclesiastical bureaucracies, which became simply irrelevant or were rendered finally defunct by regional instability? In short, 'the much loved topic of "continuity" can now come off the agenda altogether' (Carver 1993: 61). 'Our real research objective is the story of the role of towns rather simply the story of the individual towns themselves' (ibid.: 78). Paul Arthur has postulated a sequence of models for Naples to illustrate this cycle of urban circumstances in regional terms which now merit testing (Arthur 2002). His model charts the dramatic collapse and slow revival of regional interaction between the seventh and tenth centuries which merits testing in other Byzantine regions closer to Constantinople.

It is relatively straightforward to identify the moment of economic revival. Klavs Randsborg's illuminating graph of church-building in Constantinople (1992: fig. 22) between c. 300 and 1500 depicts a deep trough from the seventh to ninth centuries followed by revival under the Macedonian emperors after the 860s. New churches went hand in hand with renewed military and economic activity. Evidence of this comes not only from Corinth (Sanders 2003) in Greece as well as Butrint and Otranto in the southern Adriatic, but also from western Russia, the Baltic and emporia such as Birka in Sweden and Haithabu in north Germany (Piltz 1998, esp. fig. 3). In Constantinople itself (Randsborg 1991: fig. 74) as at Butrint and Corinth, the striking number of coins of the later ninth and tenth centuries appear to indicate a surge in marketing probably of a periodic kind as the low value bronze *folles* are seldom associated with obvious urban structures. This apparent reflation, judging from the coins, was sponsored by the Byzantine state and surely must have given rise to regional investment that in certain respects resembled the economic strategy of the Carolingians. Testing this and other hypotheses in modern excavations at Istanbul and major centres like Thessalonika as well as, of course, in Byzantine regions, is long overdue.

Conclusion

Our theme must be discontinuity; the only issue is which. People have argued for millennia over exactly what changed as the Roman world turned into the Middle Ages in the different parts of the empire; but what no one has ever been able to argue away is that there *was* a break of some kind, perhaps of many kinds, at the end of Antiquity (Wickham 1994: 99).

185

Archaeology now depicts the sheer scale of the discontinuity marking the end of antiquity, and equally throws into sharp relief the rise of the Merovingian North Sea as well as, a century later, the vaunting ambition of Charlemagne. The discontinuity lays emphasis upon a Europe of variegated regions operating at different rhythms and frequently finding commonalities through the Church and, in the case of Scandinavia, outside it. The discontinuity lays emphasis too upon the will to rediscover antiquity either by imitating its forms, as in the case of the palatine chapel at Aachen, or to obtain lost ancient technologies from the Abbasid Caliphate, such as were practised in the short but significant succession of workshops at San Vincenzo al Volturno. Re-reading the archaeology of the past sixty years or so which permitted us to reach these conclusions, it is fair to say that we are only slowly coming to appreciate the complex, sometimes puzzling character of this era. Plainly we are acquainting ourselves with an archive of new chronicles, often from the unlikeliest places, which permit us to re-read the making of the Middle Ages.

Bibliography

Alcock, L. (1963) *Dinas Powys*. University of Wales Press, Cardiff.

Alcock, L. (1971) *Arthur's Britain*. Penguin Books, Harmondsworth.

Alcock, L. (1995) *Cadbury Castle Somerset: The Early Medieval Archaeology*. University of Wales Press, Cardiff.

Alcock, L. (2003) *Kings and Warriors. Craftsmen and Priests in Northern Britain AD 550-850*. Society of Antiquaries of Scotland, Edinburgh.

Alcock, S. (1993) *Graecia Capta. The Landscapes of Roman Greece*. Cambridge University Press, Cambridge.

Ambrosiani, B. and H.L. Clarke (1992) *Early Investigations and Future Plans*. Birka Studies series vol. 1, Stockholm.

Ammerman, A.J. (2003) 'Venice before the Grand Canal', *Memoirs of the American Academy of Rome* 48: 141-58.

Anamali, S. (1989): 'L'état actuel des recherches sur l'origine des villes du moyen âge en Albanie', *XIe Congrès International d'Archéologie Chrétienne*: 2617-35.

Anamali, S. and M. Korkuti (1971) 'Les Illyriens et la genèse des Albanais à la lumière des recherches archéologiques albanaises', in M. Korkuti, S. Anamali & J. Gjinari (eds), *Les Illyriens et la genèse des Albanais*. Tirana: 7-39.

Anderton, M. (1999) (ed.) *Anglo-Saxon Trading Centres. Beyond the Emporia*. Cruithne Press, Glasgow.

Andreolli, B. and M. Montanari (1983) *L'Azienda Curtense in Italia. Proprietà della Terra e Lavoro Contadino nei Secoli VIII-XI*. CLUEB, Bologna.

Andrews, D. (1982) 'Architecture and Archaeology. Medieval Domestic Architecture in Northern Lazio', in D. Andrews, J. Osborne and D. Whitehouse (eds), *Medieval Lazio. Studies in Architecture, Painting and Ceramics (Papers in Italian Archaeology III)* (BAR International Series 125): 1-122. British Archaeological Reports, Oxford.

Andrews, P. (1995) 'Excavations at Redcastle Furze, Thetford 1989-90', *East Anglian Archaeology* 72.

Angold, M. (1985) 'The Shaping of the Medieval Byzantine City', *Byzantische Forschungen* 10: 3-4.

Arnold, C.J. (1988) *An Archaeology of the Early Anglo-Saxon Kingdoms*. Routledge, London.

Arbman, H. (1937) *Schweden und das karolingische Reich*. Almqvist & Wiksell, Stockholm.

Arthur, P. (2002) *Naples. From Roman Town to City-State: An Archaeological Perspective*. British School at Rome, London.

Arthur, P. (2004) 'From *Vicus* to Village: Italian Landscapes, c. AD 400-1000', in N. Christie (ed.) *Landscapes of Change. Rural Evolutions in Late Antiquity and the Early Middle Ages*: 103-34. Ashgate, Aldershot.

Arthur, P., M.P. Gaggia, G.P. Ciongoli, V. Melissano, H. Patterson and P. Roberts (1992) 'Fornaci medievali ad Otranto. Nota preliminare', *Archeologia Medievale* 19: 91-122.

187

Bibliography

Astill, G. (1985) 'Archaeology, Economics and Early Medieval Europe', *Oxford Journal of Archaeology* 4: 215-31.

Augé, M. (1995) *Non-Places. Introduction to an Anthropology of Supermodernity* (trans. John Howe). Verso, London.

Augé, M. (1998) *A Sense for the Other. The Timeliness and Relevance of Anthropology.* Stanford University Press, Stanford.

Baçe, A. (1981) 'Kështjella e Paleokastrës', *Iliria*, 11.2: 165-235.

Bachrach, B.S. (1998) 'Pirenne and Charlemagne', in A. Callander Murray (ed.), *After Rome's Fall*: 214-31. University of Toronto Press, Toronto.

Baldassarri, M. and Favilla, M.C. (2004) 'Forme di Tesaurizzazzione in Area Italiana tra Tardo Antico e Alto Medioevo', in S. Gelichi and C. La Rocca (eds), *Tesori. Forme di Accumulazione della Ricchezza nell'Alto Medioevo*: 143-206. Viella, Rome.

Balzaretti, R. (1996) 'Cities, Emporia: Local Economics in the Po Valley, c. 700-875', in N. Christie and S. Loseby (eds), *Towns in Transition*: 212-34. Scolar Press, Aldershot.

Bejko, L. (1998) 'Vështrim mbi mendimin arkeologjik shqiptar dhe kontekstin e tij social', *Iliria* 28.1-2: 195-208.

Bela, M. and L. Përzhita (1990) 'Harta arkeologjike e zonës së Hasit (rrethi I Kukësit)', *Iliria* 21.2: 227-48.

Belting, H. (1968) *Studien zur Beneventanischen Malerei (Forschungen zur Kunstgeschichte und Christlichen Archäologie* 7). Franz Steiner Verlag, Wiesbaden.

Bencard, M., L.B. Jorgensen and B. Madsen (1990) *Ribe Excavations 1970-1976*, vol. 4. Sydjysk Universitetsforlag, Esbjerg.

Beresford, G. (1987) *Goltho.* HMSO, London.

Bertelli, C. (1988a) *Gli Affreschi nella Torre di Torba (I Quaderni del Fondo per l'Ambiente Italiano* 1). Electa, Milan.

Bertelli, C. (1988b) 'Castelseprio e Milano', in *Bisanzio, Roma e l'Italia nell'Alto Medioevo (Settimane di Studio del Centro Italiano di Studi sull'Alto Medioevo* 34), vol. 2: 869-917. Centro Italiano di Studi sull'Alto Medioevo, Spoleto.

Besteman, J. (1990) 'Pre-Urban Development of Medemblik', in H.A. Heidinga and H.H. van Regteren Altena (eds), *Medemblik and Monnichendam. Aspects of Medieval Urbanisation in Northern Holland*: 1-30. Amsterdam.

Biddle, M. (1976) 'The Towns', in D.M. Wilson (ed.), *The Archaeology of Anglo-Saxon England*, 99-150. Methuen, London.

Bill, J. (2003) 'Navires et Navigation en Occident á l'Epoque Viking', in A-M. Flambard Héricher (ed.), *La Progression des Vikings, dès Raids à la Colonisation*: 27-56. Publications de l'Université de Rouen, Rouen.

Binford, L.R. (1981) 'Behavioural Archaeology and the "Pompeii Premise" ', *Journal of Anthropological Research* 37: 195-208.

Bischoff, B. (1962) 'Die Entstehung des Sankt Galler Klosterplanes in Paläographischer Sicht', in J. Duff (ed.), 'Studien zum St Galler Klosterplan', *Mitteilungen zur Vaterländischen Geschichte* 42: 67-68.

Blackburn, M. (2003) ' "Productive" Sites and the Pattern of Coin Loss in England, 600-1180', in T. Pestell and K. Ulmschneider (eds), *Markets in Early Medieval Europe: Trading and 'Productive' Sites, 650-850*: 20-36. Windgather Press, Macclesfield.

Bloch, M. (1935) 'Avènement et conquêtes du moulin à eau', *Annales d'Histoire Économique et Sociale* VII: 538-63.

Bloch, M. (1964) *Feudal Society.* Routledge and Kegan Paul, London.

Böhme, H.W. (1986) 'Das Ende der Römerherrschaft in Britannien und die

Bibliography

Angelsächsische Besiedlung Englands im 5 Jahrhundert', *Jahrbuch Romisch-Germanisch Zeutralmuseums* 33: 469-574.

Boucheron, P. (2003) 'Georges Duby', in V. Sales (ed.) *Les Historiens*: 227-50. Armand Colin, Paris.

Bowden, W. (2003) *Epirus Vetus: The Archaeology of a Late Antique Province*, Duckworth, London.

Bowden, W. (2004) 'The Construction of Identities in Post-Roman Albania', in W. Bowden and L. Lavan (eds), *Late Antique Archaeology: Theory and Practice*: 57-78. E.J. Brill, Leiden.

Bowden, W. and L. Përzhita (2004) 'Archaeology in the Landscape of Roman Epirus: Preliminary Report on the Diaporit Excavations, 2002-3', *Journal of Roman Archaeology* 17: 413-33.

Bowden, W., R. Hodges, and K. Lako (2004) *Byzantine Butrint: Excavations and Surveys 1994-99*. Oxbow Books/Butrint Foundation, Oxford.

Bowden, W., L. Lavan and C. Machado (2004) (eds), *Recent Research on the Late Antique Countryside*. E.J. Brill, Leiden.

Bowden, W., C. Coutts, R. Hodges, and F. Marazzi (1996) 'Excavations at San Vincenzo al Volturno: 1995', *Archeologia Medievale* XXIII: 467-76.

Bowden, W. et al. (forthcoming)' Excavations at the New Abbey', in K. Bowes and R. Hodges (eds), *San Vincenzo al Volturno 4. From Text to Territory: Excavations and Surveys in the Monastic Terra*. British School at Rome, London.

Bowersock, G. (1990) 'Review of J. Matthews – The Roman Empire of Ammianus', *Journal of Roman Studies* 80: 244.

Bowes, K. and R. Hodges (2002) 'Santa Maria in Civita Revisited', *Papers of the British School at Rome* 70: 359-61.

Bowes, K., K. Francis and R. Hodges (eds) (forthcoming) *San Vincenzo al Volturno 4. From Text to Territory. Excavations and Surveys in the Monastic Terra*. British School at Rome, London.

Braudel, F. (1977) *Afterthoughts on Material Civilisation and Capitalism*. John Hopkins University Press, Baltimore.

Braudel, F. (1984) *Capitalism and Material Life 1400-1800*. William Collins & Son, London.

Brogiolo, G.P. (1987) 'A Proposito dell'Organizzazione Urbana nell'Alto Medioevo', *Archeologia Medievale* 14: 27-46.

Brogiolo, G.P. (1989) 'Brescia: Building Transformations in a Lombard City', in K. Randsborg (ed.), *The Birth of Europe. Archaeology and Social Development in the First Millennium AD* (Analecta Romana Istitutum Danici Supplementum 16): 156-65. L'Erma di Bretschneider, Rome.

Brogiolo, G.P. (1992) 'Trasformazioni Urbanistiche nella Brescia Longobarda: Dalle Capanne in Legno al Monastero Regio di S. Salvatore', in C. Stella and G. Brentegani (eds), *S. Giulia di Brescia. Archeologia, Arte, Storia di un Monastero Regio dai Longobardi al Barbarossa*: 179-210. Comune di Brescia, Brescia.

Brogiolo, G.P. and S. Gelichi (1997) *La Città nell'Alto Medioevo Italiano*. Laterza, Rome.

Brooks, N. (1984) *The Early History of the Church of Canterbury, Christ Church from 597 to 1066*. Leicester University Press, Leicester.

Brown, E. (1974) 'The Tyranny of a Construct: Feudalism and Historians of Medieval Europe', *American History Review* 79: 1063-88.

Brown, P. (1981) *The Cult of Saints. Its Rise and Function in Latin Christianity*. Chicago University Press, Chicago.

Brown, P. (1982) *Society and the Holy in Late Antiquity*. University of California Press, Berkeley.

Bibliography

Brown, P. (1996) *Authority and the Sacred: Aspects of the Christianisation of the Roman World.* Cambridge University Press, Cambridge.

Brown, T. (1978) 'Settlement and Military Policy in Byzantine Italy', in H. McK. Blake, T. Potter and D.B. Whitehouse (eds), *Papers in Italian Archaeology* 1: *The Lancaster Seminar. Recent Research in Prehistoric, Classical and Medieval Archaeology* (BAR Supplementary Series 41 (i)): 323-38. Oxford.

Brown, T. (1984) *Officers and Gentlemen. Imperial Administration and Aristocratic Power in Byzantine Italy, AD 554-800.* British School at Rome, London.

Budina, Dh. (1971) 'Harta arkeologjike e bredetit jon dhe e pellgut të Delvinës', *Iliria* I: 275-342.

Budina, Dh. (1975) 'La carte archéologique de la vallée de Drino', *Iliria* III: 355-82.

Cabanes, P. (1976) *L'Epire, de la mort de Pyrrhos à la conquête romaine (272-167 av. J.-C.).* Paris.

Cabanes, P. (1997) 'From the Roman Conquest to the Great Crisis of the Third Century AD', in M.B. Sakellariou (ed.), *Epirus*: 114-27. Athens.

Campbell, E. (1996) 'The Archaeological Evidence for External Contacts: Imports, Trade and Economy in Celtic Britain AD 400-800', in K.R. Dark (ed.), *External Contacts and the Economy of Late Roman and Post-Roman Britain*: 83-96. Boydell and Brewer, Woodbridge.

Campbell, E. and Lane. A. (2003) *Dunadd: An Early Dalriadic Capital.* Oxbow Books, Oxford.

Cantini, F. (2003) *Lo Scavo Archeologico del Castello di Montarrenti (Siena). Per la Storia della Formazione del Villaggio Medievale in Toscana (Secc. VII-XV).* All' Insegna del Giglio, Florence.

Cantino Wataghin, G. (1985) 'L'Abbazia di Novalesa alla Luce delle Indagini Archeologiche: Verifiche e Problemi', in *Dal Piemonte all'Europa: Esperienze Monastiche nella Società Medievale (XXXIV Congresso Storico Subalpino 1985)*: 569-85. Deputazione Subalpina di Storia Patria – Regione Piemonte, Turin.

Cantino Wataghin, G. (2000) 'Monasteri tra VIII e IX Secolo: Evidenze Archeologiche per l'Italia Settentrionale', in C. Bertelli and G.P. Brogiolo (eds), *Il Futuro dei Longobardi. L'Italia e la Costruzione dell' Europa di Carlo Magno*: 129-42. Skira, Milan.

Carandini, A. (1985) *Settefenestre. Una Villa Schiavistica nell' Etruria Romana*, vol. 2: *La Villa nelle Sue Parti.* Panini, Modena.

Carbonara (1979) Iussu Desiderii. *Monte Cassino e l'Architettura Campano-Abruzzese nell'Undicesimo Secolo.* Istituti di Fondamenti dell'Architettura – Università degli Studi 'La Sapienza' di Roma, Rome.

Carelli, P. (1997) 'Thunder and Lightning, Magical Miracles: On the Popular Myth of Thunderbolts and the Presence of Stone Age Artefacts in Medieval Deposits', in H. Andersson, P. Carelli and L. Ersgård (eds), *Visions of the Past: Trends and Traditions in Swedish Medieval Archaeology*: 393-417. Central Board of Antiquities, Lund Studies in Medieval Archaeology, Lund/Stockholm.

Carocci, S. (1998) 'Signori, Castelli, Feudi', in C. Fumian (ed.), *Storia Medievale*: 247-67. Donzelli, Rome.

Carver, M.O.H. (1989) 'Kingship and Material Culture in Early Anglo-Saxon East Anglia', in S. Bassett (ed.), *The Origins of the Anglo-Saxon Kingdoms*: 141-58. Leicester University Press, Leicester.

Carver, M.O.H. (1993) *Arguments in Stone. Archaeological Research and the European Town in the First Millennium.* Oxbow Books, Oxford.

Carver, M.O.H. (1998) *Sutton Hoo: Burial Place of Kings?* British Museum Press, London.

Bibliography

Carver, M.O.H. (1996) 'Transitions to Islam: Urban Roles in the East and South Mediterranean, Fifth to Tenth Centuries AD', in N. Christie and S.T. Loseby (eds), *Towns in Transition. Urban Evolution in Late Antiquity and the Early Middle Ages*: 184-212. Scolar, Aldershot.

Castellani, A., (2000) 'Riutilizzo, Rilavorazione dei Marmi Romani nell'Abbazia Altomedievale di S. Vincenzo al Volturno', in G.P. Brogiolo (ed.), *Il Congresso Nazionale di Archeologia Medievale*: 304-10. All'Insegna del Giglio, Florence.

Ceka, N. (1998) 'Pesëdhjet vjet studime për qytetet ilire', *Iliria* 28.1-2: 121-8.

Christie, N. (ed.) (1991) *Three South Etrurian Churches: Santa Cornelia, Santa Rufina and San Liberato*. British School at Rome, London.

Christie, N. (2000) 'Construction and Deconstruction: Reconstructing the Late Roman Townscape', in T.R. Slater (ed.), *Towns in Decline, AD 100-1600*: 51-71. Ashgate, Aldershot.

Christie, N. (ed.) (2004a) *Landscapes of Change. Rural Evolutions in Late Antiquity and the Early Middle Ages*. Ashgate, Aldershot.

Christie, N. (2004b) 'Landscapes of Change in Late Antiquity and the Early Middle Ages: Themes, Directions and Problems', in N. Christie (ed.), *Landscapes of Change. Rural Evolutions in Late Antiquity and the Early Middle Ages*: 1-38. Ashgate, Aldershot

Christie, N. and C.M. Daniels, (1991) 'Santa Cornelia: the Excavation of an Early Medieval Papal Estate and a Medieval Monastery', in N. Christie (ed.), *Three South Etrurian Churches: Santa Cornelia, Santa Rufina and San Liberato*. British School at Rome, London.

Chrysos, E. (1981) Συμβολή στήν Ἱστορία τῆς Ἠπείρου κατά τήν πρωτοβηζαντινή εποχή (Δ-ΣΤ αι)', *Epeirotika Chronika* 23: 6-111.

Cilento, N. (1966) *Italia Meridionale Longobarda*. Riccardo Ricciardi Editore, Naples.

Citarella, A.O. and H.M. Willard (1983) *The Ninth-Century Treasure of Monte Cassino in the Context of Political and Economic Developments in South Italy*. Pubblicazioni Cassinesi, Montecassino.

Clark, G. (1997) 'Monastic Economies? Aspects of Production and Consumption in Early Medieval Central Italy', *Archeologia Medievale* 24: 31-54.

Conant, K. (1968) *Cluny. Les Églises et la Maison du Chef d'Ordre (Medieval Academy of America Publication 77)*. Imprimerie Protat Frères, Mâcon.

Çondi, Dh. (1984) 'Fortesa-vilë në Malathre', *Iliria* 14.2: 131-52.

Coupland, S. (2002) 'Trading Places: Quentovic and Dorestad Reassessed', *Early Medieval Europe* 11: 209-32.

Coutts, C.M. (1995) 'The Hilltop Cemetery', in R. Hodges, *San Vincenzo al Volturno 2. The 1980-86 Excavations*, Part II: 98-118. British School at Rome, London.

Craven, K. (1838) *Excursions in the Abruzzi and Northern Provinces of Naples*. Bentley, London.

Crawford, J.S. (1990) *The Byzantine Shops at Sardis*. Harvard University Press, Cambridge.

Cunliffe, B. (2001) *Facing the Ocean. The Atlantic and its Peoples*. Oxford University Press, Oxford.

Cutler, A. (2001) 'Gifts and Gift Exchange as Aspects of the Byzantine, Arab and Related Economies', *Dumbarton Oaks Papers* 55: 245-78.

Daim, F. (2000) (ed.) *Die Awaren am Rand der Byzantinischen Welt*. Universitätsverlag Wagner, Innsbruck.

Dam, R. Van (1992) 'The Pirenne Thesis and Fifth-Century Gaul', in J. Drinkwater and H. Elton (eds), *Fifth-Century Gaul: A Crisis of Identity*: 321-33. Cambridge University Press, Cambridge.

Bibliography

Davis-Weyer, C. (1987) 'Müstair, Milano e l'Italia Carolingia', in C. Bertelli (ed.), *Il Millennio Ambrosiano. Milano, una Capitale da Ambrogio ai Carolingi*: 202-37. Electa, Milan.

Deliyannis, D. (1995) 'Church Burial in Anglo-Saxon England: The Prerogative of Kings', *Frühmittelalterlichen Studien* 29: 96-119.

Delogu, P. (1977) *Mito di una Città Meridionale (Salerno, Secoli VIII-XI)*. Liguori Editore, Naples.

Delogu, P. (1988) 'The Rebirth of Rome in the Eighth and Ninth Centuries', in R. Hodges and B. Hobley (eds), *The Rebirth of Towns in the West, 700-1050 (Research Report 68)*. Council for British Archaeology, London.

Delogu, P. (1990) 'Longobardi e Romani: Altre Congetture', in S. Gasparri and P. Cammarosano (eds), *Longobardia*: 111-67. Casamassima, Udine.

Delogu, P. (1992) 'Patroni, Donatori, Committenti nell'Italia Meridionale Longobarda', in *Committenti e Produzione Artistico-Letteraria nell'Alto Medioevo Occidentale* (Settimane di Studio del Centro Italiano di Studi sull'Alto Medioevo 39), vol. 1: 303-39. Centro Italiano di Studi sull'Alto Medioevo, Spoleto.

Delogu, P. (1996) 'I Monaci e l'Origine di San Vincenzo al Volturno', in P. Delogu, R. Hodges and J. Mitchell, *San Vincenzo al Volturno. La Nascita di una Città Monastica*: 45-61. Institute of World Archaeology/ University of East Anglia, Norwich.

Delogu, P. (1997) 'Considerazioni Conclusive,' in L. Paroli (ed), *L'Italia Centro-Settrentrionale in EtáLongobarda*, 425-30. All'Insegna del Giglio, Florence.

Delogu, P. (2000) 'L'Importazione di Tessuti Preziosi e il Sistema Economico Romano nel IX Secolo,' in P. Delogu (ed.) *Roma Medievale. Aggiornamenti*: 123-42. Edizioni All'Insegna del Giglio, Florence.

Del Treppo, M. (1955) 'La Vita Economica e Sociale in una Grande Abbazia del Mezzogiorno: San Vincenzo al Volturno nell'Alto Medioevo', *Archivio Storico per le Province Napoletane* 74/35: 31-110.

Del Treppo, M. (1968) 'Terra Sancti Circenci', *L'Abbazia di San Vincenzo al Volturno nell'Alto Medioevo*. Libreria Scientifica, Naples.

Deniaux, E. (1987) 'Atticus et l'Epire', in P. Cabanes (ed.), *L'Illyrie Méridionale et l'Empire dans l'Antiquité. Actes du 1er Colloque International de Clermont Ferrand (octobre 1984)*: 245-54. Clermont Ferrand.

Deniaux, E. (1998) 'Buthrote, Colonie Romaine. Recherches sur les Institutions Municipales', in G. Paci (ed.), *Epigrafia Romana in Area Adriatica. Actes de la IXe rencontre Franco-Italienne sur l'Épigraphie du Monde Romain*: 39-49. Pisa-Rome.

De Vogüé, A. (1984) 'Le Plan de Saint-Gall, Copie d'un Document Officiel? Une Lecture de la Lettre à Gozbert', *Revue Bénédictine* 94: 295-314.

Devroey, J-P. (1985) 'Reflexions sur l'Economie des Premiers Temps Carolingiens (768-877): Grand Domaines et Action Politique entre Seine et Rhin', *Francia* 13: 475-88.

Devroey, J-P. (1993) '*Ad Utilitatem Monasterii*. Mobiles et Preoccupations de Gestion dans l'Economie Monastique du Monde Franc', *Revue Bénédictine* 103: 224-40.

Devroey, J-P. (2003) *Économie Rurale et Société dans l'Europe Franque (VIe-IXe Siècles)*. Éditions Belin, Paris.

Dewing, H.B. (ed. and trans.) (1935) *Procopius, The Anecdota*. Loeb Editions, London.

Doukellis, P.N. (1988) 'Cadastres Romains en Grèce: Traces d'un Réseau Rural à Actia Nicopolis', *Dialogues d'Histoire Anciennes* 14: 159-66.

Duby, G. (1974) *The Early Growth of the European Economy. Warriors and Peasants from the Seventh to the Twelfth Century*. Weidenfeld and Nicolson, London.

Duby, G. (1980) *The Three Orders, Feudal Society Imagined*. University of Chicago Press, Chicago/London.

Bibliography

Duncan, D.E. (1998) *The Calendar*. Fourth Estate, London.

Dunn, A. (1994) 'The transition from *polis* to *kastron* in the Balkans (III-VIIcc.): general and regional perspectives', *Byzantine and Modern Greek Studies* 18: 160-80.

Dunn, A. (1997) 'Stages in the transition from the late antique to the middle Byzantine urban centre in S. Macedonia and S. Thrace', in *Αφιέρωμα στον N.G.L. Hammond*: 137-50. ΠΑΡΑΡΤΗΑ ΜΑΚΕΔΟΝΙΚΟΝ, Thessalonika.

Durrenberger, E.P. (ed.) (1984) *Chayanov, Peasants and Economic Anthropology*. St Martin's Press, New York.

Dutton, P.E. (2004) *Charlemagne's Mustache*. Palgrave, London.

Ellis, S.P. (1988) 'The End of the Roman House', *American Journal of Archaeology* 92: 565-76.

Ellis, S.P. (1991) 'Power, Architecture and Decor: How the Late Roman Aristocrat Appeared to his Guests', in E.K. Gazda, *Roman Art in the Private Sphere*: 117-56. University of Michigan, Ann Arbor.

Emerick, J.J. (1998) *The Tempietto del Clitunno near Spoleto*. Pennsylvania State University Press, Philadelphia.

Es, W.A. van (1967) 'Wijster – A Native Village beyond the Imperial Frontier, 150-425 AD', *Paleohistoria* 11. Groningen.

Es, W.A. van (1969) 'Excavations at Dorestad. A Pre-Preliminary Report: 1967-1968', *Berichten ROB* 19: 183-207.

Es, W.A. van (1973) 'Die neuen Dorestad-Grabungen 1967-1972', in H. Jankuhn, W. Schlesinger and H. Steuer (eds), *Vor- und Frühformen der europäischen Stadt im Mittelalter*: 202-17. Abhandlungen der Akademie der Wissenschaften: Philologisch-Historische Klasse, Göttingen.

Es, W.A. van (1990) 'Dorestad Centred', in J.C. Besteman, J.M. Bos and H.A. Heidinga (eds), *Medieval Archaeology in the Netherlands*: 151-82. Van Gorcum, Assen.

Es, W.A. van and W.J.H. Verwers (1980) 'Excavations at Dorestad 1. The Harbour: Hoogstraat I', *Nederlandse Oudheden* 9. Amersfoort.

Es, W.A. van and W.J.H. Verwers (1993) 'Le Commerce de Ceramiques Carolingiennes aux Pays-Bas', in *Travaux du Groupe de Recherches et d'Études sur la Céramique dans le Nord – Pas-de-Calais*: 227-36. Centres de Recherches et d'Études sur la Céramique dans le Nord – Pas-de-Calais, Bethune.

Evison, V.I. (1965) *The Fifth-Century Invasions South of the Thames*. Athlone Press, London.

Ewert, C. (2002) Das kalifale Córdoba – seine Aufsenresidenz Madînat az-Zahrâ – sein Hafen Almería', in J. Henning (ed.), *Europa im 10 Jahrhundert. Archäologie einer Aufbruchszeit*: 11-18. Von Zabern, Mainz.

Fabech, C. (1994) 'Reading Society from the Cultural Landscape. South Scandinavia between Sacral and Political Power', in P.O. Nielsen, K. Randsborg and H. Thrane (eds), *The Archaeology of Gudme and Lundeborg*: 169-83. Akademisk Forlag/Universitetsforlaget i København, Copenhagen.

Faulkner, N. (2002) 'The Debate about the End: A Review of New Evidence and Methods', *Archaeological Journal* 159: 59-76.

Fentress, E. (1996) 'San Vincenzo al Volturno in the Middle Ages', *Journal of Roman Archaeology* 9: 604-10.

Finley, M.I. (1960), Review of E. Gibbon, *The Decline and Fall of the Roman Empire*, *Spectator* (7 October): 527-8.

Fleming, A. and N. Ralph (1982) 'Medieval Settlement and Land Use in Holne Moor, Dartmoor: The Landscape Evidence', *Medieval Archaeology* 26: 101-37.

Fleming, R. (1985) 'Monastic Lands and England's Defence in the Viking Age, *English Historical Review* 395: 247-65.

193

Bibliography

Foard, G. (1985) 'The Administrative Organisation of Northamptonshire in the Saxon Period', in C. Hawkes, J. Campbell and D. Brown (eds) *Anglo-Saxon Studies in Archaeology and History*: 185-222. Oxford University Committee for Archaeology, Oxford.

Foulke, W.D. (1974) *Paul the Deacon, History of the Lombards*. University of Pennsylvania, Philadelphia.

Fraenkel-Schoorl, N. (1978) 'Carolingian Jewellery with Plant Ornament', *Berichten ROB* 28: 345-97.

Francis, K.D. (1994) 'A Mousterian Lithic Assemblage from Monte Santa Croce, Molise', *Papers of the British School at Rome* 62: 305-10.

Francis, K.D. (2001) 'Worked Stone: Flint Tools and Whetstones', in J. Mitchell and I.L. Hansen (eds), *San Vincenzo al Volturno, vol. 3: The Finds from the 1980-86 Excavations*: 417-20. Centro Italiano di Studi sull'Alto Medioevo, Spoleto.

Francovich, R. (forthcoming) *The Beginnings of Hilltop Villages in Early Medieval Tuscany* (paper given at Harvard University, October 2004).

Francovich R. and R. Hodges (2003) *Villa to Village*. Duckworth, London.

Francovich, R. and M. Valenti (1996) 'The Poggibonsi Excavations and the Early Medieval Timber Building in Europe', in G.P. Brogiolo, S. Gelichi, R. Francovich, R. Hodges and H. Steuer (eds), *Archaeology and History of the Middle Ages, XIII International Congress of Prehistoric and Protohistoric Sciences, Forlì, Italy, 8/14 September 1996*: 135-49.

Frandsen, L.B. and S. Jensen (1987) 'Pre-Viking and Early Viking Age Ribe. Excavations at Nikolajgade 8, 1985-86', *Journal of Danish Archaeology* 7: 164-73.

Frashëri, K. (1982) 'Les Territoires Albanais dans le Haut Moyen Âge', *Studia Albanica* 19.2: 93-107.

Fulford, M.G. (1989) 'Byzantium and Britain: A Mediterranean Perspective on Post-Roman Mediterranean Imports in Western Britain and Ireland', *Medieval Archaeology* 33: 1-6.

Gadd, D. and B. Ward-Perkins (1991) 'The Development of Urban Domestic Housing in Northern Italy. The Evidence of the Excavations on the San Romano Site, Ferrara (1981-84)', *Journal of the Accordia Research Centre* 2: 105-27.

Galetti, P. (2001) *Uomini e Case nel Medioevo tra Occidente e Oriente*. Laterza, Rome.

Ganshof, F.L. (1964) *Feudalism*. University of Toronto Press, Toronto and London.

Gardiner, M. et al. (2001) 'Continental Trade and Non-Urban Ports in Mid-Anglo-Saxon England: Excavations at *Sandtun*, West Hythe, Kent', *Archaeological Journal* 158: 161-290.

Gauthier, N. (1989) 'Rouen pendent le Haut Moyen Âge', in H. Atsma (ed.), *La Neustrie: Les Pays au Nord de la Loire de 650 à 850*: 1-20. Thorbecke, Sigmaringen.

Geary, P.J. (1978) *Furta Sacra. Thefts of Relics in the Central Middle Ages*. Princeton University Press, Princeton.

Geary, P.J. (2002) *The Myth of Nations. The Medieval Origins of Europe*. Princeton University Press, Princeton.

Gelichi, S. and C. La Rocca (2004) (eds), *Tesori. Forme di Accumulazione della Ricchezza nell'Alto Medioevo*. Viella, Rome.

Gelichi, S. and P. Novara (eds) (2000) *I Laterizi nell'Alto Medioevo Italiano*. Società di Studi Ravennati, Ravenna.

Gelichi, S., M. Librenti and R. Gabrielli (2004) 'Il Progetto Nonantola: Primi Risultati dopo Due Anni di Indagine Archeologica', *Le Missioni Archeologiche dell'Universita Ca' Foscari di Venezia, IV Giornata di Studio*: 89-96. University Ca' Foscari di Venezia, Venice.

Gem, R. (1988) 'The English Parish Church in the 11th and Early 12th Centuries: A

Bibliography

Great Rebuilding?', in J. Blair (ed.), *Minsters and Parish Churches – The Local Church in Transition*: 21-30. Oxford University Committee for Archaeology, Oxford.

Gilkes, O. and M. Moran (2001) 'San Vincenzo Without the Walls – Excavations 1996-7', *Papers of the British School at Rome* 69: 385-92.

Ginatempo, M. and A. Giorgi (2000) 'Documentary Sources for the History of Medieval Settlements in Tuscany', in J. Bintliff and K. Sbonias (eds), *Reconstructing Past Populations Trends in Mediterranean Europe (3000 BC – AD 1800)*: 173-93. Oxbow, Oxford.

Goody, J. (1983) *The Development of the Family and Marriage in Europe*. Cambridge University Press, Cambridge.

Gregory, C.A. (1982) *Gifts and Commodities*. Academic Press, London.

Gregory, T. (1982) 'The Fortified Cities of Byzantine Greece', *Archaeology* 35: 14-21.

Gregory, T. (1992) 'Kastro and *diateichisma* as responses to Early Byzantine frontier collapse', *Byzantion* 62: 235-53.

Grierson, P. and M.A.S. Blackburn (1986) *Medieval European Coinage*, vol. I: *The Early Middle Ages (Fifth-Tenth Centuries)*. Cambridge University Press, Cambridge.

Griffith, D. (2003) 'Markets and "Productive" Sites: A View from Western Britain', in T. Pestell and K. Ulmschneider (eds), *Markets in Early Medieval Europe. Trading and 'Productive' Sites, 650-850*: 62-72. Windgather Press, Macclesfield.

Guidoboni, E. (ed.) (1989) *I Terremoti Prima del Mille in Italia e nell'Area Mediterranea*. Istituto Nazionale di Geofisica, Bologna.

Gutscher, D.B. (1980) 'Mechanische Mörtelmischer', *Zeitschrift für Schweizerische Archäologie und Kunstgeschichte* 38: 178-88.

Haldon, J. (1990) *Byzantium in the Seventh Century*. Cambridge University Press, Cambridge.

Haldon, J. (1993) 'Military Administration and Bureaucracy: State Demands and Private Interests', *Byzantinische Forschungen* 19: 43-63.

Haldon, J. (1999) 'The Idea of the Town in the Byzantine Empire', in G.P. Brogiolo and B. Ward-Perkins (eds) *The Idea and Ideology of the Town between Late Antiquity and the Early Middle Ages*: 1-23. E.J. Brill, Leiden.

Hall, D. (1984) 'Fieldwork and Documentary Evidence for the Layout and Organisation of early Medieval Estates in the East Midlands', in K. Biddick (ed.), *Archaeological Approaches to Medieval Europe*: 43-68. Medieval Institute Publications, Kalamazoo.

Hall, R.A. (1988) 'York 700-1050', in R. Hodges and B. Hobley (eds), *The Rebirth of the Town in the West*: 125-32. Council for British Archaeology, London.

Hall, R.A. (1989) 'The Five Boroughs of the Danelaw: A Review of Present Knowledge', *Anglo-Saxon England* 18: 149-206.

Hall, R.A. (2000) 'The Decline of the *Wic*?', in T.R. Slater (ed), *Towns in Decline, AD 100-1600*: 120-36. Ashgate, Aldershot.

Hamerow, H. (1991) 'Settlement Mobility and the "Middle Saxon Shift": Rural Patterns in Anglo-Saxon England', *Anglo-Saxon England* 20: 1-18.

Hamerow, H. (2002) *Early Medieval Settlements*, Oxford University Press, Oxford.

Hamerow, H. (2004) 'The Archaeology of Early Anglo-Saxon Settlements', in N. Christie (ed.) *Landscapes of Change. Rural Evolutions in Late Antiquity and the Early Middle Ages*: 301-16. Ashgate, Aldershot.

Handbook of English-Albanian Conversation (1972). Tirana.

Harris, A. (2003) *Byzantium, Britain and the West*. Tempus, Stroud.

Harrison, K. (1976) *The Framework of Anglo-Saxon History to AD 900*. Cambridge University Press, Cambridge.

Bibliography

Harvey, A. (1989) *Economic Expansion in the Byzantine Empire 900-1200*. Cambridge University Press, Cambridge.

Haslam, J. (1987) 'Markets and Fortress in England in the Reign of Offa', *World Archaeology* 19 (1): 76-93.

Hayes, J. (1971) *Late Roman Pottery*. British School at Rome, London.

Heidinga, H.A. (1987a) *Medieval Settlements and Economy North of the Lower Rhine*. Van Gorcum, Assen.

Heidinga, H.A. (1987b) 'The Hunneschans at Uddel Reconsidered', *Chateau Gaillard* XIII: 53-62.

Heitz, C. (1980) *L'Architecture Religieuse Carolingienne. Les Formes et leurs Fonctions*. Picard, Paris.

Henderson, J. and I. Holand (1992) 'The Glass from Borg, an Early Medieval Chieftain's Farm in Northern Norway', *Medieval Archaeology* XXXVI: 29-58.

Henderson, J. and M. Mundell Mango (1995) 'Glass at Medieval Constantinople. Preliminary Scientific Evidence', in C. Mango and G. Dagron (eds), *Constantinople and its Hinterland: Papers from the Twenty-Seventh Spring Symposium of Byzantine Studies, Oxford, April 1993*: 333-56. Variorum, Aldershot.

Héron, C. and O. Meyer (1991) 'L'Environnement Urbain du Monastère de Saint-Denis', *Le Dossiers d'Archéologie* 158: 76-89.

Herschend, F. (1994) 'The Origin of the Hall in Southern Scandinavia', *Tor* 25: 175-99.

Higgins, V. (2001) 'The People of San Vincenzo in Late Antiquity and the Early Middle Ages', in J. Mitchell and I.L. Hansen (eds), *San Vincenzo 3: The Finds from the 1980-86 Excavations*: 425-37. Centro Italiano di Studi sull'Alto Medioevo, Spoleto.

Hills, C. (2003) *Origins of the English*. Duckworth, London.

Hill, D. et al. (1990) 'Quentovic Defined', *Antiquity* 64: 51-8.

Hill, D. (1996) *A History of Engineering in Classical and Medieval Times*. Routledge, London.

Hines, J. (1997) (ed.) *The Anglo-Saxons from Migration Period to the Eighth Century. An Ethnographic Perspective*. Boydell and Brewer, Woodbridge.

Hodges, R. (1981) *The Hamwih Pottery: The Local and Imported Wares from 30 Years' Excavations at Middle Saxon Southampton and their European Context*. Council of British Archaeology, London.

Hodges, R. (1982) *Dark Age Economics. The Origins of Towns and Trade AD 600-1000*. Duckworth, London.

Hodges, R. (1985) 'Excavations at San Vincenzo al Volturno: A Regional and International Centre from AD 400-1100', in R. Hodges and J. Mitchell (eds), *San Vincenzo al Volturno. The Archaeology, Art and Territory of an Early Medieval Monastery* (BAR International Series 252): 1-36. British Archaeological Reports, Oxford.

Hodges, R. (1988a) *Primitive and Peasant Markets*. Blackwell, Oxford.

Hodges, R. (1988b) 'Anglo-Saxon England and the Making of the Modern World System', in D. Hooke (ed.), *Anglo-Saxon Settlements*: 291-307. Blackwell, Oxford.

Hodges, R. (1988c) 'The Danish Contribution to the English Castle', *Acta Archaeologica* 59: 169-72.

Hodges, R. (1989) *The Anglo-Saxon Achievement*. Duckworth, London.

Hodges, R. (1990) 'Rewriting the Rural History of Early Medieval Italy: Twenty-Five Years of Medieval Archaeology Reviewed', *Rural History* 1 (1): 17-36.

Hodges, R. (1991) 'A Fetishism for Commodities: Ninth-Century Glass-Making at San Vincenzo al Volturno', in M. Mendera (ed.) *Archeologia e Storia della Produzione del Vetro Preindustriale*: 67-90. All'Insegna del Giglio, Florence.

Hodges, R. (1992a) 'An Old European: Ralegh Radford', *Current Archaeology* 128: 30-3.

Hodges, R. (1992b) 'The Eighth-Century Pottery Industry at La Londe, near Rouen, and

its Implications for Cross-Channel Trade with Hamwic, Anglo-Saxon Southampton',
Antiquity 65: 882-87.

Hodges, R. (1992c) 'Villaggi Altomedioevali nell'Alta Valle del Volturno', *Almanacco del Molise* (2): 71-96.

Hodges, R. (ed.) (1993a) *San Vincenzo al Volturno I: The 1980-86 Excavations*, Part I: 31-2. London, British School at Rome.

Hodges, R. (1993b) 'Il Declino e la Caduta: San Vincenzo al Volturno', in A. Carandini, L.C. Ruggini and A. Giardina (eds), *La Storia di Roma III* (*ii*): 255-78. Einaudi, Turin.

Hodges, R. (1993c) 'The Riddle of St Peter's Republic', in L. Paroli and P. Delogu (eds), *La Storia Economica di Roma dell'Alto Medioevo alla Luce dei Recenti Scavi Archeologici*: 353-66. All'Insegna del Giglio, Florence.

Hodges, R. (1994) 'In the Shadow of Pirenne: San Vincenzo al Volturno and the Revival of Mediterranean Commerce', in R. Francovich and G. Noyé (eds), *La Storia dell'Alto Medioevo Italiano* (*VI-X Secolo*) *alla Luce dell'Archeologia*: 109-28. All'Insegna del Giglio, Florence.

Hodges, R. (ed.) (1995a) *San Vincenzo al Volturno 2. The 1980-86 Excavations*, Part II: 153-75. British School at Rome, London.

Hodges, R. (1995b) 'The late Roman Settlement at San Vincenzo al Volturno', in R. Hodges (ed), *San Vincenzo al Volturno 2: The 1980-86 Excavations*, Part II: 127-8. British School at Rome, London.

Hodges, R. (1995c) 'San Vincenzo al Volturno and the Plan of St. Gall', in R. Hodges (ed.) *San Vincenzo al Volturno 2: The 1980-86 Excavations*, Part II: 153-75. London, British School at Rome.

Hodges, R. (1996) 'Dream Cities: Emporia and the End of the Dark Ages', in N. Christie and S. Loseby (eds), *Towns in Transition*: 289-305. Scolar, Aldershot.

Hodges, R. (1997a) *Light in the Dark Ages. The Rise and Fall of San Vincenzo al Volturno*. Duckworth, London.

Hodges, R. (1997b) '10 October 881. The Sack of San Vincenzo al Volturno', in B. Magnusson, S. Renzetti, P. Vian and S.J. Voicu (eds), *Vltra Terminum Vagari: Scritti in Onore di Carl Nylander*: 129-41. Quasar, Rome.

Hodges, R. (1998) 'Henri Pirenne and the Question of Demand in the Sixth Century', in R. Hodges and W. Bowden (eds) *Sixth Century Europe: Production, Distribution and Demand*: 3-12. E.J. Brill, Leiden.

Hodges, R. (2000) *Towns and Trade in the Age of Charlemagne*: 69-92. Duckworth, London.

Hodges, R. and W. Bowden (eds) (1998) *Sixth-Century Europe: Production, Distribution and Demand*. E.J. Brill, Leiden.

Hodges, R. and J. Mitchell (eds) (1985) 'San Vincenzo al Volturno. The Archaeology, Art and Territory of an Early Medieval Monastery', *British Archaeological Reports International Series* 252: 37-60. Oxford.

Hodges, R. and J. Mitchell (1996) *The Basilica of Abbot Joshua at San Vincenzo al Volturno*. Abbazia di Montecassino, Monteroduni.

Hodges, R. and S.J. Mithen (1993) 'The "South Church": a Late Roman Funerary Church and the Hall for Distinguished Guests', in R. Hodges (ed.), *San Vincenzo al Volturno I: The 1980-86 Excavations*, Part I: 123-91. British School at Rome, London.

Hodges, R. and D. Whitehouse (1983) *Mohammed, Charlemagne and the Origins of Europe*. Duckworth, London.

Hodges, R. and D. Whitehouse (1996) *Mahomet, Charlemagne et les Origines de l'Europe*. P. Lethilleux, Paris.

Hodges, R. and C.J. Wickham (1995) 'The Evolution of Hilltop Villages (AD 600-1500)',

Bibliography

in G. Barker (ed.), *A Mediterranean Valley. Landscape Archaeology and Annales History in the Biferno Valley*: 254-287. Leicester University Press, Leicester.

Hodges, R., G. Barker and K. Wade (1980) 'Excavations at D85 (Santa Maria in Civita): an Early Medieval Hilltop Settlement in Molise', *Papers of the British School at Rome* 48: 70-124.

Hodges, R., W. Bowden and K. Lako (eds.) (2004) *Byzantine Butrint. Excavations and Surveys 1994-99*. Oxbow Books, Oxford.

Hodges, R., R. Buckley and A. Sennis (1994) 'An Early Medieval Building Tradition? A Pagliaio at Colli a Volturno', *Papers of the British School at Rome* 62: 311-21.

Hodges, R., S. Gibson and A. Hanasz (1990) 'Campo la Fontana: A Late Eighth-Century Triconch and the Ponte Latrone at the Entrance to the Territory of San Vincenzo al Volturno'. *Papers of the British School at Rome* 52: 148-94.

Hodges, R., S. Gibson and J. Mitchell (1997) 'The Making of a Monastic City. The Architecture of San Vincenzo al Volturno in the Ninth Century', *Papers of the British School at Rome* 65: 233-86.

Hodges et al. (P. Grierson, P. Herring, V. Higgins, J. Nowakowski, H. Patterson and C.J. Wickham) (1984) 'Excavations at Vaccereccia (Rocchetta Nuova): A Later Roman and Early Medieval Settlement in the Volturno Valley, Molise', *Papers of the British School at Rome* 52: 148-94.

Hodges, R. et al. (1995) 'The Refectory', in R. Hodges (ed.) *San Vincenzo al Volturno 2: The 1980-86 Excavations*: 65-83. British School at Rome, London.

Hodges, R., G. Saraçi, W. Bowden, P. Chiles, O. Gilkes, K. Lako, A. Lane, S. Martin, J. Mitchell, J. Moreland, S. O'Hara, M. Pluciennik and L. Watson (1997) 'Late-antique and Byzantine Butrint: Interim Report on the Port and its Hinterland', *Journal of Roman Archaeology* 10: 207-34.

Hodges, R., W. Bowden, O. Gilkes and K. Lako (2000) 'The Anglo-Albanian Project at Butrint', *Archeologia Medievale* 27: 241-57.

Hodges, R., K. Lako, W. Bowden, A. Crowson, O. Gilkes, L. Përzhita, P. Reynolds and J. Vroom (2003) 'Roman and Byzantine Butrint: Excavations and Survey 2000-2001', *Journal of Roman Archaeology*, 15: 199-229.

Hooke, D. (1985) *The Anglo-Saxon Landscape: The Kingdom of the Hwicce*. Manchester University Press, Manchester.

Hope-Taylor, B. (1977) *Yeavering: An Anglo-British Centre of Early Northumbria*. HMSO, London.

Hordern, P. and N. Purcell (2000) *The Corrupting Sea. A Study of Mediterranean History*. Blackwell, Oxford.

Horn, W. and E. Born (1979) *The Plan of Saint Gall. A Study of the Architecture and Economy of, and Life in, a Paradigmatic Carolingian Monastery*, 3 vols. Berkeley, University of California Press.

Horton, M. (1987) 'Early Muslim Trading Settlements of the East African Coast: New Evidence from Shanga', *Antiquaries Journal* LXVII: 290-323.

Hoxha, E. (1985) 'Mbi arkeologjinë historinë e lashtë të Shqipërisë', *Iliria* 15.1: 29-47.

Hvass, S. (1986) 'Vorbasse: eine Dorfsiedlung während des 1. Jahrtausends n. Chr. in Mitteljütland, Dänemark', *Bericht der römisch-germanischen Kommission* 67: 529-42

Hvass, S. (1988) 'The Status of the Iron Age Settlement in Denmark', in M. Bierma, O. Harsema and W.A. van Zeist (eds) *Archeologie en Landschaap*: 97-132. Rijksuniversiteit Groningen, Groningen.

Jacobsen, W. (1992) *Der Klosterplan von St. Gallen und die karolingische Architektur*. Deutscher Verlag für Kunstwissenschaft Berlin, Berlin.

Bibliography

Jeanne-Rose, O. (1996) 'Trouvailles Isolées de Monnaies Carolingiennes en Poitou: Inventaire Provisoire, *Revue Numismatique* 151: 241-83.

Jensen, O. (2000) 'The Many Faces of Stone Artefacts', in O. Jensen and H. Karlsson (eds), *Archaeological Conditions. Examples of Epistemology and Ontology*: 129-43. Göteborg University, Göteborg.

Jørgensen, L. (2003) 'Manor and Market at Lake Tissø in the Sixth to Eleventh Centuries', in T. Pestell and K. Ulmschneider (eds) *Markets in Early Medieval Europe. Trading and the 'Productive' Sites, 650-850*: 175-207. Windgather Press, Macclesfield.

Karagiorgou, O. (2001) 'Demetrias and Thebes: the Fortunes and Misfortunes of Two Thessalian Port Cities', in L. Lavan (ed.), *Recent Research in Late-Antique Urbanism*: 182-215. Journal of Roman Archaeology, Supplementary Series no. 42), Portsmouth, RI.

Karaiskaj, G. (1980) 'Gradishta e Symizës në periudhën e vonë antike dhe mesjetë', *Iliria* IX-X: 171-210.

Keeley, E. and P. Sherrard (1975) *C.P. Cavafy: Collected Poems*, Princeton University Press, Princeton.

Keynes, S. and M. Lapidge (eds) (1983) *Alfred the Great (Including Asser's Life of King Alfred)*. Penguin Books, Harmondsworth.

Klaus, R.W. and Steinmüller, U. (2001) *Monemvasia. The Town and its History*. Agia Paraskevi, Athens.

Komata, D. (1976) 'Forteresses hautes-medievales Albanaises', *Iliria* V: 183-203.

Komata, D. (1980) 'Varreza arbërore e Shurdahut', *Iliria* IX-X: 105-22.

Korkuti, M. (1971) *Shqipëria Arkeologjike*. Tirana.

Korkuti, M., J.L. Davis, L. Bejko, M.L. Galaty, S. Muçaj and S.R. Stocker (1998) 'The Mallakastra Regional Archaeological Project: First Season, 1998', *Iliria* 28.1-2: 253-73.

Krautheimer, R. (1980) *Rome: Profile of a City, 312-1308*. Princeton University Press, Princeton.

La Regina, A. (1989) 'I Sanniti', in G. Pugliese Carratelli (ed.), *Italia Omnium Terranum Parens*: 299-432. Scheiwiller/Credito Italiano, Milan.

La Rocca Hudson, C. (1986) ' "Dark Ages" a Verona: Edilizia Privata, Aree Aperte e Strutture Pubbliche in una Città dell'Italia Settentrionale', *Archeologia Medievale* 13: 31-78.

Laiou, A.E. (2002) 'Exchange and Trade, Seventh-Twelfth Centuries,' in A.E. Laiou (ed.) *The Economic History of Byzantium from the Seventh through the Fifteenth Century*: 697-770. Dumbarton Oaks Research Library and Collection, Washington.

Lako, K. (1982) 'Kështjella e antiketit të vonë në Çuken e Ajtoit', *Iliria* 12.1: 207-19.

Le Begue, J. (1967) *Eraclius de Coloribus et Artibus Romanorum*, in M.P. Merrifield, *Original Treatises dating from XII-XVIII Centuries on the Arts of Painting*, vol. 1: 166-257 (reprint of 1849 edition). New York, Dover Publications.

Lebecq, S. (1983) *Marchands et Navigateurs Frisons du Haut Moyen Âge*. Presses Universitaires de Lille, Lille.

Lebecq, S. (1986) 'Dans l'Europe du Nord des VIIe-IXe Siècles: Commerce Frison ou Commerce Franco-Frison?', *Annales ESC*: 183-93.

Lebecq, S. (1991) 'Pour une Histoire Parallèle de Quentovic et Dorestad', in J-M. Duvosquel and A. Dierkens (eds), *Villes et Campagnes au Moyen Âge. Mélanges Georges Despy*: 415-28. Liège.

Lebecq, S. (2000) 'The Role of the Monasteries in the Systems of Production and Exchange of the Frankish World', in I.L. Hansen and C. Wickham (eds) *The Long Eighth Century*: 121-48. E.J. Brill, Leiden.

Bibliography

Leccisotti, T. (1987) *Monte Cassino* (*Abbazia di Montecassino Scritti Vari* 1). Abbey of Monte Cassino, Montecassino.

Levison, W. (1946) *England and the Continent in the Eighth Century*. Clarendon Press, Oxford.

Le Goff, J. (1980) *Time, Work and Culture in the Middle Ages*. University of Chicago Press, Chicago.

Le Goff, J. (1988) 'The Wilderness in the Medieval West', in J. Le Goff (ed.), *The Medieval Imagination*: 233-45. University of Chicago Press, Chicago and London.

Lombard, M. (1972) *Espaces et Reseaux du Haut Moyen Âge*. Mouton, Paris.

Loseby, S.T. (1998) 'Marseille and the Pirenne Thesis, 1', in R. Hodges and R. Bowden (eds) *The Sixth Century*: 203-29. E.J. Brill, Leiden.

Louis, E. (2004) 'A De-Romanised Landscape in Northern Gaul', in W. Bowden, L. Lavan and C. Machado (eds), *Recent Research on the Late Antique Countryside*: 479-504. E.J. Brill, Leiden.

Loveluck, C.P. (2002) 'Wealth, Waste and Conspicuous Consumption: Flixborough and its Importance for Middle and Late Saxon Rural Settlement', in H. Hamerow and A. McGregor (eds) *Image and Power in the Archaeology of Early Medieval Britain*, 78-130. Oxbow Books, Oxford.

Loyn, H. (1984) *The Governance of Anglo-Saxon England*. Edward Arnold, London.

Maddicott, J.R. (1989) 'Trade, Industry and the Wealth of King Alfred', *Past and Present* 123: 3-51.

Magoun, F.B. (1940) 'The Rome of Two Northern Pilgrims', *Harvard Theological Review* 33: 268-77.

Manacorda, D. (2001) *Crypta Balbi. Archeologia e Storia di un Paesaggio Urbano*. Electa, Milan.

Mango, C. (1989) 'Review of G. Bradshaw: The Colour of Power', *Times Literary Supplement* December: 22-8.

Marazzi, F. (1991) 'Il Conflitto fra Leone III Isaurico e il Papato fra il 725 e il 733, e il "Definitivo" Inizio del Medioevo a Roma: Un'Ipotesi in Discussione', *Papers of the British School at Rome* 59: 231-57.

Marazzi, F. (1994) 'Le "Città Nuove" Pontificie e l'Insediamento Laziale nel IX Secolo', in R. Francovich and G. Noyé (eds), *La Storia dell'Alto Medioevo Italiano* (*VI-X Secolo*) *all Luce dell'Archeologia*: 251-78. All'Insegna del Giglio, Florence.

Marino, L., D. Guerrizio and B. Libertucci (2001) *Materiali e Tradizioni Costruttive nel Molise*. Cierre Edizioni, Verona.

May, J. and P. Weddell (2001) 'Bantham: A Dark Age Puzzle', *Current Archaeology* 178: 420-2.

Mazza, S. (1978-79) 'Il Complesso Fortificato di Torba', *Sibrium* 14: 187-215.

McClendon, C.B. (1987) *The Imperial Abbey of Farfa. Architectural Currents of the Early Middle Ages*. Yale University Press, New Haven and London.

McCormick, M. (1986) *Eternal Victory. Triumphal Rulership in Late Antiquity, Byzantium and the Early Medieval West*. Cambridge University Press, Cambridge.

McCormick, M. (2001) *The Origins of the Medieval Economy*. Cambridge University Press, Cambridge.

McKitterick, R. (1983) *The Frankish Kingdoms under the Carolingians*. Longmans, London.

McKitterick, R. (ed.) (1994) *Carolingian Culture: Emulation and Innovation*. Cambridge University Press, Cambridge.

McKitterick, R. (ed.) (2001) *The Early Middle Ages*. Oxford University Press, Oxford.

McNeill, W. (1986) 'Mythistory or Truth, Myth, History and Historians', *Speculum* 61: 1-10.

200

Bibliography

Meneghini, R. and R. Santangeli Valenziani (2001) 'La Trasformazione del Tessuto Urbano tra V e IX Secolo', in M.S. Arena, P. Delogu, L. Paroli, M. Ricci, L. Saguì and L. Vendittelli (eds), *Roma dall' Antichità al Medioevo. Archeologia e Storia*: 20-33. Electa, Milan.

Metcalf, D.M. (1986) 'The Monetary History of England in the Tenth Century Viewed in the Perspective of the Eleventh Century', in M.A.S. Blackburn (ed.) *Anglo-Saxon Monetary History*: 133-58. Leicester University Press, Leicester.

Metcalf, D.M. and J.P. Northover (1989) 'Coinage Alloys from the Time of Offa and Charlemagne to *c.* 854', *Numismatic Chronicle* 149: 101-20.

Metcalf, D.M. (1994) 'The Beginnings of Coinage in the North Sea Coastlands: A Pirenne-Like Hypothesis', in B. Ambrosiani and H. Clarke (eds), *The Twelfth Viking Congress*, vol. 3: 196-214. Birka Studies, Stockholm.

Metcalf, M. (1999), 'The Monetary Economy of Ninth-Century England South of the Humber: A Topographical Analysis', in M. Blackburn and D. Dumville (eds), *Kings, Currency and Alliances: History and Coinage of Southern England in the Ninth Century*: 167-99. Boydell Press, Woodbridge.

Metcalf, M. (2003) Variations in the Composition of the Currency at Different Places in England, in T. Pestell and K. Ulmschneider (eds), *Markets in Early Medieval Europe. Trading and 'Productive' Sites, 650-850*: 37-47. Windgather Press, Macclesfield.

Meyer, O. (1993) 'Le Bourg Monastique de Saint-Denis', in M. Petit and M. Deprarère-Dargery, *L'Ile-de-France de Clovis à Hugues Capet du Vᵉ Siècle au Xᵉ Siècle*: 91-6. Editions du Valhermeil, Condé-sur-Noireau.

Meyvaert, P. (1980) 'Review of the "Plan of St Gall" ', *University Publishing* 9: 18-19.

Millett, M. (1990) *The Romanisation of Britain*. Cambridge University Press, Cambridge.

Milošević, A. (2005) 'Ogetti Preziosi, Segni Distintivi Carolingi della Croazia', in G.P. Brogiolo and P. Delogu (eds) *L'Adriatico della Tarda Antichità all'Età Carolingia*: 245-70. All'Insegna dell'Giglio, Florence.

Millett, M. with S. James (1983) 'Excavations at Cowdery's Down, Basingstoke, Hampshire', *Archaeological Journal* 140: 151-279.

Mitchell, J. (1990) 'Literacy Displayed: The Use of Inscriptions at the Monastery of San Vincenzo al Volturno in the Early Ninth Century', in R. McKitterick (ed.), *The Use of Literacy in Early Medieval Europe*: 186-225. Cambridge University Press, Cambridge.

Mitchell, J. (1992) 'A Carved Ivory Head from San Vincenzo al Volturno', *Journal of the British Archaeological Association* CXLV: 66-76.

Mitchell, J. (1994) 'The Display of Script and the Uses of Paintings in Longobard Italy', *Testo e Immaginazione nell'Alto Medioevo* (*Settimane di Studio del Centro Italiano di Studi sull'Alto Medioevo* 41): 887-951. Centro di Studi sull'Alto Medioevo, Spoleto.

Mitchell, J. (1996) 'Monastic Guest Quarters and Workshops: The Example of San Vincenzo al Volturno', in H-R. Sennhauser (ed.), *Wohn- und Wirtschaftsbauten Frühmittelalterlicher Klöster*: 127-55. VDF, Zurich.

Mitchell, J. (1997) 'Spatial Hierarchy and the Uses of Ornament in an Early Medieval Monastery', in D. Paris-Poulain (ed.), *Le Rôle de l'Ornament dans la Peinture Murale du Moyen Âge*: 35-55. Université de Poitiers, Poitiers.

Mitchell, J. (2000) 'Diffusione dello Smalto Cloisonne', in C. Bertelli and G.P. Brogiolo (eds) *Il Futuro dei Longobardi. L'Italia e la Costruzione dell'Europa di Carlo Magno*: 454-63. Skira, Milan.

Mitchell, J. (2001a) 'The Early Medieval Tiles and Modillions', in J. Mitchell and I.L. Hansen (eds), *San Vincenzo al Volturno 3: The Finds From the 1980-86 Excavations*: 83-122. Centro Italiano di Studi sull'Alto Medioevo, Spoleto.

Bibliography

Mitchell, J. (2001b) 'An Early Medieval Enamel', in J. Mitchell and I.L. Hansen (eds) *San Vincenzo al Volturno 3: The Finds From the 1980-86 Excavations*: 279-86. Centro Italiano di Studi sull'Alto Medioevo, Spoleto.

Mitchell, J. (2001c) 'A Set of Sword-Belt Mounts of Iron Inlaid with Silver and Associated Bridle-Furniture', in J. Mitchell and I.L. Hansen (eds) *San Vincenzo al Volturno 3: The Finds From the 1980-86 Excavations*: 393-406. Centro Italiano di Studi sull'Alto Medioevo, Spoleto.

Mitchell, J. (2003) 'San Vincenzo al Volturno: The Archaeology of the Arts and Magic at an Early Medieval Monastery', in *I Longobardi dei Ducati di Spoleto e Benevento*: 1099-1125. Centro Italiano di Studi sull'Alto Medioevo, Spoleto.

Mitchell, J. (2004) 'The Archaeology of Pilgrimage in Late Antique Albania', in W. Bowden, L. Lavan and C. Machado (eds), *Recent Research on the Late Antique Countryside*: 145-88. E.J. Brill, Leiden.

Mitchell, J. and I.L. Hansen (eds) (2001) *San Vincenzo al Volturno 3: The Finds from the 1980-86 Excavations*. Centro Italiano di Studi sull'Alto Medioevo, Spoleto.

Mitchell, J., L. Watson, F. de Rubeis, R. Hodges and I. Wood (1997) 'Cult, Relic and Privileged Burial at San Vincenzo al Volturno', *Atti del I Convegno Nazionale di Archeologia Medievale, Pisa 29-31 May 1997*: 315-21. All'Insegna del Giglio, Florence.

Moreland, J. (1985) 'A Monastic Workshop and Glass Production at San Vincenzo al Volturno, Molise, Italy', in R. Hodges and J. Mitchell (eds), *San Vincenzo al Volturno. The Archaeology, Art and Territory of an Early Medieval Monastery* (BAR International Series 252): 37-60. British Archaeological Reports, Oxford.

Moreland, J. (2000) 'Concepts of the Early Medieval Economy', in I.L. Hansen and C. Wickham (eds) *The Long Eighth Century*: 1-34. E.J. Brill, Leiden.

Moreland, J. (2002) *Archaeology and Text*. Duckworth, London.

Morra, G. and F. Valente (1993) *Il Castello di Venafro. Storia-Arte-Architettura*. Edizioni Enne, Campobasso.

Morris, C.D. and R. Harry (1997) 'Excavations on the Lower Terrace, Site C, Tintagel Island, 1990-94', *The Antiquaries Journal* 77: 1-143.

Morris, R. (1985) 'The Church in the Countryside: Two Lines of Enquiry', in D. Hooke (ed.), *Medieval Villages*: 47-60. Oxford University Committee for Archaeology, Oxford.

Morris, R. (1989) *Churches in the Landscape*. Dent, London.

Morrisson, C. and Sodini, J-P. (2002) 'The Sixth-Century Economy', in A.E. Laiou (ed.) *The Economic History of Byzantium from the Seventh through the Fifteenth Century*: 171-220. Dumbarton Oaks Research Library and Collection, Washington.

Morton, A.D. (1992) *Excavations at Hamwic*, vol. I. Council of British Archaeology, London.

Mucaj, S. (1980) 'Vendbanime të antikitetit të vonë në krahinën e Mallakastrës', *Iliria* IX-X: 279-99.

Munch, F.S., O.S. Johansen and E. Roesdahl (2003), *Borg in Lofoten. A Chieftain's Farm in North Norway*. Arkeologisk Skriftserie 1, Tapir Academic Press, Trondheim.

Näsman, U. (1998) 'The Justinianic Era of South Scandinavia: An Archaeological View', in R. Hodges and W. Bowden (eds) *The Sixth Century*: 255-79. E.J. Brill, Leiden.

Nees, L. (1986) 'The Plan of St Gall and the Theory of the Program of Carolingian Art', *Gesta* 25 (1): 1-8.

Nelson, J.L. (1986) ' "A King across the Sea": Alfred in the Continental Perspective', *Transactions of the Royal Historical Society* 36: 45-68

Newman, J. (1992) 'The Later Roman and Anglo-Saxon Settlement Pattern in the

Bibliography

Sandlings', in M. Carver (ed.), *The Age of Sutton Hoo. The Seventh Century in North-West Europe*: 25-38. Boydell, Woodbridge.

Newman, J. (2003) 'Exceptional Finds, Exceptional Sites? Barham and Coddenham, Suffolk', in T. Pestell and K. Ulmschneider (eds) *Markets in Early Medieval Europe*: 97-109. Windgather Press, Macclesfield.

Nielsen, P.O., K. Randsborg and H. Thrane (eds) (1994) *The Archaeology of Gudme and Lundeborg*. National Museum, Copenhagen.

Nitz, H-J. (1988) 'Settlement Structures and Settlement Systems of the Frankish Central State in Carolingian and Ottonian Times', D. Hooke (ed) *Anglo-Saxon Settlements*: 249-74. Blackwell, Oxford.

Noble, T.P.X. (1976) 'The Monastic Ideal as a Model for Empire: The Case of Louis the Pious', *Revue Bénédictine*: 235-50.

Noonan, T.S. (1994) 'The Vikings in the East: Coins and Commerce', in B. Ambrosiani and H. Clarke (eds), *The Twelfth Viking Congress. Developments Around the Baltic and the North Sea in the Viking Age*, vol. 3: 215-36. Birka Studies 4, Stockholm.

Pagan, H. (1986) 'Coinage in Southern England', in M.A.S. Blackburn (ed.), *Anglo-Saxon Monetary History*: 45-65. Leicester University Press, Leicester.

Panella, C. (1993) 'Merci e Scambi nel Mediterraneo Tardoantico', in A. Carandini, L.C. Ruggini and A. Giardina (eds), *Storia di Roma* III/ii: 613-97. Einaudi, Turin.

Panofsky, E. (1960) *Renaissance and Renascences in Western Art*. Almqvist and Wiksell, Stockholm.

Pantoni, A. (1973) *Le Vicende della Basilica di Montecassino Attraverso la Documentazione Archeologica* (*Miscellanea Cassinese* 36). Badia di Montecassino, Montecassino.

Pantoni, A. (1980) *Le Chiese e gli Edifici del Monastero di San Vincenzo al Volturno* (*Miscellanea Cassinese* 40). M. Pisani, Montecassino.

Patterson, H. (2001) 'The Soapstone', in J. Mitchell and I.L. Hansen (eds), *San Vincenzo al Volturno 3: The Finds From the 1980-86 Excavations*: 327-8. Centro Italiano di Studi sull'Alto Medioevo, Spoleto.

Patterson, J. (1985) 'A City Called *Samnium*', in R. Hodges and J. Mitchell (eds), *San Vincenzo al Volturno. The Archaeology, Art and Territory of an Early Medieval Monastery* (BAR International Series 252): 185-200. British Archaeological Reports, Oxford.

Pavan, G. (1990) 'Architettura del Periodo Longobardo', in G.C. Menis (ed.), *I Longobardi*: 236-98. Electa, Milan.

Peduto, P. (1990) 'Insediamenti Longobardi del Ducato di Benevento', in S. Gasparri and P. Cammarosano (eds), *Longobardia*: 307-74. Casamassima, Udine.

Périn, P. (2004) 'The Origin of the Village in Early Medieval Gaul', in N. Christie (ed.), *Landscapes of Change. Rural Evolutions in Late Antiquity and the Early Middle Ages*: 255-78. Ashgate, Aldershot.

Përzhita, L. (1986) 'Kështjella e Bushaitit', *Iliria* 16.2: 187-213.

Përzhita, L. (1990) 'Kështjella e Pecës në periudhëm e antikitetit të vonë', *Iliria* 20.1: 201-41.

Përzhita, L. (1995) 'Kështjella e vonë antike e Domajve (Umishjt)', *Iliria* 25.1-2: 267-77.

Pestell, T. and K. Ulmschneider (2003) (eds) *Markets in Early Medieval Europe. Trading and 'Productive' Sites, 650-850*. Windgather Press, Macclesfield.

Petralia, G. (1995) 'A Proposito dell' Immortalità di Maometta e Carlomagno (o di Constantino)', *Storica* 1: 37-87.

Pietri, C. (1986) 'Chiesa e Comunità Locali nell' Occidente Cristiano (IV-VI d.C.): L'Esempio della Gallia', in A. Giardina (ed.), *Società Romana e Impero Tardoantico*, vol. 3: *Le Merci, gli Insediamenti*: 761-95. Laterza, Rome.

Bibliography

Piltz, E. (1998) 'Varangian Companies for Long Distance Trade', in E. Piltz (ed.) *Byzantium and Islam in Scandinavia*: 85-106 Paul Åströms Forlag, Jonsered.

Pluciennik, M. et al. (K. Lako, L. Përzhita and D. Williams) (2004): 'The Environs of Butrint 2: The 1995-96 Field Survey', in R. Hodges, W. Bowden & K. Lako (eds), *Butrint: Excavations and Survey 1994-99*: 47-63. Oxbow Books, Oxford.

Pohl, W. (1991) 'Conceptions of Ethnicity in Early Medieval Studies', *Archaeologia Polona* 29: 39-49.

Pohl, W. (2001) 'History in Fragments: Montecassino's Politics of Memory', *Early Medieval Europe* 10: 343-74.

Polci, B. (2003) 'Some Aspects of the Transformation of the Roman Domus between Late Antiquity and the Early Middle Ages', in L. Lavan and W. Bowden (eds) *Theory and Practice in Late Antique Archaeology*: 79-122. E.J. Brill, Leiden.

Popovic, V. (1984) 'Byzantines, Slaves et Autochthones dans les Provinces de Prévalitaine et Nouvelle Épire', in V. Popoviç (ed.), *Villes et Peuplement dans l'Illyricum Protobyzantin. Actes du Colloque Organisé par l'École Française de Rome (Rome, 12-14 mai 1982)*: 181-213. École Française de Rome, Rome.

Potter, T.W. (1995) *Towns in Late Antiquity. Iol Caesarea and its Context*. Ian Sanders Memorial Committee, Oxford.

Poulter, A. (1983) 'Town and Country in Moesia Inferior', in A. Poulter (ed.), *Ancient Bulgaria*, Part 2, Nottingham: 74-118.

Poulter, A. (1992) 'The Use and Abuse of Urbanism in the Danubian Provinces during the Late Roman Empire', in J. Rich (ed), *The City in Late Antiquity*: 99-135. Routledge, London.

Powell, A. (2004) 'The Faunal Remains', in R. Hodges, W. Bowden and K. Lako (eds), *Butrint: Excavations and Survey 1994-99*: 305-20. Oxbow Books, Oxford.

Procopius (1935) *The Anecdota or Secret History* (trans. H.B. Dewing) (Loeb Classical Library). Heinemann, London.

Provero, L. (1998) *L'Italia dei Poteri Locali. Secoli X-XII*. Carocci, Rome.

Prummel, W. (1983) 'Excavations at Dorestad 2 : Early-medieval Dorestad, an Archaeozoological Study', *Nederlandse Oudheden* 11. Amersfoort.

Radford, R. (1956) 'The Imported Pottery Found at Tintagel', in D.B. Harden (ed.) *Dark-Age Britain*: 59-70. Methuen, London.

Randsborg, K. (1983) 'Les Activités Internationals des Vikings: Raids ou Commerce?' *Annales: Economies, Sociétés, Civilisations* 36 (5): 862ff.

Randsborg, K. (1991) *The First Millennium AD in Europe and the Mediterranean*. Cambridge University Press, Cambridge.

Randsborg, K. (1992) *Archaeology and the Man-Made Reality*. Aarhus University Press, Aarhus.

Randsborg, K. (1998) 'The Migration Period: Model History and Treasure', in R. Hodges and W. Bowden (eds), *The Sixth Century*: 61-88. E.J. Brill, Leiden.

Renfrew, C. (1986) 'Introduction, Peer-Polity Interaction and Socio-Political Change', in C. Renfrew and J.F. Cherry (eds), *Peer-Polity Interaction and Socio-Political Change*: 1-18. Cambridge University Press, Cambridge.

Renfrew, C. and J.F. Cherry (ed.) (1986), *Peer-Polity Interaction and Socio-Political Change*. Cambridge University Press, Cambridge.

Reuter, T. (2000) ' "You Can't Take It with You": Testaments, Hoards and Moveable Wealth in Europe, 600-1100', in E.M. Tyler (ed.) *Treasure in the Medieval West*: 11-24. York Medieval Press, York.

Reynolds, P. (2005) 'Hispania in the Late Roman Mediterranean: Ceramics and Trade', in K. Bowes and M. Kulikowski (eds), *Hispania in Late Antiquity. Twenty-First Century Approaches*: 369-486. E.J. Brill, Leiden.

Bibliography

Riché, P. (1978) *Daily Life in the World of Charlemagne*. Liverpool University Press, Liverpool.

Riddle, J.M. (1977) *Marbode of Rennes' (1035-1123) DE LAPIDIBUS. Considered as a Medical Treatise with Text, Commentary and C.W. King's Translation. Together with Marbode's Minor Works on Stones*. Franz Steiner, Wiesbaden.

Riddler, I. (1993) 'The Distinguished Guests Refectory', in R. Hodges (ed.) *San Vincenzo al Volturno I: The 1980-86 Excavations*, Part I: 210-15. British School at Rome, London.

Roffe, D. (1981) 'The Lincolnshire Hundred', *Landscape History* 3: 27-36.

Rogerson, A. (2003) 'Six Middle Anglo-Saxon Sites in West Norfolk', in T. Pestell and K. Ulmschneider (eds) *Markets in Early Medieval Europe. Trading and 'Productive' Sites, 650-850*: 110-21. Windgather Press, Macclesfield.

Romano, D. (2000) 'A Tale of Two Cities: Roman Colonies at Corinth', in E. Fentress (ed.), *Romanization and the City. Creation, Transformations and Failures*: 83-104. Journal of Roman Archaeology, Supplementary Series, Portsmouth, RI.

Rovelli, A. (1993) 'Usi Monetari nell' Italia Altomedievale: L'Esempio della Documentazione Farfense', *Annali dell'Istituto Numismatico* 40: 547-56.

Rovelli, A. (2000) 'Some Considerations on the Coinage of Lombard and Carolingian Italy', in I.L. Hansen and C. Wickham (eds), *The Long Eighth Century*: 195-224. E.J. Brill, Leiden.

Rovelli, A. (2004) 'I Tesori Monetali', in S. Gelichi and C. La Rocca (eds) *Tesori. Forme di Accumulazione della Ricchezza nell'Alto Medioevo (Secoli V-XI)*: 241-56. Viella, Rome.

Saguì, L. (1993) 'Produzione Vetraria a Roma tra Tardoantico e Alto Medioevo', in L. Paroli and P. Delogu (eds), *La Storia Economica di Roma nell' Alto Medioevo alla Luce dei Recenti Scavi Archeologici*: 113-36. All'Insegna del Giglio, Florence.

Saguì, L. (1998) (ed.) *Ceramica in Italia: VI-VII Secolo*. All'Insegna del Giglio, Florence.

Sahlins, M. (1985) *Islands of History*. Chicago University Press, Chicago.

Sanderson, W. (1985) 'The Plan of St Gall Reconsidered', *Speculum* 60 (3): 615-32.

Sanders, G.D.R. (2003), 'Byzantine Corinth', in C.K. Williams II and N. Bookidis (eds) *Corinth. The Centenary 1896-1996*: 385-400. American School of Classical Studies at Athens, Athens.

Sawyer, P. (1965) 'The Wealth of England in the Eleventh Century', *Transactions of the Royal Historical Society* 15: 145-64.

Sawyer, P. (1986) 'Anglo-Scandinavian Trade in the Viking Age and After', in M.A.S. Blackburn (ed.), *Anglo-Saxon Monetary History*: 185-200. Leicester University Press, Leicester.

Scaccia Scarafoni, E. (1946) 'La "Torre di S. Benedetto" e le Fabbriche Medioevali di Montecassino (Ricerche di Topografia)', *Bullettino dell'Istituto Storico Italiano per il Medio Evo e Archivio Muratoriano* 59: 137-83.

Schmid, K. (1972) 'Zur Ablosung der Langobardenherrschaft durch den Franken', *Quellen und Forschungen aus Italienischen Archiven und Bibliotheken* 52: 1-36.

Schutz, H. (2004) *The Carolingians in Central Europe, their History, Arts and Architecture*. E.J. Brill, Leiden.

Sénac, P. (2002) *Les Carolingiens et Al-Andalus (VIIIᵉ-IXᵉ Siècles)*. Maisonneuve et Larose, Paris.

Settia, A.A. (1991) 'Chiese, Strade e Fortezze nell'Italia Medievale', in *Italia Sacra. Studi e Documenti di Storia Ecclesiastica* 46. Herder Editrice e Libreria, Rome.

Shaw, B.D. and R.P. Saller (1983) 'Editors' Introduction', in M.I. Finley, *Economy and Society in Ancient Greece*: ix-xxvi. Penguin Books, Harmondsworth.

Bibliography

Silber, I.F. (1995) 'Gift-giving in the Great Traditions: the Case of Donations to Monasteries in the Medieval West', *Archives of European Sociology* XXXVI: 209-43.

Sims-Williams, P. (1983a) 'The Settlement of England in Bede and the Chronicle', *Anglo-Saxon England* 12: 1-42.

Sims-Williams, P. (1983b) 'Gildas and the Anglo-Saxons', *Cambridge Medieval and Celtic Studies* 6: 1-30.

Skre, D. and Stylegar, F-A. (2004) *Kaupang. The Viking Town*. University of Oslo, Oslo.

Small, A.M., J. Robert and R.J. Buck (1994) *The Excavations of San Giovanni di Ruoti*. University of Toronto Press, Toronto.

Smart, V. (1985) 'The Moneyers of St. Edmund', *Hikuin* 11: 83-90.

Smart, V. (1986) 'Scandinavians, Celts and Germans in Anglo-Saxon England: The Evidence of Moneyers' Names', in M.A.S. Blackburn (ed.), *Anglo-Saxon Monetary History*: 171-84. Leicester University Press, Leicester.

Smith, C.A. (1976) 'Exchange Systems and the Spatial Distribution of Elites: the Organisation of Stratification in Agrarian Societies', in C.A. Smith (ed.), *Regional Analysis*, vol. 2: *Social Systems*: 309-74. Academic Press, New York.

Smyth, A.P. (1998) 'The Emergence of English Identity, 700-1000' in A.P. Smyth (ed.) *Medieval Europe. Studies in Ethnic Identity and National Perspective in Medieval Europe*: 24-52. Macmillan, London.

Spahiu, H. and D. Komata (1974) 'Shurdhahu-Sarda, qyteti fortifikuar mesjetar shqiptar', *Iliria* III: 257-328.

Stafford, P. (1989) *Unification and Conquest – A Political and Social History of England in the Tenth and Eleventh Centuries*. Edward Arnold, London.

Steuer, H. (1987) 'Der Handel der Wikingerzeit zwischen Nord- und Westeuropa aufgrund Archäologischer Zeugnisse', in K. Duwel et al. (eds), *Untersuchungen zu Handel und Verkehr der Vor- und Frühgeschichtlichen Zeit in Mittel- und Nordeuropa, IV, Der Handel der Karolinger und Wikingerzeit*: 113-97. Vandenhoeck and Ruprecht, Gottingen.

Steuer, H. (1989) 'Archaeology and History: Proposals on the Social Structure of the Merovingian Kingdom', in K. Randsborg (ed.), *The Birth of Europe. Archaeology and Social Development in the First Millennium AD* (Analecta Romana Institutum Danici Supplementum 16): 100-22. L'Erma di Bretschneider, Rome.

Stevenson, J. (2001) 'The Vessel Glass', in J. Mitchell and I.L. Hansen (eds), *San Vincenzo al Volturno 3: The Finds From the 1980-86 Excavations*: 203-78. Centro Italiano di Studi sull'Alto Medioevo, Spoleto.

Szöke, B.M., K.H. Wedepohl and A. Kronz (2004) 'Silver-stained Windows at Carolingian Zalavár, Mosaburg (Southwestern Hungary)', *Journal of Glass Studies* 46: 85-108.

Stubbs, W. (ed.) (1874) 'Memorials of St. Dunstan, Archbishop of Canterbury', *Rolls Series* 63.

Sullivan, R. (1998) 'What Was Carolingian Monasticism? The Plan of St. Gall and the History of Monasticism', in A. Callander Murray (ed.) *After Rome's Fall*: 251-87. University of Toronto Press, Toronto.

Taylor, H.M. (1975) 'Tenth-Century Church Building in England and on the Continent', in D. Parson (ed.), *Tenth-Century Studies. Essays in Commemoration of the Millennium of the Council of Winchester and 'Regularis Concordia'*: 141-68. Phillimore, London.

Téreygeol, F. and C. Dubois (2003) 'Mines et Métallurgie Carolingienne à Melle', *Archéologie Médiévale* XXXIII: 91-102.

Theuws, F. (1991) 'Landed Property and Manorial Organisation in Northern Austrasia: Some Considerations and a Case Study', in N. Roymans and F. Theuws (eds), *Images*

Bibliography

of the Past. Studies on Ancient Societies in Northwest Europe: 299-407. Instituut voor Pre- en Protohistorische Archeologie Albert Egges van Giffen (IPP), Amsterdam.

Thomas, C. (1981) *A Provisional List of Imported Pottery in Post-Roman Western Britain and Ireland*. Institute of Cornish Studies, Redruth.

Thomas, C. (1998) *Christian Celts. Messages and Images*. Tempus, Stroud.

Thomas, N. (1991) *Entangled Objects. Exchange, Material Culture, and Colonialism in the Pacific*. Harvard University Press, London.

Thorndike, L. (1923-58) *A History of Magic and Experimental Science: During the First Thirteen Centuries of Our Era*, 8 vols. Columbia University Press, New York.

Thurston, T.L. (2001) *Landscapes of Power, Landscapes of Conflict: State Formation in the South Scandinavian Iron Age*. Kluwer Academic Plenum, New York.

Toubert, P. (1973) *Les Structures du Latium Médiéval. Le Latium Méridional et le Sabine du IXe Siècle à la Fin du XIIe Siècle (Bibliothèque des Écoles Françaises d'Athèns et de Rome 221)*. École Française de Rome, Rome.

Toubert, P. (1976) 'Pour une Historie de l'Environnement Economique et Social du Mont-Cassin (IXe-XIIe Siècles)', *Comptes Rendus de l'Académie des Inscriptions et Belles-Lettres*: 689-702.

Toubert, P. (1995) *Dalla Terra ai Castelli: Paesaggio, Agricoltura e Poteri nell'Italia Medievale*. Einaudi, Turin.

Toubert, P. (2004) *L'Europe dans sa Première Croissance. De Charlemagne à l'An Mil*. Fayard, Paris.

Ugolini, L.M. (1932) *Albania Antica*, vol. II: *L'Acropoli di Fenice*. Rome.

Ugolini, L.M. (1942) *L'Acropoli di Butrinto*. Rome.

Ulriksen, J. (1994) 'Danish Sites and Settlements with a Maritime Context, AD 200-1200', *Antiquity* 64: 797-811.

Valenti, M. (ed.) (1996) *Poggio Imperiale a Poggibonsi: dal Villaggio di Capanne al Castello di Pietra*. All'Insegna del Giglio, Florence.

Valenti, M. (2004) *L'Insediamento Altomedievale nelle Campagne Toscane Paesaggi. Popolamento e Villaggi tra VI e X secolo*, All'Insegna del Giglio, Florence.

Veen, M. Van der (1985) 'An Early Medieval Hilltop Settlement in Molise: The Plant Remains', *Papers of the British School at Rome* 53: 211-24.

Verhulst, A. (1989) 'The Origins of Towns in the Low Countries and the Pirenne Thesis', *Past and Present* 122: 3-35.

Verhulst, A. (1994) 'The Origins and Development of Medieval Towns in Northern Europe', *Economic History Review* XLVII: 362-73.

Verhulst, A. (2002) *The Carolingian Economy*. Cambridge University Press, Cambridge.

Vince, A. (1990) *Saxon London. An Archaeological Investigation*. Seaby, London.

Wade, K. (1988) 'Ipswich', in R. Hodges and B. Hobley (eds), *The Rebirth of Towns in the West, AD 700-1050*: 93-100. Council for British Archaeology, London.

Wallerstein, I. (1974) *The Modern World-System*. Academic Press, London.

Walmsley, A. (1996) 'Byzantine Palestine and Arabia: Urban Prosperity in Late Antiquity', in N. Christie and S.T. Loseby (eds), *Towns in Transition*: 126-58. Scolar, Aldershot.

Ward-Perkins, B. (1981) 'Two Byzantine Houses at Luni', *Papers of the British School at Rome* 49: 91-8.

Ward-Perkins, B. (1996) 'Urban Continuity?', in N. Christie and S.T. Loseby (eds), *Towns in Transition*: 4-17. Scolar, Aldershot.

Wheeler, R.E.M. (1935) *London and the Saxons*. London Museums Catalogues 6. London.

Bibliography

White, H. (1973) *Metahistory: The Historical Imagination in Nineteenth-Century Europe*, Johns Hopkins University Press, Baltimore.

White, L. (1962) *Medieval Technology and Social Change*. Oxford University Press, Oxford.

Whitelock, D. (1979) *English Historical Documents* (2nd edn). Sidgwick and Jackson, London.

Whyman, M. (2002) 'Emporia and Early Medieval Settlement', in D. Perring (ed.), *Town and Country in England: Frameworks for Archaeological Research*: 92-106. Council for British Archaeology, London.

Wickham, C.J. (1981) *Early Medieval Italy. Central Power and Local Society 400-1000*. Macmillan, London.

Wickham, C.J. (1985a) *Il Problema dell'Incastellamento dell'Italia Centrale: L'Esempio di San Vincenzo al Volturno* (*Studi sulla Società degli Appennini nell'Alto Medioevo II; Quaderni dell'Insegnamento di Archeologia Medievale della Facoltà di Lettere e Filosofia dell'Università di Siena* 5). All'Insegna del Giglio, Florence

Wickham, C.J. (1985b) 'The *Terra* of San Vincenzo al Volturno in the Eighth to Twelfth Centuries: The Historical Framework', in R. Hodges and J. Mitchell (eds), *San Vincenzo al Volturno. The Archaeology, Art and Territory of an Early Medieval Monastery* (BAR International Series 252): 227-58. British Archaeological Reports, Oxford.

Wickham, C.J. (1994) *Land and Power. Studies in Italian and European Social History, 400-1200*. British School at Rome, London.

Wickham, C.J. (1995) 'Monastic Lands and Monastic Patrons', in R. Hodges (ed.) *San Vincenzo al Volturno 2: The 1980-86 Excavations*, Part II: 138-52. British School at Rome, London.

Wilkes, J. (1992) *The Illyrians*. Blackwell, Oxford.

Williams, D. and C. Carreras (1995) 'North African Amphorae in Roman Britain: A Re-Appraisal', *Britannia* XXVI: 240-1.

Wilson, D. and C. Blunt (1961) 'The Trewhiddle Hoard', *Archaeologia* 98: 75-122.

Wiseman, J. (2001) 'Landscape Archaeology in the Territory of Nikopolis', in J. Isager (ed.), *Foundation and Destruction. Nikopolis and Northwestern Greece: The Archaeological Evidence for the City Destructions, the Foundation of Nikopolis and the Synoecism*: 43-63. Monographs of the Danish Institute in Athens, Athens.

Wood, I. (1983) *The Merovingian North Sea*. Viktoria Bökforlag, Alingås.

Wood, I. (1993) *The Merovingian Kingdoms*. Longman, London.

Wormald, P. (1983) 'Bede, the Bretwaldas and the Origins of the *Gens Anglorum*', in P. Wormald (ed.), *Ideal and Reality in Frankish and Anglo-Saxon Society*. Blackwell, Oxford.

Wormald, P. (1994) '*Engla Lond*', *Journal of Historical Sociology* 7: 1-24.

Wrigley, E.A. (1985) 'Urban Growth and Agricultural Change: England and the Continent in the Early Modern Period', *Journal of Interdisciplinary History* 15: 683-728.

Zadoro-Rio, E. (2003) 'L'Habitat Rural au Moyen Âge', *Les Nouvelles de l'Archéologie*, 92: 5-33.

Zettler, A. (1988) *Die Frühen Klosterbauten der Reichenau: Ausgrabungen – Schriftenquellen – St Galler Klosterplan* (*Archäologie und Geschichte. Freiburger Forschungen zum Ersten Jahrtausend in Südwestdeutschland* 3). Jan Thorbecke Verlag, Sigmaringen.

Zettler, A. (1990) 'Der St Galler Klosterplan: Überlegungen zu seiner Herkunft und Entstehung', in P. Godman and R. Collins (eds), *Charlemagne's Heir. New Perspectives on the Reign of Louis the Pious (814-840)*: 655-87. Clarendon Press, Oxford.

Index

Index

Index

211